GAMBLING FOR LOVE

Gambling for Love

John Killick

Australia's first decimal currency bank robber

Connor Court Publishing

Connor Court Publishing Pty Ltd

Copyright © John Killick 2015

ALL RIGHTS RESERVED. This book contains material protected under International and Federal Copyright Laws and Treaties. Any unauthorised reprint or use of this material is prohibited. No part of this book may be reproduced or transmitted in any form or by any means, electronic or mechanical, including photocopying, recording, or by any information storage and retrieval system without express written permission from the publisher.

PO Box 224W
Ballarat VIC 3350
sales@connorcourt.com
www.connorcourt.com

ISBN: 9781925138603 (pbk)

Cover design by Ian James

Printed in Australia

*Dedicated to the memory
Of my mother
Laurie Vivian "Peggy"
(Too little too late)*

Foreword

It is not often one gets invited to write the Foreword of an autobiography like *Gambling for love*. This is a rollicking yarn, the autobiography of one of Australia's best-known criminals: John Killick. Like many men with charm, intelligence, humour and the gift of the gab, he was a ladies' man but he had one great love in his life: Cathy. A message loud and clear comes from this book: Don't gamble. Gambling cost John Killick everything: his first love, his freedom and the best years of his life.

It all started with a dreadful childhood with the associated pain, violence, lack of guidance and mentoring and the lack of exploitation of his talents. If John's first bet on the horses had lost him money, things might have been different. If someone had actually taken John Killick under his or her wing early in his life, he could have been a useful member of society. Without the disadvantages of his early life, there is no doubt that John Killick could have been a great sportsman, chess player and articulate barrister.

However, it is not too late. John Killick is highly intelligent and is starting a writing career late in life after decades on the dark side. Former prisoners can change for the better and can still inspire and motivate those around them. Killick should be writing weekly columns or blogs and interacting with young people to show from first hand experience the consequences of gambling, drugs, crime and violence. He has realised late in in the day how he has wasted much of his life and wants to show people that, as a result of his gambling, grim experiences and prison isolation, there is no future in gambling and robbery. He should have been taught this while a teenager in prison rather than being bashed.

John's life evolved from gambling to petty theft, imprisonment and all of the brutalities associated with prison life. There is another message in this book: prison is not a holiday. Don't go to prison. The chances of being buggerised, bashed, brutalised, bullied, tortured, stabbed and killed are high. In John Killick's time, prison was not for rehabilitation. It was for brutal punishment and retribution that could only lead to resentment, hatred and recidivism and it is only extraordinarily strong willed people like John Killick who could have survived decades of prison hardships half a century ago.

Petty crime and imprisonment in his formative teenage years and continual unsuccessful gambling evolved to numerous bank robberies, periods of imprisonment, escape attempts and the pain of a love affair that just could not be realised into a meaningful relationship. John Killick has done some pretty stupid things in his life and in this book explains the background to these actions. On a number of occasions, John Killick was Australia's most wanted man with Australian police and Interpol searching for him.

One wonders how many children in today's fatherless single parent drug-addled world of chronic unemployment will turn out? Already the prison population, as John Killick shows, has changed from old style crims to prisoners profoundly psychiatrically damaged by drugs. Decades ago, prisoners had a crim's sense of ethics and morality, as John explains, but with most prisoners now druggies, no such honour amongst thieves exists. John shows that his disdain for homosexuals changes over time as a result of seeing their brutalisation in the prison system. His disdain for drug peddlers does not change.

Many years before I met John, he had been publishing short stories. He had been taught to write well by an outstanding person, the late Ian Mudie. Just think of what John Killick could have been if he had met Ian Mudie in his teenage years. On one of his periods outside, a former school and university friend contacted me. She was a Commonwealth Employment Services officer case managing John Killick and was charmed by this colourful bank robber larrikin. She asked whether I could help him to grow a writing career and, in the '90s, I met John a number of times and tried to help him. A subsequent bank robbery and an escape from prison in a hijacked helicopter put a spanner in the works for a while but during incarceration, John and I kept contact by mail and later by telephone. And he kept reading, writing and improving his skills.

I have given my publishers, Anthony and Julie Cappello of Connor Court Publishing, a couple of painful Chinese burns to persuade them to publish a book that is not really the genre of Connor Court. Over the last five years, Connor Court has grown into one of Australia's most successful small publishers. They took a great risk with my 2009 book *Heaven and Earth* and were rewarded with a best seller. My thanks go to Anthony for taking another risk and giving John Killick the break in life he should have had sixty years ago.

This is John Killick's first book. The second is on the way; I have read it and just could not put it down. Watch this spot.

Emeritus Professor Ian Plimer
Adelaide, Australia

Preface

Life has taught me that man
has an inherent, often subconscious,
drive for self-destruction
and unless he identifies and harnesses it,
he will eventually succumb to it.

John R. Killick

ACKNOWLEDGEMENTS

I am grateful to Emeritus Professor Ian Plimer who assured me six years ago that we would get this book published. His tireless efforts – between frequent overseas trips – have been a major contributing factor to this book being on the shelves. The publisher Anthony Cappello took a gamble by publishing his first 'true' crime book – although I still think of it as a true 'love story' – and he is thanked. Gloria has always believed in my ability to write books. She had to put up with a lot, including my pedantic insistence on retyping various pages and chapters on numerous occasions and to her I owe my thanks. Lucy read the original manuscript and made some pertinent suggestions re content which were implemented. I thank both the late Ian Mudie who, under difficult circumstances, encouraged me and taught me how to write and Carla Molino, who helped to polish my technique and believed in this book. Dean Ryan, my good friend, also believed in this book to the extent that he said he would publish it himself if he couldn't get a publisher and John Kerr supported and encouraged me for years. Both are thanked. My friend Louis Kovacs, who has a new heart and a new life, is also thanked for his support.

My legal team, Joe Crowley and Eidan Havas, fought hard to get me out of gaol, free of shackles, to enable me to publish this book. These two are thanked and show that stories about lawyers are not always true. One can learn and receive help and encouragement while in prison. In prison, many people helped me. Bunty Ellis-Freeman, one time education officer at Goulburn, encouraged me to do courses against overwhelming odds prevailing at the time. Bertie Kidd, Bernie Matthews, Gary Hughes and Ted Havorka and other prisoners – too many to name – encouraged me to ensure that this book saw the light of day. Officer Karen Williams, at Nowra Correctional Centre, also encouraged me to continue writing during difficult times. The educational staff – both civilian and custodial – in Wellington, Parklea, Nowra and Dawn de Loas gave me help and positive feedback. All the girls at Dawn de Lois 'Shine For Kids', they do a marvellous job and they promised to buy this book. I'm checking up on you. Psychologists Aleesha Gorton, Fiona Mason and Georgina helped me evolve into who I am despite my long history in prison. Geoff Turner, the fearless Official Visitor at Parklea and Head Teacher at Randwick TAFE, gave me unwavering support.

My brother David and my niece Rebecca both believed in this book when others didn't. My son John, teacher in China, and linguist extraordinaire, never gave up on his Dad and these family members have my heartfelt thanks.

Lyn Warner, my dear friend, gone but not forgotten who did so much to help me, and the young typist, Jess Williams, who did her best to type a manuscript the content of which must have shocked her. The late David Hart meticulously typed up the original manuscript. Reader Bobby Mackay not only gave the book a pass but a glowing recommendation and it is so heartening to have a complete stranger support my work. And all of those people over the years who I have not mentioned who encouraged and urged me to publish this book.

Gary Stevens said this book won't sell 5,000 copies. I'm counting on you readers to prove him wrong.

And finally to Cathy. Where are you? Maybe you will read this book and realise that we came closer than you think.

1

Family Life
(1942-1955)

I was born in Sydney on Friday 13 February 1942. Two days later Singapore fell to the Japanese. Over 15,000 Australians were imprisoned.

On 19 February, the Japanese launched their first and second attacks on the Australian mainland. Twice, within two hours, 180 Japanese planes bombed Darwin and nearby military bases. The official death toll was 244, mostly US sailors, with more than 400 wounded. Twenty-one ships were sunk or badly damaged and 20 warplanes destroyed. A higher tonnage of bombs was dropped on Darwin than on Pearl Harbour.

Australians were fearful that their great county could soon fall to the seemingly unstoppable Japanese. It wasn't a good week to be born in Australia. On 3 March the Japanese bombed Broome and Wyndham, killing seventy people.

My mother, whoever she was, handed me over for adoption. I have no memory of her and no information about her. Maybe I was born out of wedlock. In those days, unwed mothers were often forced to give up their babies for adoption. It's possible that my biological father never knew of my existence. The mother I do remember was the mother I loved, but my feelings towards the father I knew were ambivalent. As a small boy I thought of him as two people: the sober, decent, hardworking man; and the drunken, violent tyrant who terrorised all of us. He was the nightmare of my childhood.

I was eight and my brother, David five, when Dad, during one of his drunken rages, told me: "You're not my son, you little black bastard! Your mother can't have kids, so we adopted you because no one else wanted you."

At the time I displayed no emotion but inside I was shattered. Who was I? My mother comforted me, insisting that it wasn't true. But this type of abuse occurred on numerous occasions and I soon realised it was true. I was adopted and I had jet-black hair, so I was a little black bastard. In contrast, David's hair was blonde and curly. People often commented on how different we looked.

For most of his working life, Dad, a powerfully built man, was a truck driver. Some demon inside him pushed him to do the work of two men. When I was nine, I watched him lift, unassisted, a refrigerator on to the back of his truck. As a young man he had been a champion amateur boxer. When he was drunk he loved to fight.

By the time I was thirteen, we had moved house seven times. Mum always said we had to move because of the neighbours. Each time we moved into a new place the neighbours, to begin with, were friendly towards us; within a month they avoided us. All of them were frightened and outraged by Dad's violent drunken rages and abuse. During the Christmas holidays in 1951, I watched with my mother from her bedroom window while he fought one of our neighbours on the front lawn. The neighbour, a fit-looking, hot-tempered young man had had enough of my father's abuse.

Mum, in an agitated state, was barracking for the neighbour. "Kill the bastard," she mumbled.

But even drunk, Dad was formidable. He knocked the neighbour down twice before the young man gave up and staggered away, defeated. When drunk, Dad would turn on anyone. Most of the time Mum was the target. He would call her the vilest of names and accuse her of being a slut and a mad woman. Sometimes she would snap and start smashing crockery and glassware. A few times she came at him with a bread knife. Once, when she menaced him with a knife, he backhanded her with such force she fell halfway across the room. It was one of the rare times I saw him actually hit her.

Usually, when she began smashing things he would shout at me: "Johnny, your mother's gone insane again! Try and stop her."

I was the only one who could stop her, but it wasn't easy. Sometimes she would look at me and I'm sure she didn't know who I was. She had once been a plump, jovial woman; but over the years she had become frail, distraught and totally reliant on Bex powders and sleeping pills.

I remember nights, in the middle of winter, when Mum, David and I huddled together under the house rather than go inside and be abused by Dad. Although he never abused David, who was his favourite, David was just as frightened of him as we were. Sometimes the three of us would walk the streets until the early hours of the morning, when we could stealthily return to our beds.

Until 1955, the hotels closed at 6.00 pm so he'd bring home bottles of beer or go to a mate's place and share booze and stories for hours. Somehow he always managed to drive his truck home. There were no breathalysers in those days. Friday and Saturday nights were the worst. With no work the next day he would drink until he fell into a drunken sleep. Sometimes Mum gave me crushed sleeping pills to slip into his beer.

He used the fact that she wouldn't sleep with him as an excuse to drink; she always said she wouldn't sleep with him because he drank. It was an impossible situation. The two were totally incompatible. He said that the only reason the two of them stayed together was for the well being of David and I. In later years he admitted that it was the wrong decision.

Born Reginald Gladstone Killick in 1909, he had, as a child, experienced bullying and harsh punishments from his stepfather, whose surname was Huxley. When he was 20 the Great Depression exacted its toll on everyone, but particularly the working class. He couldn't get work and often went hungry. Until he got a job driving trucks in the mid thirties, he went through tough times. I think he suppressed a deep rage at the way his life had thus far been spent and alcohol triggered the rage.

My mother, born Laurie Vivian Richards in 1916, also suffered at the hands of her stepfather, a stern disciplinarian devoid of a sense of humour. He never forgave her for marrying Dad. She told me that when she met Dad he had been handsome, attentive to her, and most importantly, he rarely drank. It had been financially impossible for her to leave him and take David and I with her. In those days a woman on her own with two kids had no support system to which she could turn. The only way she could make extra money was to sew clothes on her sewing machine. She was good at it and a lot of neighbours paid her to make alterations for them. She always ensured that David and I were neatly dressed and well nourished. It was a rare night when we didn't have meat, vegetables and dessert for dinner.

On most Fridays she would go to Paddy's Markets in Haymarket and buy used clothing. Afterwards she would alter it on her machine until it fitted one of us. Sometimes, after she had tailored a dress to fit her, she would put it on and call me in and ask how it looked. I would always tell her she looked beautiful and that it was perfect for her. This always pleased her. Sometimes, to me, she did look beautiful as she pirouetted around the room like a young girl. The sad part was when she had to sell them. I don't know how many times she gave me one of her best dresses and told me to take it to one of the neighbours and ask if the lady wanted to buy it. She always sold them cheaply and I usually came home with the money.

It distressed me to do this and I would often plead with her: "Not that dress, Mum. That's your best one."

"I'm tired of it," she would say. "Don't fret, I'll get some new ones on Friday."

I always did as she asked. At times I knew that if I didn't come back with the money she wouldn't be able to serve up a hot meal; then there would be trouble when Dad came home. Occasionally, he would get inebriated on a working day. If he wasn't home for dinner by seven, I became hopeful that he had been arrested for drunkenness or fighting. I dreaded the moment when he would come staggering through the door demanding dinner, even if it was after midnight.

I found it difficult to study at school and was referred to as a daydreamer. I took days off from school and neglected all homework. I retreated into a fantasy world of radio serials, comics and books. I listened to most of the serials on the radio; *Superman* (played by Leonard Teale) and *Biggles* were my favourites. I also read all of the *Biggles* books by Captain W E Johns. I borrowed books from the library twice a week and collected as many comics as I could, swapping them with other boys. *Superman*, *Batman*, *Captain Marvel* and *The Phantom* were my heroes, all of whom had mild-mannered second personalities.

Eventually I developed my own personal hero. I called him Paleface. It began in the backyard while I played imaginary cowboys and Indians. I became the Paleface who fought hordes of Indians and always won. I also fought outlaws, ruthlessly killing them. During these games I was invincible. Some nights while waiting for my father to come home, fearing it and dreading it, I wished I could become Paleface and confront him.

2

The Singer and the Storyteller
(1948-1956)

In 1948 I started school at Ryde Primary, just after we had moved from a rat-infested flat in Balmain to Arthur Street, North Ryde. Every day I would walk the 500 yards (about 450 metres) to the bus stop where I'd catch a bus to Top Ryde. From there it was a short walk to school. On the way home a bigger, older boy began to terrorise me. He would get off the bus at the same stop, chase me up the hill catch me and give me a thumping.

When I told my parents about it, Dad insisted I fight the boy. "Attack him with your schoolbag," he advised.

Afraid, but determined to stop the bullying, I spent all day at school trying to psyche myself into an aggressive frame of mind. That afternoon, instead of running as soon as I got off the bus, I waited for the bully to alight. As he stepped from the bus I belted him as hard as I could with my schoolbag, which was packed with books. Shocked and unprepared, he went into a defensive stance, covering his head with his hands. Without hesitation I hit him with a frenzy of blows with my bag. He fell to the ground crying. He was eight years old and he never bothered me again.

The family next door, the Kellys, were a rough bunch. The father claimed to be a cousin of John Kelly who, at Long Bay Penitentiary in 1939, became the last man to be hanged in New South Wales. There were five boys and one girl, Maureen. She could fight as well as any boy. She was about five years older than me and she took it upon herself to protect me from bullying by her brothers. On more than one occasion she thrashed one of them after I had copped a bit of a slap around. The youngest child was Terry who died of diphtheria when only two. I remember Dad leaning over the back porch one night talking to Terry's father who was leaning over his porch. Both were drinking beers.

"He'll pull through, mate," Dad said. "He's a Kelly."

But a Kelly or not, the kid didn't make it. I don't think anyone in Australia dies of diphtheria these days.

Until I was 14 I suffered from asthma. Sometimes the attacks were so severe that I had difficulty breathing and I was certain I was going to die. I can recall occasions when I was clawing at the window, trying to open it in the middle of winter, desperate to get more air. My parents would restrain me and give me the asthmatic spray. I can still recall the berry taste of that panacean mist as I made horrible gasping sounds trying to suck in air. I also came down with the usual illnesses of childhood at that time: measles, pneumonia, mumps, bronchitis, chicken pox, cold and flu. Consequently I missed a lot of schooling. I enjoyed staying at home all day reading comics and books. School bored me. When I wasn't sick I would often feign illness and Mum usually allowed me to stay home.

At one stage I had more than 400 comics. I collected soft drink bottles, cashed them and bought comics. Every Friday, Mum would give me two shillings (20 cents) to buy lunch. Instead I'd buy four or five new comics. To give an indication of the value of two shillings in the early '50s, the first *Sun Herald* newspaper was published in 1952 and cost sixpence (5 cents). Sixty-three years later it cost 60 times that amount.

Another hobby I spent a lot of time with was my Meccano set. Sometimes I would spend the entire day building model trucks, jeeps, bridges etc with the perforated metal strips and plates, wheels and axles all held together by nuts and bolts. It was the only toy I was interested in. For Christmas or my birthday I always asked for additions to my set. When the plastic Lego building bricks became popular in the late '50s, the steel Meccano sets dramatically dropped in popularity. Probably, today, most kids would find it boring; the wonderful world of computers has too many lures.

One of the highlights of the year was Empire Day. Although the British Empire was defunct and had long ago been replaced by the

Commonwealth, Empire Day was held on 24th May every year until 1966 to commemorate Queen Victoria's birthday. We celebrated her birthday, although she had been dead for more than 50 years, by burning a huge bonfire in the middle of a nearby paddock and setting off hundreds of fireworks. At least 50 people would attend. At daybreak the next morning, the Kelly kids and I would go to the paddock to search for fizzers, fireworks that had failed to ignite. We always found plenty.

I was good at marbles. Most of the time when I played marbles at school I would win. One day a boy who had lost all his marbles accused me of fudging, by failing to keep my fist on the ground as I flicked the marble. We began to fight until a couple of prefects came over and marched us off to the headmaster's office. He wasn't interested in who started the fight; he caned both of us with six strokes on the hand with a bamboo cane. Before my schooldays were over I was caned dozens of times. In those days corporal punishment was still an acceptable penalty. Some of the states were still punishing criminals by flogging them with a cat-o'-nine-tails. I would later meet and fight the last man in Australia to be flogged with a cat-o'-nine-tails, the cop killer, William John O'Mealley.

Not long after my tenth birthday we moved to Slade Street, Rozelle. One of the last memories I have of Ryde Primary School was a week before my birthday when we were all paraded in the school ground and the headmaster gravely announced that the King was dead. King George VI had died of lung cancer. Then they played the national anthem, *God Save the King*, even though it was too late to save him and we returned to our classrooms. A few boys were crying.

When Queen Elizabeth II was inaugurated, the national anthem became *God Save the Queen*. It was traditional to stand up in movie theatres before the session began and stare at a picture of the monarch on the screen while the national anthem played. No one dared to sit down before it ended. In Thailand today, you can be gaoled for up to 15 years if you remain seated at the movies during the playing of the Royal Anthem.

I started school at Rozelle Primary. I also joined the Christian Endeavour Boys' Society and was chosen to sing at one of their concerts.

From the radio I had learned dozens of songs sung by popular artists such as Frank Sinatra, Bing Crosby, Perry Como, Guy Mitchell, Frankie Laine and Nat 'King' Cole. At the time the American crooner Johnny Ray had a string of recent hits and when he visited Australia the radio stations bombarded the airwaves with his songs. He also became the first crooner to throw himself around the stage and cry.

I chose to sing his latest hit, *Walking My Baby Back Home*. The hall was packed and even Mum, Dad and David came to watch me enthusiastically hurl myself around the stage in a fair imitation of the singer. But I didn't cry. I received a rousing reception and Dad talked about it for years. For him, it was my one outstanding achievement.

For me, it was proof that I could psyche myself into taking on daunting tasks, just like Paleface. Due to my flair for telling stories, aided by a vivid imagination, I soon became popular with the kids in Rozelle. They would often come to my place and ask me to come out and tell them a story. Sometimes as many as a dozen girls and boys would sit on the grass at the rear of Slade Street (a no through road) and I would enthral them with stories I made up as I went along. Most of my stories involved monsters and super-heroes.

Sometimes I brought my all-powerful hero, the Paleface, into the action. He was, of course, invincible. But at this stage he was a mere figment of my imagination.

3
DAD VERSUS FREDDY SANDS
(1953)

After the end of World War II there was a huge influx of immigrants to Australia. We called them New Australians. Although a large percentage was British, by 1947 thousands of continental Europeans began arriving with hopes of a better life in the land of largesse. To a lesser degree, Eastern Europeans followed them. I met kids who came from Russia, Hungary, Malta, Yugoslavia, Austria, Czechoslovakia, Poland and a couple of Germans who pretended to be Austrians. And all the Russians I knew claimed to be white Russians.

"What's a white Russian?" I asked Dad.

"A bloody Russian wog who's not a Commo," he said.

Communism was used as a scare tactic by the government at the time, similar to terrorism now. The Menzies Government tried to have the Communist Party outlawed in Australia but was thwarted by the High Court.

The White Australia Policy still existed, so no Asians or Africans could immigrate. Until 1960, the iconic national magazine *The Bulletin* used the proud masthead slogan 'Australia for the White Man'. In the 1850s about 40,000 Chinese arrived in Australia to work in the goldfields. By the end of the century numerous restrictions were placed on Chinese immigrants, but thousands remained in Australia, particularly Sydney where they established a strong Chinese community.

Between 1945 and 1959 more than one and a half million immigrants had arrived in Australia. These New Australians proved to be a great asset to the country and helped to shape its now multicultural nature. Most of them were hard workers and it was mainly these New Australians who built the Snowy Mountains hydroelectric project and slaved tirelessly in the steelworks at Port Kembla's giant mills.

The economy began to boom. There was no thought for the environment. People were buying cars (instead of walking and using buses and trains), refrigerators (instead of relying on the iceman to deliver a block of ice every day for the ice box), vacuum cleaners (instead of carpet sweepers) and washing machines (instead of boiling clothes in coppers and using manual wringers). Milk was delivered in bottles instead of being poured into billy cans or saucepans. Bakers, in their horses and carts, who delivered delicious hot fresh bread and rolls, were being replaced by men in vans and wrapped, sliced bread sold in shops. The rich even had air conditioning.

The outer suburbs of Sydney were being supplied with sewerage systems and flush toilets instead of using sanitary pans that were emptied and replaced once a week by sanitary workers. At North Ryde, we often joked that we could smell the dunny cart a mile away. Blackouts were still a regular occurrence in the late '40s and early '50s and we always stocked up with candles and kerosene to fuel the kerosene lamps and heaters.

Most suburbs had a picture theatre. Balmain had two: Hoyts and Kings. Rozelle had one, Hoyts. Saturday afternoon matinees were always packed out. The kids got great value for their money: cartoons, serials and two movies. Some of us even got to sit next to the girl we fancied.

We all had our favourite movie stars. Mine was James Stewart. My friend, Les, idolised Marilyn Monroe. In 1953 she posed nude for a new magazine in the US, *Playboy*. You couldn't get *Playboy* then in Australia but it didn't stop Les from fantasising about Marilyn Monroe. One day he told me that George, a 19-year-old who boarded at his place, had tried to get it for him. Unable to do so, he had shown him other magazines with naked women in them.

"Was Marilyn Monroe in any of them?" I asked.

"No," he said. "But he showed me what spunk looks like."

"Ugh, he's a creep!"

"No, he's not. Do you want me to get him to show you?"

"No way! You should tell your parents."

"Dad would flog me. Don't tell anyone, will you?"

Apparently Les wasn't the only kid who received free semen demonstrations from George. He had another four or five students. When the father of one of the boys found out about it, he bashed George so badly he was admitted to hospital. Shortly afterwards, he left town and, it was rumoured, the state. Les and I never discussed it again.

At school I surprised myself by being chosen for the soccer team. But after a few games, I was dropped. I didn't have much luck at football. A year earlier, at Ryde Primary, I had broken my left arm playing rugby league.

Dad brought home a punching bag and I practised boxing on it. Boxing was the only sport Dad was interested in. He taught me to box and took me to see a few fights at the old Leichhardt Stadium. In November 1954, I fought a tough kid called George Spencer in a lane after school. He picked the fight. Both of us took off our shoes and fought for a long time. Both of us had large blisters on our feet. Eventually he sat down on the gutter and cried. The fight had been even, but I refused to give in. I learnt a lot about myself that day. My favourite boxer was the American Negro, Freddy Dawson. I listened to most of his fights on the radio and he always won. He was unbeaten in about 20 fights in Australia. I had a scrapbook full of clippings of his fights.

One afternoon when I was eleven, Dad came home and said: "Johnny, I've got a surprise for you."

I could see that he'd had a few drinks, but he wasn't drunk. He had a big grin on his face as he walked across to the front door, opened it and said, "Come in, Freddy."

A half-drunk Aboriginal with a potbelly walked in.

Dad put his arms around his shoulder and said: "Johnny, this is Freddy Dawson. He's over here to fight George Barnes. I told him you're his number one fan and he wanted to meet you."

I was outraged. "That's not Freddy Dawson!"

Fred stood staring at the floor.

Dad shrugged. He was disappointed that the clumsy ruse had failed. "You can't fool this kid," he said, winking at Mum. "I only said he was Freddy Dawson as a joke. But, and I swear this on my dying oath, this is Freddy Sands, one of Dave Sands' brothers. He can fight like a thrashing machine."

Until he had been killed in a road accident in 1952, Dave Sands, an Aboriginal, had been classed by many as the uncrowned middleweight champion of the world. I knew he'd had three or four brothers, some of them fighters. I accepted Dad's word that this man was Freddy Sands.

"How are you, brother?" Fred said.

I shook his hand and asked him whom he had fought. He said he hadn't fought for a while and had forgotten the names of most of his opponents. Dad explained that he'd had a lot of hard fights and was a bit punch-drunk, that's why he couldn't remember things. Mum seemed a bit sceptical about Fred, David was overawed, and I was thrilled to think that a real boxer had come to visit us. After a couple of beers and a bit of reminiscing about some of Dave Sands' fights, Dad and Fred decided to give an exhibition bout on the patio. I asked Dad if I could get a few of my friends to come and watch. He was all for it, deciding that he and Fred would have another beer while they waited for us.

I rushed out to tell Les. Between us we rounded up about a dozen kids to come and watch "Mr Killick fight Freddy Sands."

When Dad saw all the kids he made them form a ring around the patio, which was about five metres by six metres in diameter.

"This is only an exhibition bout," Dad announced. "Freddy has had 36 fights for 30 wins, 18 by KO. But he hasn't fought for a while."

"And Dad used to be middleweight champion of Balmain," I said proudly.

Dad was pleased. "That's right. I've got the trophy inside if anyone wants to see it later."

All the kids looked suitably impressed. This was going to be one hell of a fight. I didn't mention that the trophy was dated 1932, 21 years ago. Dad was now a heavyweight, especially around the midriff.

Dad stepped back and shaped up to Fred. "You ready, Freddy?"

Freddy looked a bit unsteady on his feet, "I'm ready, brother."

I was a bit worried that Dad would get hurt, but it became obvious in a few seconds that Fred was the one in danger. With Fred on the back move, Dad stalked him all around the patio, throwing lefts and rights trying to belt his brains out. With the kids screaming encouragement, he finally cornered him and hit him with a powerful right to the stomach. Poor old Fred, who hadn't thrown a punch, dropped to the ground badly winded. Dad then became concerned and helped him to his feet. He told the disappointed crowd that the exhibition bout was over. He took Fred inside and they had a few more drinks, then Fred left. I never saw him again.

Afterwards, Dad often boasted about the time he had flattened one of the 'Fighting Sands' while half of Rozelle and Balmain watched.

I found out later than none of the Sands' brothers was named Fred.

John's mother at the ferry jetty of Taronga Park Zoo, c. 1957

John with his brother David and their mother outside Central Railway entrance, 1948

John's mother and friend before she met his father, outside the Palais, c. 1936

Below: John's father and friend standing by car with tram at left in background, c. 1936

David, friend Gary, John and neighbours at Arthur Street, North Ryde, 1949

Below: The Killick house at 19 Lombard Street, Fairfield, 1956

4

I'VE READ A LOT OF COMICS
(1953-1955)

In 1953 Dad took me to a Balmain dentist. I remember it was just after the Russian President, Joseph Stalin, died. Dad was happy about that. He said Stalin was a dictator and a mass murderer.

"But he was on our side in the war, wasn't he, Dad?" I asked.

"Don't be a smart arse, Johnny," Dad said.

At the dentist's surgery Dad told him: "Give him a temporary filling."

Some of my teeth were decayed and one front tooth in particular was causing me sleepless nights. Every time the dentist began to drill the tooth he hit a nerve and I screamed and tried to get out of the chair. Eventually Dad took over from the nurse and held me down while this dentist, who I can only describe as a sadist, finished his task. It was the most painful, horrific ordeal I have ever experienced. The dentist complained to Dad that if I wanted more work done he would have to put me under the gas. On the way home Dad accused me of being a sissy and said he had never been so embarrassed before in his life. While we lived at Rozelle I had a lot of problems with my teeth and we returned to the dentist four or five times, usually for a temporary filling. Each time, the dentist applied a gas mask on me and gassed me until I was unconscious. Then he would do the drilling and filling.

In February 1954, Queen Elizabeth II became the first reigning British monarch to visit Australia. School lessons were put aside and we were taken to Moore Park to get a glimpse of our young Queen. After a long wait the big moment arrived. Here she comes, the lady we stood to attention for during the national anthem. She and Prince Phillip were standing on an open, elevated platform in the back of a large jeep, waving and smiling at the crowd. As I caught a fleeting glimpse of her smiling in my direction I thought she was indeed a beautiful Queen. At that moment I realised that some people were born to stride upon the stage of life while most of us would simply look on in awe.

Not long after the Queen had returned to England, Mum had to go in to hospital for a gall stone operation. There were complications and for a while her life was in the balance. I refused to believe that she would die. Dad had to leave David and I in the care of his elder brother, Claude, a tall, wiry man with a perpetual scowl. He made it obvious he wasn't too pleased about being our minder. I heard him say to Dad: "I've already got five mouths to feed." He had three children.

The second morning I was there, he grabbed me by the scruff of the neck and dragged me into the bathroom, pointing to one of the taps.

"You left this tap dripping all night," he accused.

He was intimidating. "I'm sorry, Uncle Claude," I mumbled, uncertain of whether or not I was the offender.

"Water costs money," he said. "It's time you were taught some discipline."

He got the strap and while David and two of my cousins watched began flogging me. I covered up but his attack was ferocious and a few of the blows struck my face. Although I wouldn't give him the satisfaction of seeing me break down and cry, I eventually began yelling at him to stop.

Soon afterwards he dropped his hands by his side and, breathing heavily, muttered, "Next time I won't stop."

It was a humiliating experience for a 12-year-old. When Dad came to see us, I told him about the flogging. Incensed, he took David and I home with him. As far as I know, he never spoke to his brother again. Although Mum was out of danger, she had to remain in hospital for another week. Until she came home Dad took us to work with him in the truck. He worked for Yellow Express and made deliveries all over Sydney. He worked hard and he made a lot of pub stops. Sometimes he would go into a hotel, have a quick drink then come out and we would drive to his next scheduled stop. Other times he would bring us a soft drink and go inside for another drink or two.

All the hotels had colourful, glass covered posters displaying healthy looking cricketers, footballers, swimmers and other sportsmen with the names of beers prominent: 'Toohey's Pilsener', 'Resch's Dinner Ale', 'Tooth's KB'. The message was far from subtle in those days before television: These healthy, athletic people drink our beer, why not you? Dad didn't need the aid of the posters. He told me he knew every pub in Sydney and had drunk in most of them.

During the week I witnessed at first hand the legendary six o'clock swill. The hotels had to close at 6.00 pm and at about five to six the barmen would yell: "Five minutes!"

There were no chairs or tables in the bar and the noise was deafening as men lined up three or four deep, pushing and shoving, trying to buy one more before the taps were switched off. Dad was always in front. It puzzled me that women weren't permitted into bars and yet many of them worked as barmaids in some of the toughest pubs in Sydney's history. If a woman wanted a drink she had to go to the ladies' lounge.

For my twelfth birthday I was given my first pushbike. I had been hoping for a brand new Speedwell or Malvern Star with all the accessories but Dad could only manage a second hand bicycle that Mum painted and hid with a neighbour until my birthday. I was still thrilled and rode it for miles, exploring new suburbs. There were lots of steep hills in the area and riding a bike without gears helped to strengthen my puny legs. Eventually I fastened a carry basket to the handle bar and filling it with comics, rode around asking any boy I saw if he wanted to swap comics. It soon became difficult to find comics I hadn't read. One of the boys told me about a little second hand bookshop in Rozelle where you could exchange comics for a penny (one cent) each. The proprietor was a big, fat guy with glasses. He looked to be about forty. After I told him I wanted to swap some comics he asked me how much I had.

"Sixpence," I said, putting it and six comics on the counter.

He flicked through the comics checking to see if they were in acceptable condition. Satisfied, he took from under the counter a large bundle of comics that I estimated to be about one hundred, and placed them in front of me. I eagerly began to go through the pile. What treasures might I find here?

"Read it … read it … read it … read it …" I went on in a reiterative chant until I found one I hadn't read. Putting it aside, I continued, "Read it … read it … read it … read it."

I went through half the pile before I found another one. Then the chant began again: "Read it … read it … read it … "

I was aware the fat guy was staring at me, a strange look on his face.

When I exhausted the pile without finding another unread gem, I gave him a smile, displaying my new temporary fillings. "Could I have another bundle, please?"

I knew he had another three stacks under the counter. Without saying a word he reached under and produced another large pile. He dropped them on to the counter, none too gently.

"Thank you. Read it … read it … read it … read it …"

By the time I had chosen six comics, I was halfway through the fourth stack.

"You've read a lot of comics," he said.

"I've got more than you."

He was interested. "Do you want to sell them?"

Although I had no intention of parting with my treasured collection, I was curious as to their value. "How much would you pay?"

"A penny each."

"No thanks."

It was my first lesson in business principles. Business people can rip you off and it's called fair trade. The next time I visited the bookshop the proprietor told me he didn't have any comics.

"What about the ones under the counter?"

He gave me that strange look. "You've read them all, now piss off."

Early in 1955 we moved to a house in Lombard Street, Fairfield. In late March I began school at Fairfield High School. Already nearly two months behind the other boys, I had difficulties catching up in my studies due to my habit of taking numerous sickies and staying home. Mum would always write me a note. Later that year, the legislation was altered to allow hotels to remain open until 10.00 pm. As a result, Dad was coming home late and drunk on a lot of weeknights as well as weekends. One Sunday morning a neighbour, an Englishman, complained to Dad that he and his family had been offended by Dad's language the previous night. Sober, Dad apologised and said he couldn't remember a thing. A few nights later, drunk, Dad knocked on the Englishman's door and offered to fight him in a phone box.

The gentleman declined his offer.

5

Super Bunny

(1955-1982)

In late 1955, David and I went with Mum to Paddy's Markets and bought a puppy. He was a black and white mongrel with a playful nature. We named him Whisky. Some months later he was dead, killed by a tick.

I grieved for my little pal. Mum went to the markets and brought home another black and white pup. He was half fox terrier, half cocker spaniel. Without hesitation I named him Whisky. His cowardice became legendary in the Fairfield area. Other dogs knew a coward when they saw one, they were always chasing him. When he was fully grown, I saw dogs about half his size chasing him. It gave him a bit of a complex. To compensate for this he barked at nearly every person he saw but no one took any notice of him.

About six months after Mum had bought Whisky, a friend gave me a pet rabbit. Whisky was always sniffing around the rabbit cage, his chest puffed out, giving the occasional bark. But even the rabbit didn't seem too perturbed. Each day I'd let the rabbit out of the cage for a bit of exercise; the yard was fenced off so he couldn't escape. During the rabbit's exercise period, Whisky was leashed to his kennel. One day, while the rabbit was out, Whisky somehow slipped his collar off and began chasing the rabbit around the yard, with me in hot pursuit trying to catch Whisky. We had a trench in the yard for drainage. Across the trench was a wooden plank about 20 centimetres wide. The rabbit jumped on to the plank. Whisky came to an abrupt stop, looking at the rabbit, and then tentatively began to edge along the plank towards his prey. The rabbit had turned side on and seemed transfixed to the spot as it watched its relentless pursuer creep closer.

High noon had arrived. Whisky got to within about ten centimetres of the rabbit, then stopped. His chopped tail was stiff and erect as he puffed out his chest and gave an almighty bark. The rabbit replied by biting him on the chest. Whisky gave a startled yelp and fell into the trench in a state of shock. It was the ultimate disgrace. He crawled out of the trench a smelly, bedraggled, defeated dog. He never barked at the rabbit again.

Although he didn't see it, Dad often told the story, each time adding a bit here and there. The last time I heard him tell it, more than a quarter of a century later, the story had changed considerably. I had brought a friend of mine, Frank, around to Dad's flat in Waterloo to see him. At this stage of his life Dad, at 72, was confined to his flat; he had difficulty walking, a bad heart and took about 50 various pills a day to keep him alive. He loved nothing better than to reminisce about the good old days. If you came to his flat you were almost certain to be regaled with one of his stories.

After I had introduced Frank to him and we had chatted inanely for a few minutes, Dad said: "Tell Frank about the rabbit we had, Johnny."

I shook my head. "You tell him, Dad." I knew if I told it as it had happened without the embellishments, Dad wouldn't recognise it. He had reached a stage where, after he told them a few times, he believed his own stories. He looked at Frank, who considered himself to be a heavy in the Adelaide underworld. He was big and tough, but not overly endowed with intelligence. Dad sensed this; if Frank had looked smart, Dad probably would have modified the story a little.

Dad eased back into his chair. "We had this rabbit," he said, still staring at Frank. "It was a giant, twice the size of ordinary rabbits."

Frank looked across at me; I looked at the floor.

"Johnny had a dog that was terrified of the rabbit. The rabbit used to chase him around the yard, catch him and beat him up."

Frank was staring at Dad in disbelief, but Dad was accustomed to this when he told stories. It never discouraged him.

He went on: "We kept the rabbit in a cage, but one day he got mad about something and ripped his way out and raced down the street. Now there was this big German shepherd who lived a few doors down, a ferocious mongrel who had all the kids in the neighbourhood terrified. Well, he saw the rabbit and jumped straight over the fence after it." Dad paused for effect. He had set the stage for a big finale. He looked across at me. "You remember this don't you, Johnny?"

"I remember him beating up my dog," I said. I had to give him some support without looking ridiculous.

Dad smiled. "How could you forget it?" He turned to Frank again. "This rabbit was not only a killer, he was super cunning with it. He could have got away from the dog if he'd wanted to. But he had other plans. You know what he did?"

Frank shook his head. "What?"

"He waited until the German shepherd had almost caught up to him, then he stopped, rolled over on to his back and sprung up on to the dog's stomach, ripping him to pieces. It was all over in seconds, he ripped the dog's guts out."

Frank looked like he was choking on a boiled lolly. Dad held his gaze, defying him to say he was lying.

"The rabbit ran off into the Chinaman's cabbage patch," Dad said. He started to laugh. "This bloody Chinaman down the street was always chasing dogs out of his garden. Well, he was in for the shock of his life this day."

I stared at Dad. This Chinaman bit was a new one to me.

"The rabbit had gone crazy," Dad said, still looking at Frank. "He went berserk in the Chinaman's garden and ripped up 57 cabbages before the Chinaman ran out with his shotgun." Dad sighed. "The rabbit saw him coming, but he was fearless. He just continued to rip up the cabbages as the Chinaman pointed the shotgun at him … and do you know what?"

By now Frank was ready for anything. He stared at Dad, spellbound. "No, what?"

Dad hesitated, then looked across at me. I got the distinct impression that whatever it was he had been going to say, he thought better of it. He sighed again, and said: "He blasted the rabbit with both barrels."

I heaved a sigh of relief. Frank had braced himself for a different answer. A stupid look enveloped his face. He couldn't quite comprehend that the rabbit had met its end without putting up some sort of resistance. "Did he kill it?"

Dad pounced. "Of course he bloody killed it. It was only a rabbit, not a super bunny."

"Did the Chinaman sue you, Dad?" I cut in.

"He tried to, but he couldn't prove it was our rabbit. The bloke who owned the German shepherd came up to me and he was crying. He said, 'Your bloody rabbit just killed my dog. What are you going to do about it?' I told him he must be crazy, how could a rabbit kill a German shepherd? He threatened to go to the police and I told him, 'Do it. They'll think you're off your head. Your dog was a menace; it was only a matter of time before it hurt one of the kids around here. The rabbit did us all a favour.'"

When we left Dad's place, Frank said to me: "Was your old man having a go at me?"

"No," I said, "Dad told it the way he remembers it."

6

POPEYE, REDCRAZE AND TULLOCH
(1955-1958)

Although I was now a teenager my interest in comics hadn't diminished. Apart from the ordinary comics, I began collecting the *Classics Illustrated*. Later in life, when someone asked me if I'd read a certain classic, I'd often said yes, relying on my memory of the illustrated version. In 1955, a new series of *Popeye* comics were published. I had the entire collection until one month they skipped a number, I think it was number 15. I went to various newsagencies but no one could tell me what happened to the missing edition.

"Why don't you write to the publishers and complain?" one lady joked.

"I will", I said. And I did. I explained that by jumping from number 14 to 16 they had spoilt my collection. Where could I get a copy of number 15? They wrote back apologising, explaining that due to industrial action, number 15 hadn't been printed. But because I was a genuine *Popeye* fan, they would send me a year's subscription free of charge.

In 1974, *Man* magazine published a story I wrote called *Number One Power Puss*, based on the *Popeye* incident.

For me, 1956 was a memorable year. Apart from it being the year of the Melbourne Olympics, it was the year I took up tennis, became a gambler and overcame my asthmatic affliction. I also remember talk of a possible World War III over the farcical Suez Canal crisis, when Egypt nationalised the Canal. That incident saw the true decline of British power. It was also the year Soviet troops ruthlessly crushed the Hungarian uprising, killing more than 25,000. Hungary's attempts to break from the Warsaw Pact and become a neutral country had failed.

When I began playing tennis, two of the greatest players in history,

Ken Rosewall and Lew Hoad were both amateurs. On a few occasions I went to see them play exhibition matches. It was free admission. When they both turned professionals to play in Jack Kramer's troupe a lot of the kids in my tennis circle called them traitors.

"How will we win the Davis Cup now?" they lamented.

But we still had Ashley Cooper and Mal Anderson. Quickly followed by Neale Fraser, Rod Laver, Roy Emerson and Fred Stolle. Not long afterwards came John Newcombe and Tony Roche. It was an era of Australian tennis champions that no country has even come close to matching. One day in 1958 I watched an up-and-coming young redhead get on his knees to make a powerful smash. My friends and I were astonished at the speed and accuracy of the smash as the ball skidded off the sideline taking chalk.

"How could he do that on his knees?" I asked.

One of my friends shrugged. "A fluke shot."

It had been no fluke. We had just watched the Rockhampton Rocket, Rod Laver, future two-time Grand Slam winner and still acclaimed by many as the greatest player of all time. Naturally, we all tried to emulate the smash while on our knees without much success. Although I won trophies and tournaments and made it to A grade by the time I was 17, I knew I'd never be a champion. But I enjoyed tennis not only on a competition level, but also as a social outlet. At one stage I was playing competition tennis on Tuesday nights, Saturday and Sunday mornings and Saturday afternoons, and social tennis whenever I could manage it. After a few years the physical benefits of such a rigorous routine became apparent. From the thin, sickly child, I became a fit and athletic teenager.

My one regret was that neither Mum nor Dad would come to watch me play. Even though I often invited both of them to come and give me support during an important match, they always made excuses. I would have relished demonstrating to my parents that there was something I could do well. But neither of them had any interest in tennis. Mum, I feel, would have been embarrassed being a spectator; Dad dismissed it as a sissies' game, although he was pleased when I won the trophies.

In October 1956, I had my first bet. I was in my second year at Fairfield High School. The boy who sat next to me in class, Warwick, was already an inveterate horse bettor. He was a thin, freckled-faced kid, who wore glasses and who confided to me that sometimes he stole money from his mother's purse for betting.

"Betting on horses is a mug's game," I told him. "You can't win," was my smug advice, echoing Dad's words, who occasionally had a bet with the local SP bookie and usually lost. But in 1954 he had won a bit on *Rising Fast* in the Melbourne Cup. When it won, he told me: *"Rising Fast* is a champion. They can overcome tremendous odds to win, that's why they are champions."

Warwick fancied himself as a good distance runner. One Friday afternoon we decided to have a race, 20 times around Fairfield oval, about five miles (eight kilometres). Warwick wanted to bet on it. I was confident I could beat him. Since my asthma had ceased, running had become my forte. If I wasn't riding my bike, I was running everywhere. Playing tennis had also increased my stamina.

"All right," I said. "I'll bet you ten shillings I'll beat you."

That bet was to change my lifestyle. I trailed him for 19 laps then sprinted past him on the last lap, winning easily.

He was a bad loser. "Come to my place tomorrow and I'll pay you," he said and walked away.

The following afternoon, I went to his house. He was in the lounge room; the radio was on, the floor strewn with race guides. His parents were out.

"I had a few bets on the trots last night," he said. "The bookie owes me 18 shillings and I'll collect it after the races today. I'll pay you then, John."

I was worried he would lose it all and I wouldn't get paid. "Can't you go and see him and get it now?"

He shook his head. "I can't now. Don't worry, you'll get paid."

I knew that if he started losing he would bet the lot. "I might have a couple of bets myself," I said.

He stared at me. "Come on, who's the one who said you couldn't win?"

I smiled. "Give me a look at the race guide. There might be a champion running."

It was Caulfield Cup day, 1956. I read the form for the race. The top weight was a champion named *Redcraze*. He had to carry nine stone 13 pounds (63 kg) on a mud-drenched track. If he could win, it would be the highest weight ever carried to victory in a Caulfield Cup. The legendary *Rising Fast* had won the past two Cups and *Redcraze* had to carry more weight than *Rising Fast* had carried.

"He must be good!" I thought.

I told Warwick to put ten shillings to win on *Redcraze*.

He gave me a shocked look. "You'll lose your money. It's been raining all week in Melbourne. The track's a bog. He'll have to be *Phar Lap* to win with the weight he's got."

I'd won the money on a race and I was prepared to lose it the same way. "Champions can do anything," I said, promising myself that if *Redcraze* was beaten I'd never bet on a horse again. "Put it on the nose."

Warwick had no option but to put the bet on. When the race began, *Redcraze* dropped out to last. Halfway through the race he was still last. I cursed myself for being a fool. Then the champion made his run. I felt the adrenalin charge through me as the race caller shouted excitedly: "And here comes *Redcraze*."

He won by about four lengths! I was on an adrenalin-fuelled high. "What a horse! He's another *Rising Fast*."

Warwick, who had backed another horse, was scowling: "If it hadn't been a heavy track I would have backed him myself."

I collected more than £2. It was equivalent to two month's pocket money. My attitude to betting changed. I decided to have a few bets each week. Perhaps if I had lost immediately afterwards, I would have given it away, but I continued to win. It was an era of true champions and they captured my imagination: *Rising Fast*, *Redcraze*, *Sailor's Guide*, revered names even now; and a two-year-old colt trained by the legendary T J Smith which either ran first or second every time I backed him. He now ranks alongside *Phar Lap* as the greatest Australasian horse of all time, his name was *Tulloch*. I listened on the radio as another two-year-old colt named *Todman* won his first race by ten lengths in Australasian record time. He now rates as one of the greatest sprinters in Australasian history.

In the 1957 Caulfield Cup I reasoned champions had won the past three Caulfield Cups, why not a fourth? I backed *Tulloch*. Rushing from the tennis courts I rode to a pub in Fairfield to listen to the race, as there were no TABs in those days. Blocked for a run, *Tulloch* got out late and won by four lengths in Australasian record time! While other kids talked about Sputnik, the forerunner of satellite technology, which earlier that month the Russians had launched into orbit, I raved about Haley's Comet because a man named Haley owned *Tulloch*. To me, he was the greatest horse of all time. *Tulloch*, *Todman*, *Redcraze* and other top class gallopers, with their incredible performances, stirred my blood and set my pulse racing as nothing else could. Today, nearly sixty years later, I still thrill at the performances of champions in all sports. There's something about greatness that stirs the blood in all of us.

Although, from the time I was fourteen, gambling on horses became an integral part of my life, I was, until my early twenties, able to control it. On most Saturdays I would place a few bets with the SP bookmarker and then go play tennis, rarely hearing the races. I never bet beyond my means. The only chances I had to go to the races were during the off-season between winter and summer tennis competitions. Once, during the off-season, a group of us from the tennis club went to Warwick Farm races. One of the boys, Charlie D'Amore, a good tennis player, lost all his money. He was devastated.

"I'm never going to bet again," he declared.

He went on to become one of Sydney's leading bookmakers.

7
ENCOUNTER WITH POLICE
(1956-1957)

One day I said to Dad: "When I grow up, I'm going to become a policeman."

He glared at me: "Don't you ever step foot in this house again if you join the police force. No son of mine will be a copper."

I was shocked by his attitude and questioned it. He went on to tell me why cops were no good. They would arrest their own mothers, they took bribes, they bashed drunks, they arrested the poor and looked after the rich. Cops were no good. I declared then that, whatever else I became, I'd never be a cop. To my knowledge the only trouble Dad had with the police was at Fairfield one Saturday afternoon when I was fourteen. I was riding my bike home from the nearby tennis courts where I had been playing that afternoon, when I saw Dad come out of the hotel opposite the railway station. He began to stagger across the road towards the taxi rank. I could see that on a one-to-ten scale of drunkenness he was about a nine and a half. Before I could reach him, three uniformed cops who had been standing beside a paddy wagon nearby, rushed across and dragged him to the vehicle. Although he tried to offer some resistance, one of them punched him in the stomach and then they bundled him in to the back of the wagon.

Jumping off my bike I rushed over to them and shouted: "That's my father! Let him go!"

But they slammed the door and told me to shove off.

I heard Dad yelling: "Johnny! Go and get your mother. Tell her your old man has been kidnapped and bashed for nothing and she has to come bail me out."

I pedalled home as fast as I could.

When I told Mum what had happened she said, "Good, he can stay there. Looks like we're in for a peaceful night."

"But Mum," I protested, "I think they're going to bash him. I saw one of them hit him."

She was unperturbed. "They won't touch him anymore. Let him sleep it off for the night."

He never forgave her for leaving him there. Sometimes, when he was drunk, he would rave on and on about the time Mum left him in gaol to be bashed by the coppers when she could have bailed him out for two quid (four dollars). After witnessing the way the police manhandled Dad that day, I lost a lot of respect for them. About 15 months later, I lost all respect. A friend of mine, Bob, and I decided to go to Orange and pick cherries. It had been a snap decision, made one night on the way home from the movies. I'm not sure whether it was my idea or his. At the time both of us were 15 and the idea seemed exciting. On arrival we could ring Bob's parents to let them know we were okay, and they could tell my parents. After catching a train to Penrith, we trekked along the highway trying to hitch a ride. The first vehicle to stop was a police car. As it came alongside us, one of the two cops inside put his head out of the window. He looked tough.

"Where are you two going?"

"We're off to Orange," Bob said.

"Off to Orange, eh," the cop said. He sounded suspicious. "Where do you live?"

"Fairfield," Bob said.

"Then why are you going to Orange at one o'clock in the morning?"

"We only decided to go a few hours ago," Bob said. "We want to get a job picking cherries."

"Picking cherries, eh," the cop said, implying by his tone that he didn't believe it. "You'd both better get in the car and we'll talk about it at the station."

"I don't want to go to the station," I said. "We haven't done anything wrong."

The cop must have decided that we were dangerous criminals and about to run. He got out of the car. I noticed his hand on his gun.

"How much money have you got?" he asked.

"About six shillings," I said.

"Then I can charge you with vagrancy, you smart little cunt. Now both of you get in the back of the car."

He was menacing. We got in. At Penrith Police Station we were taken to separate rooms. The menacing cop was one of the two who questioned me. He was tall and solidly built, his rugged good looks spoilt by thick, cruel lips perpetually twisted into a sneer. When I stuck to my story he became aggressive. The other cop, thin and nondescript, played the nice guy. He told the tough cop to go easy on me. Then he would try to persuade me to tell the truth. When I wouldn't change my story, the other cop took over. He was certain I was running away from home because we had committed some type of crime. While I was sitting on a chair he grabbed me by the hair and shook my head from side to side until tears were running down my face.

"You little liar," he said. "Tell me the truth or I'll belt it out of you!"

"Better tell him the truth, John," the nice guy advised.

"I am telling the truth!" I shouted.

The tough cop continued to grip my hair. "I'm running out of patience with you."

The two cops who had been in the other room questioning Bob, came in. "Looks like they're clean," one of them said. "I've rung the other kid's father and he's coming to pick them up."

The bully cop looked disappointed. "I've got a feeling about this one," he said. Reluctantly, he released his grip on my hair. "If you ever try this caper again, wasting out valuable time, I'll personally put you in hospital. Understood?"

"Yes," I said. I was sure he meant it.

When Bob's father arrived, Dad was with him. As soon as we were outside Dad backhanded me hard across the face. Neither of us said a word. Bob's father said he thought it would be a good idea if Bob and I didn't see each other for a while. When we arrived home, Mum hugged me and started to cry. It made me realise how irresponsible and thoughtless I had been.

"Promise me you'll never run away again," she said.

I promised her I would never do anything like that again.

8
FIRST JOB, FIRST GIRLFRIEND
(1957-1959)

In 1957, my schoolwork deteriorated to the point where I regularly finished near the bottom of the class in most subjects, although, due to all the reading I did, I was always at the top of my class in English and spelling. I also had a natural flair for mathematics. But, overall, I was a poor student. Eventually, I failed my Intermediate Certificate exam. Without it employers were reluctant to employ school leavers, except in most menial of jobs. But I managed to get a job working behind the counter at Coles Variety Store in Auburn after I scored high marks in some type of test they gave me. Taking the job prevented my playing Saturday morning tennis but I had no choice. Working for a wage began a new era for me. I now considered my childhood days were gone.

Within a month of beginning work at Coles I made an appointment with an Auburn dentist. I still had numerous temporary fillings instead of permanent fillings. These began to fall apart, leaving my mouth full of rotting teeth. The dentist extracted all my remaining ten teeth from my top jaw and immediately inserted a full plate of false teeth. I went home by train and the next morning went to work. The dentist managed to save all my bottom teeth. I even had a gold-capped tooth in the front. Finally, I was able to smile at people without being self-conscious of displaying decaying teeth. It was a huge confidence booster for me.

In January 1958 I met Sonia, a beautiful, dark-haired girl of gentle nature. She worked at Winns, a department store next door to Coles. I had noticed her sometimes when she came into Coles to look around. One day she came up to where I was serving on the hardware counter and bought something. After chatting to her for a few moments I asked her to lunch and she accepted. It was my first date. We got along well and began to meet every day for lunch. Eventually she took me home to meet her parents, two sisters and a brother. Her mother, a lovely lady with premature white hair, always made me feel special.

Sonia wanted to meet my family but I always made excuses. How could I take her home to my dysfunctional family? I preferred to live the lie. I took her to movies, and once I brought her along to watch me play tennis. I hit the ball as hard as I had ever hit it, I scurried for every ball, focussed on every point: "Look at me!" was the message. But she was unimpressed. Tennis skills didn't interest her. She was a special girl and I knew it. She was also the marrying kind and I was too immature to maintain a steady relationship, let alone marriage.

In June 1958, I resigned from Coles, explaining to the perplexed manager that I needed to play Saturday morning tennis competition. This was the first major mistake of my life. I had no qualifications for another job. Coles had offered great career opportunities for me. Simply walking out so I could play tennis was an irresponsible act and I had no realistic plan for the future. But tennis hadn't been my only motivation for leaving Coles. At that stage I felt the need to distance myself from Sonia. We were meeting every work day in a little café before work, at lunchtime, after work and I was visiting her place regularly as well as taking her out. Combined with work and all the tennis, it was wearing me down.

Within weeks of my leaving Coles, Sonia and I split up. It was a mutual agreement. In July I started working for Wrenches, a dog biscuit factory in Lidcombe. With shift work and overtime I was earning about £13 a week, which was almost twice my wage at Coles. But the switching from night shift to morning shift then back to night shift made it difficult to have a social life. With overtime, I was working twelve-hour shifts and I was also secretly ashamed that I had been reduced to baking dog biscuits for a living. I endured it for eight months before resigning. Dad was furious. He made it clear that if I didn't find another job and pay my board, he didn't want me home. He wasn't going to support a bludger.

In 1957, Dad had been forced to give up his job with Yellow Express due to a slipped disc he had incurred while loading his truck. The injury became progressively worse. Although he had worked for the firm since 1938, they tried to force him out without a penny. But the union intervened. Dad took a job as a storeman/cleaner with Scottish Tailoring, a trendy men's wear shop in the city. The wages were poor, but Yellow Express had agreed, as part of the union negotiated compensation plan, to top up his wages to those he had earned as a truck driver. Although he hated the job and was plagued by increasing pain in his back, he stuck it out for nearly three years until he was forced to give up work completely. He spent the remainder of his life on workers' compensation. To a man like Dad, not being able to work was a cruel blow.

I started work at Arnotts in Homebush. I had progressed from dog biscuits to people biscuits. Most of the workers were women, some of them as rough as any man I'd met. I endured it for nearly two weeks before resigning. My next job was a clerical position with the New South Wales Railways. This time I lasted for nearly three weeks. I had to start as 6.00 am at Darling Harbour. It necessitated my getting up at 4.15 am, scoffing down a bowl of cereal and then riding my bike a few miles to the Fairfield railway station where I'd chain it to a post and catch a train for the 50 minutes journey to Town Hall station. From there I'd jog to the office at Darling Harbour. After a few weeks I began arriving late for work. When the boss complained, I resigned. During the next month I applied for numerous jobs without success. In 18 months I'd resigned from four jobs, the last three in quick succession. It didn't read well with future employers, especially as I didn't have an Intermediate Certificate. I refused to apply for a job in a factory.

"Never be afraid to get your hands dirty," Dad said. "Hard work never hurt anyone."

It was a policy he had lived by, but as far back as I could remember we had always been in debt. We had never owned a car or gone away for a holiday. All our clothes were second hand and neither David nor I ever had a school uniform. We could rarely afford to go to the dentist. We always owed the local shopkeeper money. Sometimes debt collectors would come knocking on our door and Mum would indicate for us to be quiet, pretending no one was at home. Once, a guy came around to the back door, which wasn't closed, and he stood there staring at us as Mum peeked through the front curtains. He belittled her, reducing her to tears.

The simple fact was she had no money to pay him. I concluded that you had to be more than a labourer to get anywhere. Dad had worked his guts out all his life and all he had to show for it was a crippled spine. Surely I could do better than that.

For a while I had aspirations of becoming a successful singer. In 1954, Bill Haley had burst onto the scene with his immortal hit *Rock Around the Clock* that sold over 20 million copies. The song also contributed to making the movie *Blackboard Jungle* a box office smash. Popular music underwent a dramatic change. Rock'n'roll began to dominate the airwaves. In 1956, Elvis Presley had replaced Haley as the number one rocker, but there soon followed a plethora of singers and groups who inspired imitators around the world. Australia had some of the best. In 1958, I went to a dance at Auburn where the dynamic Johnny O'Keefe was performing. When he was on stage he had magnetism about him that most other performers lacked. During the next 12 months I went to see a number of top Australian singers including Col Joye, Dig Richards, Lonnie Lee and soon to be internationally famous Frank Ifield. But O'Keefe was the one who impressed me most.

"I can do it, too," I thought.

I sang at a few tennis functions and received a lot of encouragement. But I was just one of hundreds of kids with the same aspirations, some of whom had more talent than I did. Very few were successful. Ten days before my 17th birthday, three of the biggest names in pop star history at the time were killed in a plane crash: Buddy Holly, Richie Valens and J P Richards (The Big Bopper). The tragedy motivated Don Maclean to write his classic *American Pie*, a mega hit a decade later. It was about this time that Sonia and I decided to give our relationship another try. She had been dating another boy, Ken, who also worked at Coles. One day I was in the same carriage with him on a train. He told me that he and Sonia had split.

"Any reason?" I asked, secretly pleased.

He shrugged. "I couldn't get anywhere with her."

The next day I called into Winns and she agreed to have lunch with me.

As we chatted during lunch I realised that I missed her. She seemed prettier than ever. "Too bad about you and Ken," I said.

She gave me an amused look. "How did you know?"

"Met him on a train. He told me."

"Did he tell you why?"

"Said you had too many boyfriends."

She laughed. "Not at the moment." She met my gaze. "What have you been up to?"

"Not much. I'm out of work."

"That's not good, John. You should never have left Coles. You were doing well there."

"Oh well, too late to worry about that. How about coming to Lidcombe Baths with me on Saturday afternoon?"

She didn't hesitate. "All right." She paused. "Any reason why you've chosen the baths?"

"I want to see you in a swimsuit."

She smiled. "You haven't changed."

I really did intend to meet her at the swimming pool. I was standing on the platform at Fairfield railway station waiting for the train to Lidcombe. I was reading the race guide, as there seemed to be a few good things running at Warwick Farm that day. Suddenly the train to Warwick Farm approached on the other side. I rushed out the gate up the stairs of the archway and ran down and jumped onto the moving train. The good things were beaten. I left the races penniless. On Monday I went to see Sonia and tried to explain what had happened.

"If you really cared about me, you would have been there," she said.

"It doesn't mean I don't care about you. I honestly thought the horses would win. It won't happen again."

"No, it won't. I met someone else. When you didn't come I accepted his invitation to go to the movies that night."

I was shocked. "He's a fast worker, isn't he? Who is he?"

"He's a butcher. He's asked me out again on Saturday."

And that was that! I heard she married the guy a few years later.

9

THE WORST DAY OF MY LIFE
(1959)

June arrived and I was still without a job. Desperate, I called in at Wrenches and asked the boss for my old job back. He said I had a hell of a nerve but, because I was a good worker, I could fill the next vacancy. When I returned home to give Mum the good news I found her sitting in the lounge room crying. Her sister, Zelma, had written to her predicting that it wouldn't be long before I left home and never returned. She cited the aborted trip to Orange the previous year to support her prophecy. She had never liked me and she despised Dad.

I realised with a shock that Mum didn't look well. I hugged her. "Don't take any notice of her, Mum. You know she's always trying to cause trouble."

"You're all I've got," she said, holding my hand and looking into my eyes, searching for reassurance. "Promise me you'll never leave me on my own."

It was a pathetic scene. At 43, she should have had more in life to look forward to. At the time I couldn't foresee what was coming. Although the signs were there, I was oblivious to them. I had no intention of leaving her on her own. Her mother was dead from cancer and her stepfather would have nothing to do with her because of Dad. I thought that by simply reassuring her that I loved her and would never leave her, she would regard the letter with the contempt it deserved. It was the second major mistake of my life.

About a week later, at about 2.00 am, on a cold June morning in 1959, I was awakened by a thump. Rolling over in bed, I tried to go to sleep again. But I could hear voices coming from Mum's bedroom. Some lights were on. Getting up, I went to see what had happened. Mum was lying on the floor at the side of her bed. Dad and David were kneeling beside her.

I hurried over to them. "What's wrong with Mum?"

Dad looked at me. He was white. "Get your bike and go ring Doctor Ferguson. Hurry. Tell him your mother's seriously ill and ask him to come straight away."

Grabbing some coins, I ran out to the shed, got on my bike and pedalled as fast as I could towards the nearest phone booth. The phone was broken, vandals had struck again. Swearing, I rode to another phone booth about 600 metres away. This one was working. I rang Doctor Ferguson's home number. His wife answered.

"I'm ringing for Mrs Killick," I said. "She's terribly sick and needs a doctor immediately. Could you ask Doctor Ferguson …"

She cut in. "Doctor Ferguson is asleep. You'll have to ring another doctor." She hung up.

I was stunned. In those days most doctors made house calls, and in an emergency, would come at any hour. I knew we owed Doctor Ferguson money, but this was an emergency. There was no phone book in the booth. I rang information. The woman who answered sounded half asleep. She was slow, but eventually she gave me the number for another doctor. When I told him the situation he said he would come immediately. Returning home I went to Mum's bedroom. Dad had lifted her onto the bed. She was still unconscious.

"Where have you been?" he asked, in an agitated manner. "Your mother's in a bad way."

I took Mum's hand and felt her pulse: it was faint, and slow. "A different doctor's coming," I said and explained why.

"Bloody Ferguson!" Dad slammed his right fist into his palm in frustration. "I'll bet he didn't come because your mother hadn't paid him for all the bloody pills he gave her."

When the doctor came, I could tell by his manner that my mother was critically ill. He drove off to order an ambulance.

It arrived within ten minutes. I kissed Mum on the cheek. "I love you, Mum," I said. Never had I meant it more than at that moment.

Dad and David went with the ambulance. I stayed at home. I knew my going to the hospital wouldn't help her. There was nothing I could do. She would either come through, or she wouldn't. Deep down, I feared she wouldn't, because I knew she didn't want to. All of us had let her down, but especially me. I should have done more for her. She had often told me I was her reason for living. Now she felt I wasn't worth it. I sat on the front steps and waited in the dark and the cold. I did my crying then. I cried for hours. It was after 7.00 am when Dad and David got out of a taxi in front of the house. Both of them were crying. Dad came through the gate and saw me.

"Be brave, Johnny."

I stared straight ahead, not looking at him. My mind was numb. I had stopped crying.

"We lost her!" Dad said. They walked past me, too preoccupied with their own grief to notice that I was sitting there emotionless.

I sat there for about another hour and then two detectives arrived. I went inside with them. They wouldn't tell me anything. They took Dad into the bedroom and spoke to him for a few minutes. Then they had a look around the house, took some empty pill bottles and left. The visit by police confirmed what I had suspected, that my mother had committed suicide. I confronted Dad with it, but he denied it.

"Your mother's heart gave out," he told me. He was still visibly upset. It was obvious that, in his own way, he had loved Mum.

I went into Mum's room. Her purse was sitting on the bedside table. I opened it, there was £12 ($24) in it. I put it in my pocket. I had never stolen anything before. This time it was different. I was 17, I had no other money, and I would soon be on my own. I knew she would want me to have it. I went to my room and packed a large suitcase with my clothing and few belongings. Dad asked me what I was doing.

"I'm leaving," I said.

He was shocked. "What do you mean you're leaving? Your mother has just died."

"I can't bear to live in this house any longer, Dad. I have to be on my own for a while."

He stared at me, shock replaced by anger. "If you walk out of this house, don't come back."

I picked up my suitcase. "All right," I said, and walked out the front door.

Dad followed to the door. "Don't go, Johnny. Don't leave your old man and the little fellow."

I kept walking. I didn't look back.

That terrible day I lost my mother, something within me died. Perhaps it was my childish belief that if you are good then everything will turn out all right. Although I was numb with the shock of my mother's death, I was terribly bitter that she, a good woman in every sense of the word, should die the way she had. Despite her excellence as a mother and a person, life had given her little. Now, at 43, she was dead. But the thing which was to gnaw at me for years, was my belief that if we had not been poor, perhaps even had a phone, my mother would have lived.

10

Arrest!
(June/July 1959)

The day my mother died, the boy John Killick died with her, leaving a bitter youth with a couldn't-give-a-damn attitude.

I booked into a boarding house in Burwood. Because it was cheaper I took a share room. My roommate was a big, well-built, blonde-haired guy of about 30 named Joe. For the first few days, although he seemed an amicable type, I made it clear that I wasn't interested in socialising, not even to the extent of polite conversation. I was in a confused state of shock and I tried to block out all thoughts of Mum. About 12 family and friends attended the funeral service. I was standing with Dad and David when Zelma and her husband, Tony, came over and began talking in a consolatory manner. Tony, a wiry, balding ex-serviceman, was wearing his uniform. I gave Zelma a look of contempt and began to walk away.

Tony grabbed me by the arm and said: "What's the matter with you, John?"

Jerking my arm free, I stared at him the pent up rage close to exploding. "Ask your wife," I said and walked away.

Before they closed the coffin I went over and, for the last time, gazed at my mother's face. Ineffable grief engulfed me as the realisation that my mother was gone forever penetrated the limbo type state of mind I had lived with since her death. I bent and kissed her on the forehead, then recoiled in shock. She was cold. No one had told me she would be like that. That last kiss is entrenched forever in my memory.

As they closed the coffin, Zelma, sobbing, flung herself on to it and cried out: "What have they done to you, my poor darling! What have they done?"

Tony pulled her away. This woman who had written the malicious letter was oblivious of the effect her unfounded accusations had had on my vulnerable mother. All of us had contributed to her despair and I couldn't blame anyone else. After leaving the cemetery, despite pleas from Dad to come home, I returned to Burwood. That night Joe propositioned me sexually. Shocked, I angrily rebuffed him and told him I'd ask for a room change the next morning.

He apologised three or four times. "It will never happen again," he said. "I totally misjudged you."

After that we got along okay. I was naïve about homosexuality and the fact that he was far from effeminate persuaded me that, due to my grief, I'd misinterpreted his intentions. Eventually he confided to me that he was ripping off social security and he was collecting the dole using six aliases.

My immediate reaction was that Dad would have hated this guy. "You're doing the wrong thing, Joe," I said. "You're robbing the working man." I was reiterating Dad's words.

Joe gave me a condescending smile. "The working man has got nothing to do with it," he said. "You'll learn soon enough that the government is run by clever crooks, it robs the poor to pay the rich. When you know enough about politics you'll understand what I'm talking about."

We didn't discuss it again. Money was a problem for me. From the time I had left Wrenches my attitude towards employment had been irresponsible. Now my prospects of securing a good job seemed bleak and I had no special talents. I had discarded my grandiose dreams of being a singer. I was bitter and incapable of applying myself to the twelve hours a day shift work I knew would be required of me if I returned to Wrenches. I pawned my watch and tennis racquet, postponing the inevitable for a few days. Crime was on my mind and I knew I was on the verge of becoming a criminal. I thought of my mother and searched my soul for the reins of moral restraint, but nothing was there. My mother was dead and it was me against the world.

Joe considered himself to be my mentor. He often gave me advice: "If you can rip off the system, do it before it rips you off."

No one had ever spoken to me in that way before. I decided that instead of ripping off the system, I'd rip off my mentor. I'd be robbing a robber rather than a friend. At least that was the way I justified it to myself. Looking back, more than half a century later, I can't blame my dysfunctional background for my criminality. I found it too easy to cross the line. Until then, the criminality had lain dormant inside me, but like a cancer, it was there. A bad gene, perhaps? Joe was going to Brisbane for the weightlifting championships. He would be gone for two weeks. On the eve of his departure I asked him to be my guarantor for a new tennis racquet I wanted to buy on terms.

Although he agreed to do it, he gave me a lecture about buying things on credit. "It only leads to trouble," he said.

I told him I didn't have an application form but if he gave me a specimen signature I would trace over it.

He gave me a questioning look, then shrugged. "Okay, I can't see any harm in it. If there are any queries about it, I can always say I signed it."

The next afternoon I helped him pack, taking note of which suitcase he put his bank books in. When he went downstairs to ring for a taxi I opened the suitcase and took the bank book with his correct name on it. After he had gone I checked the balance. He had £80. At the time the average weekly wage was less than £20. I immediately moved out of Burwood and rented a single room in a similar type of residence in Strathfield. It took dozens of attempts before I was satisfied with my efforts to forge Joe's signature.

When I entered the bank at Burwood my heart was pounding. My mother had been dead for a month and I was about to become a criminal. As I handed the teller the passbook my hand was unsteady. Without giving me a second glance, he checked the signature then gave me the money. In high spirits I returned to the rooming house. The lady in charge, a thin, beak-nosed woman of about forty, gave me a hard stare as I walked up the stairs. It concerned me a bit. I was already beginning to acquire an instinct for danger, an instinct that, in later years, would develop to an almost animal level.

About ten minutes later the cops arrived and arrested me. I later learned that while I had gone to make the withdrawal the lady had gone snooping around in my room and found the discarded withdrawal slips in the wastebasket. She had immediately rung the police. They told her to ring them when I returned, which she had promptly done. I was taken to Burwood Police Station where I made a statement admitting the crime. A cop asked me if I had someone who would bail me out. I told him I had no one.

"What about your father?" he asked.

"He won't bail me," I said adamantly. I had no idea whether Dad would bail me or not but I had made the decision to go it alone because I couldn't come crawling back as soon as things went wrong.

About an hour later I was taken to the Albion Street Boys' Remand Centre. I can't remember much about the juvenile gaol. When I arrived it was almost dinner time. Meals were served in a large room with lots of tables and chairs. The boys on my table were younger and smaller than me. I was surprised to find that I was one of the biggest kids in the place as anyone 18 or over was sent to prison. Later we were taken about six at a time to the shower room where we were ordered to strip and shower while the guards watched. One of the boys told me this supervision was to prevent some of the bigger boys raping the smaller ones. At the time I thought he was kidding. I was a bit embarrassed about having to strip naked and shower with others, but I had no choice and I did as I was told. Not long after everyone had finished showering and we were all dressed in pyjamas, we were ordered to bed. My bed was in the middle of a row of about 20 beds in a dormitory. I was tired and thought I'd go to sleep immediately the lights were out, instead I was overcome by depression and I began to cry into my pillow. I cried for my mother and all the things that could have been. I felt totally alone in the world. It was hours before I slept. At about 6.00 am I was woken by the sound of loud bells ringing and guards yelling at us to get up and make our beds. After breakfast I was put on work duty. Cold and miserable I sat in a corner and, for the first time in my life, peeled potatoes. I had been at it for about an hour when I was called to the office.

Dad and David were there.

"G'day, Johnny," Dad said. "I've come to take you home."

Stunned, I could only say: "Thanks, Dad."

On the way home Dad explained that the police had called on him the previous night and told him where I was. By then it had been too late to bail me out.

"What was it like in gaol, John?" David asked.

"Boring," I said, trying to give the impression that it hadn't bothered me.

"Make sure you keep your nose clean after this," Dad said.

It was a much milder rebuke than I had expected. It was late July, a Saturday at the end of the 1958/59 racing season. The legendary Billy 'Last Race' Cook who had made a habit of winning the last race, retired and unable to win his last race.

As soon as we arrived home I was overcome with the pervading presence of Mum. I knew immediately I couldn't live there. I tried to explain my feelings to Dad but it was hard for him to understand. Tempers became frayed and we had a heated discussion about it. The underlying unstated fact was that we didn't like each other. He was making a belated effort to be a good father but it was far too late. A few days later I moved out, renting a room with an Italian family in Guildford.

For the forgery, technically my first bank robbery, I was placed on a 12 months good behaviour bond.

11

BEATING THE BOOKIE
(August/September 1959)

I took a job machine cutting lawn mower axles in a factory at Surry Hills. While there I met Jim who was the same age as me. He had come down from Orange to try his luck in the big city. Three days after I had started, the factory burnt down. Jim suggested we each put in a claim for £50 for clothes we had left in our lockers.

"I didn't leave any clothes in my locker," I said.

"But they don't know that, do they?" he said.

He had a point. I asked for £20 and promptly received it. Jim went for £50 and had hassles; he eventually settled for £20. Jim had a bit of resemblance to the film star, James Dean, who had died in a car crash in 1955. Jim took advantage of the resemblance in his constant pursuit of girls. Sometimes he would stop a girl in the street and ask her for a date. More often than not, the girl would accept. After the factory burnt down, I teamed up with him. His hedonistic lifestyle intrigued me. We spent our days going to town, checking out the milk bars and fun parlours with the sole purpose of picking up girls. With the irrepressible Jim making the overtures we often succeeded.

Money was our big problem. Sometimes we would go to a café, order a meal and run off without paying. One night in Burwood, a big, angry Greek café owner chased us and caught Jim. When I heard Jim screaming I stopped and looked behind me. The guy gave Jim a couple of whacks and took his pullover off him. After that, Jim wasn't game to try it again.

In those days security in the big department stores was slack. We decided to try our hands at shoplifting. We took turns at walking into a store, picking up a piece of merchandise, usually an item of clothing, and walking out with it. Then we would go to various hotels and sell the goods, with the price tags still attached and ask for about a third of the retail price. It annoyed me to part with our stolen property so cheaply. Despite Jim and I being the ones risking our freedom, these beer-swilling knockabouts who bought the merchandise were profiting more than we were. I had an idea. Why couldn't we take the stolen items back to the store and get a refund?

"You need a cash receipt docket to get a refund," Jim said.

But I had figured a way around it. To test the plan we chose the majestic Anthony Hordens. The building had eight or nine levels and, at the time, was the largest department store in the Southern Hemisphere. I went to the sporting goods department and bought a tennis racquet for about £5 ($10). I paid the lady cashier in silver. "I had to raid my piggy bank," I said, giving her an embarrassed grin.

"It's all money," she said.

Outside, I gave Jim the docket. He went inside, picked up a racquet and walked out. If someone challenged him he had the docket to prove ownership.

Later, I returned to the store with one of the racquets and took it to the lady cashier. "I raided my piggy bank for nothing," I said. "Dad had already bought me a new racquet."

She smiled. "Aren't you the lucky one? I'll get you a refund. Do you have your docket there?"

"Oh, sorry. I don't know what I did with it."

"That's okay. I remember you."

She gave me a refund with a smile. The next day, during the lady's lunchtime break, Jim returned the other racquet with the official docket to a different cashier. We used the same trick in other stores. One day we got refunds from three different departments at Anthony Hordens. For nearly two weeks we had a charmed run, making good money. We also bought items on credit using false names. Apparently they didn't bother checking the bogus information we supplied. Eventually the stores' personnel woke up to what we were doing and they put out a red alert on us. It culminated with me bursting out of Mark Foys, now the Downing Centre Court Complex, with an overweight store detective chasing me until he stopped, clutching his chest. That was the end of our shoplifting days.

One Friday night we decided to rob an SP bookmaker who operated a few streets from where Jim rented a room in Newtown. Our logic was sound. We figured that the bookie, being an illegal operator, wouldn't report a robbery to the police. We had been there a few times. The bookie conducted business from a shed in an enclosed backyard of a house. The only way in or out for punters was via the back gate, which was situated halfway up a long lane. Jim and I walked in about two minutes before the starting time of the last race. We mingled with about 15 punters who were crowded around a loudspeaker in the far corner.

When the race caller on the radio said: "There's only one to come into line and they'll be ready to go," I rushed over to the guy taking the bets and waved a ten shilling note at him.

"Ten bob on the favourite!" I shouted.

The announcer said the words everyone was waiting for: "He hits the lever and they're racing in the last."

"Get on earlier next time," the bookie growled, grabbing my money and writing down the bet.

I glanced around, hesitating. The punters were preoccupied with listening to the race. The bookie had stacks of money laid out in front of him. Behind him stood a huge moronic type of guy, obviously a protector. With my arms moving like pistons I snatched two bundles of money, the fives and tens, and spun around and dashed towards the gateway. It was closed. Jim, whose job it had been to open the gate for me, had panicked and gone without me.

"Quick! Stop the bastard!" shouted the shocked bookie as I fumbled with the lock, opened the gate and leapt out just evading a punter who made a desperate lunge at me. I could hear shouts of abuse and outrage as I ran down the lane clutching the money.

I glanced over my shoulder; there was a small army of punters chasing me! At the time Newtown was one of the toughest areas in Sydney.

"If they catch me, they'll kick me to death," I thought, running as fast as I had ever ran in my life.

I turned the corner and I saw Jim jogging ahead of me about 30 metres away. "This way, mate!" he yelled.

I could still hear the chasers behind me. I risked another look over my shoulder and two guys were only about five metres behind me.

"Stupid idiots," I thought. "They should be on my side for robbing a bookie."

After another few hundred metres they gave up. "We'll get you, you bastard!" one of them yelled.

I gave them the thumbs up sign. "Mug punters! I got yours!"

Jogging, I caught up to Jim.

"Good on you, mate!" he said. "I knew they couldn't catch you. Come on, let's go to my place."

"You nearly got me killed," I gasped, out of breath.

"Sorry, mate. But when you didn't grab the money straight away I didn't think you were going to do it. I looked too suspicious standing near the gate on my own, the big bloke was staring at me."

"I don't see why I should split the money with you," I said.

"Mate! If they'd caught you, I would've been in like Flynn to help. But there's no one in Sydney who could catch you. I knew that."

"I had to get out the bloody gate," I said.

But I found it impossible to remain irate with him, as we had been partners in crime for a while now. I still felt guilty over his thumping by the Greek café owner. If I'd have stayed close the two of us could have overpowered him. Jim wasn't a fast runner. Our ill-gotten gain totalled more than £200, which I shared with Jim.

I had no remorse about the robbery. The way I saw it, bookies were legitimate targets.

12

Lucky to be Alive
(September/November 1959)

A few days after the bookie robbery, Jim flush with money returned to Orange. He tried to persuade me to go with him, claiming all the young guys go to the city, resulting in girls outnumbering guys by four to one. But at the time I wasn't interested. I wanted to take up competition tennis again.

I began dating an attractive Austrian girl named Lilo. Although she didn't play tennis, she often came along to watch me play. Ironically, the short break from tennis proved to be a positive thing. I was now playing the best tennis of my life. In a competition match I beat one of the best players in Fairfield 6-2. In October my appendix burst. By the time I got to St Vincent's Hospital I was in a bad way. The doctor told me the poison was in my system and they would have to operate immediately.

"How old are you?" he asked.

"Seventeen."

He gave me a concerned look. "We can't operate on anyone under 18 without their parents' written consent. Where can we contact your parents?"

"My mother's dead. My father lives at Fairfield but he's not on the phone."

"Is there anyone we can ring to let him know?" I sensed the urgency in his voice as he went on: "And give me his address so we can send the police around."

The police! The realisation that I could die frightened me. Until now I had, with the illogical confidence of youth, always regarded myself as invincible.

"What sort of law have we got when you're going to let me die because my father is 20 miles away! What's the difference if I'm 17 or 18!"

He knew I was right. It upset him. "I'm not going to let you die, you little fool! Now will you give me the information I need to save your life?"

I still remember the number I gave him that probably saved my life: UB2119. At the time letters prefixed phone numbers. It was the phone number of Sandra Sparkes, one of my tennis teammates. I also gave him Dad's address.

A short time later a nurse gave me a needle. "This will stop the pain," she said.

I felt myself drifting off into unconsciousness, a dark void was enveloping me. Far off into the distance I could see bright light and my mother, dressed in white, was floating towards me softly calling my name. I knew she wanted me to join her.

My last thought before I fell into the black void, was: "No! I don't want to die!"

When I regained consciousness I was lying in bed in a hospital ward. I had an intravenous drip inserted in my left arm and a drainage tube in my stomach. My mind was hazy. I remembered that I had to play in a tennis semi-final on Saturday afternoon! I struggled to get out of bed.

"What are you doing, mate?" the guy in the bed next to me asked.

"I have to go play a tennis semi-final," I said. "What time is it?"

He got out of bed and grabbed me as I tried to stand up. I had torn the drip out of my arm and the tube from my stomach.

"Hey, you'd better get back into bed, mate. You're pretty sick."

One of the other patients began to yell for a nurse. A young, plump nurse rushed in, pushed me back into bed and re-inserted the drip and tube.

"You're a naughty boy," she admonished. "Where did you think you were going?"

The guy who grabbed me laughed. "He said he had to go and play tennis."

The nurse smiled. "You won't be playing tennis for a while. You're lucky to be alive. It's amazing you were able to get out of bed."

"What time is it?" I asked.

"It's ten past eleven, Monday morning."

Monday! I had been unconscious for nearly 48 hours! Later that day a doctor came to examine me. He told me that by the time I had been brought into the operating theatre my appendix had been burst for many hours. The poison had penetrated my entire system and it was a miracle I had been able to survive. He asked me if I played a lot of sport.

"Only tennis," I said. "But I play a lot."

"Well, your fitness probably saved your life."

His words had a lifetime effect on me. Until that time fitness hadn't been something I had strived for as it had come as a natural result of playing a lot of tennis, riding a bike and often running instead of walking. But from the moment that doctor told me that fitness had saved my life, I have, without being fanatical, made the effort to maintain a reasonable level of fitness no matter where I am. On the Tuesday I was allowed visitors. Dad came with Lilo. She told me she had driven the staff crazy ringing up to enquire about how I was progressing.

"They said you only had a 50-50 chance of surviving," she said, looking at me with soft brown eyes that were close to tears.

"She really does care about me," I thought. She looked beautiful and I wondered why I wasn't in love with her.

"You're lucky to be alive, Johnny," Dad said. "The coppers and half the kids in Fairfield were racing around trying to find me. I was in Britains when they rushed in and said: 'Mr Killick, Johnny's in hospital and they need you to sign the papers before they can operate.' Your old man didn't ask any questions, I didn't even finish my schooner. I rushed straight out and got into a copper's car they had waiting."

He began to laugh as Lilo, a few patients and I and their visitors stared at him. He was talking loudly, reliving the event. "You should have seen the look on the copper's face when I said to him: 'What's wrong, Flatfoot, you frightened of getting booked? Put your foot on the bloody pedal and if you get pinched by one of your mates, I'll pay the fine'. He went red as a tomato and revved it to the floor, the sirens blaring. But by the time we got here you were nearly dead. I abused the doctors. If I hadn't arrived when I did you'd be dead now, all because of their stupid red tape."

Eleven years later in a case similar to mine (*Younts v St Francis Hospital and School of Nursing, 1970*), the Court ruled that a minor who receives an explanation of the procedures and risks and who is capable of making an intelligent decision can give his/her own consent, especially in an emergency, when waiting for a parent's consent could endanger his/her life, limb or function.

That night a few of my teammates, including Sandra Sparkes, came to see me. She told me that when she had relayed the news of the crisis to a lot of the teams, they immediately postponed their matches and set out to find Dad. Hearing this, I felt humble. Despite some of the stories that I knew had been circulating about me throughout the Fairfield tennis circles since the forged bank book incident, my friends had stuck by me. During the time I spent in hospital, I received numerous visits. They kept me there for six weeks. While I was there the dynamic radio personality, Jack Davey, was admitted to a private ward. He had cancer. He was a legend in the radio world and the nurses often talked about him. Apparently, as sick as he was, he was always wisecracking with them and making them laugh. I had always been a fan of his and his programme *Give it a Go* had been one of my favourites.

One day one of the nurses came to me. She had been crying. "Jack Davey has just died," she said.

"Gee, I'm sorry to hear that."

"He was only forty nine," she said, "but he looked so old at the end."

A few hours later on the other side of the world in Vancouver another Aussie legend, the film star Errol Flynn, died. He was only a few months older than Davey. Davey's funeral was one of the largest ever in Sydney. He made me aware of the adulation, even in death, a true celebrity commands from the multitude. A week after Davey died, the NSW Premier, Joe Cahill, died. He was 68. Another state funeral was held. I thanked God that I had somehow survived. I doubted Dad could afford to bury me.

The day I was discharged from hospital an old nun called to me as I was leaving. "Excuse me," she said, "but it's customary to pay at least half the bill before you leave."

I was stunned. I had always assumed that hospitals were free. "I'm sorry," I said, embarrassed. "I don't have any money at the moment."

She stared at me for a few moments, then said: "What about your parents? Will they pay?"

I shrugged. "Mum's dead. I doubt if Dad would have it. How much is it?"

She mentioned some three-figured amount. I decided to be truthful with her. "Sister, you people have been good to me. You saved my life. But I have no money. All I can do is give you my word that if I get the money I'll bring it to you personally."

She regarded me with eyes that would be impossible to deceive. Then she nodded. "All right, young man. I believe you will try to meet your commitment. I suppose we can't ask for more than that. Even if you can't come by all of it, send us what you can. I'll keep my eye on your account from time to time and see what efforts you are making." She held out her hand. "Be careful. You aren't entirely healed yet."

I took her hand. "Thank you, sister. Don't worry, I'll get the money for you." She was a nice old lady; I was determined to get the money for her somehow.

13

MELBOURNE AND BACK
(November/December 1959)

The day I was discharged from hospital I returned home to live with Dad and David. Although memories of Mum still pervaded every room, the five months since her death had blunted the intensity of my feelings. Dad tried hard to establish a normal father and son relationship but, at that stage of my life, I found it difficult to live in the same house with him particularly as he was now boozing nearly every day.

"As soon as you are well enough, go and get a job," he said. "It doesn't matter if you have to cart shit, it's a job. Without a job a man is nothing."

The fact that his working days were behind him was gnawing away at him. Although I didn't say it, I felt I'd rather be dead than to finish up like him. To my surprise he told me to apply for the dole. He said that, until I could work, I was entitled to it. Although it was only about £2 a week, it would help. A friend confided to me that Lilo had been dating a guy named Colin who was 21. When I confronted her about it, she admitted it, but assured me it wasn't serious. Nevertheless, we had a heated argument. She took off the friendship ring I had given her and handed it to me. Angrily, I threw it in the grass. Upset, she stormed off. That was the last time I saw her. The following Friday night I went to watch some of my friends play social tennis. After a while I became depressed at having to be a spectator rather than a participant. I felt out of place, particularly when a few of them remarked on how much weight I had lost.

"Don't worry," I said. "I'll soon be back winning tournaments."

But that animal instinct, which I was beginning to develop, told me that my days as a competition player were over. I decided that I'd had enough of Lilo, Dad, tennis and, in fact, Sydney. It was time to travel. I would give Melbourne a try. Full of confidence I went to Randwick races. My luck was in and I won more than £20. I didn't hesitate. I went to Central railway station and bought a ticket to Melbourne for travel the next day.

When I told Dad, who was slightly drunk, he ordered me to pack my bags and get out. "From now on it's me and the little fella against the world," he declared.

I walked over to the little fella (David) who, at fourteen, was nearly as tall as me. "I'll be back, Dave. When I get a nice place of my own you can come and live with me."

"He'll stay with his old man," Dad yelled. "The only place you'll have of your own is a cell."

It was an accurate assessment of my future.

That night I slept on Burwood railway station. Sunday night I was on the train to Melbourne arriving at Spencer Street railway station at about 9.30 am. Although I had little money and no friends in Melbourne, I was excited at being in another city for the first time. Melbourne, the home of the Melbourne Cup and, only three years ago, the Olympic Games. For a while I walked around, savouring the new sights. Suddenly a shortish guy of about 40, dressed in a suit and a hat, came alongside me and said: "I'll bet you're from Sydney."

I frowned. "That's right. How did you know?"

He smiled, displaying perfect teeth. He stank of perfume. "Sydney boys have a way about them, the way they walk and talk." He paused. "Wow, look at her, isn't she something?" He indicated a pretty girl walking past.

"She's okay."

"Okay? I'll bet you'd like to give her a bit, wouldn't you?"

Ignoring him, I began to walk on. This guy gave me the creeps.

He walked beside me. "A good-looking boy like you, I'll bet you could give her plenty, too. How many inches could you give her?"

I stopped and glared at him. "Piss off you poofter, before I smash your teeth down your throat."

He scurried off like a rat. Thinking about it, I concluded that he had probably followed me from the railway station. I had heard about perverts like him who wait around the interstate train stations and bus depots, preying on lonely kids who were new to the city.

I rented a cheap room in Albert Park, opposite a park and some tennis courts. After a few days I managed to get a job in a milk bar in town. Already I was feeling homesick. I missed Lilo and the Fairfield tennis scene. I was so lonely that often, after I had finished work, I would stay in town and go to a movie. Afterwards, instead of catching the train, I'd jog home trying to get back into condition. I began dating a pretty blonde, blue-eyed girl named Jutta. She was also Austrian. Incredible odds: my Sydney girlfriend, Lilo, and my Melbourne girlfriend, Jutta, both Austrian born. Jutta was 15. When the school holidays began I took a day off work and spent most of the day at her place listening to records while her parents were at work. Both of us were Elvis fans but she was almost fanatical about him. She had an extensive collection of most of his LP albums. When I took a second day off work the boss sacked me. It was a new experience for me, usually I resigned from jobs. I had a back-up plan. I would sell raffle tickets. At school when they held fund-raising raffles I had always been one of the top sellers.

I bought two books of raffle tickets and a toy printing set. After making a rubber stamp with the words 'Box Hill Judo Club' embossed on it, I stamped each ticket and caught a train on the Box Hill line. Getting off a few stations before Box Hill I went from door to door selling the tickets for a shilling each or three for two shillings. The non-existent prize was a transistor radio. Commercially, transistor radios were relatively new to Australia and a lot of people bought a ticket or tickets in the hope of winning one. When someone asked me about the Judo Club, I replied: "We've just started it up and we're raising money for equipment."

I sold all the tickets and collected about £8, only £2 less than I had been earning weekly at the milk bar. I had again crossed the line into criminality but reasoned that a shilling or two wouldn't break anyone.

While waiting for the train I began talking to the railway attendant, a tall, thin, sallow-faced guy of about 23. Inviting me into his office for a coffee he complained that he had the world's most boring job. As we sat sipping our coffees I noticed the cash drawer was full of money. My mind began to race. I'd have to sell a lot of raffle tickets to get that amount of money. This guy wasn't too bright; maybe I could get the money. A few minutes before the train was due I said: "I could probably get you a job working with me. I make at least £8 a day." I showed him the money I had. "This is my day's pay."

He stared at me, open-mouthed. "Eight pound a day! Gee, that's big money. What do you do?"

I could hear the train coming. I walked over to the electric jug. "I'll make us another cup of coffee while you collect the tickets. I'll tell you all about it when you get back."

He hesitated, and then hurried to the door. "I'd appreciate it, mate. I won't be long." He went outside, leaving the door open.

Rushing over to the cash drawer I grabbed all the notes and stuffed them into my pockets before walking out. Only a few people had got off the train. The ticket collector immediately saw me.

I walked up to him "We've got time before the next train. Let's get something to eat, I'm starved."

He nodded. "I'll close the door first."

"Oh, I forgot to turn the jug off," I said as he hurried towards the door.

"I'll do it," he yelled.

As soon as he had gone inside I ran from the station and down the street as fast as I could. Although I was nowhere near peak fitness, I figured I had enough start to elude him if he came after me. When I reached the corner, I looked back. He wasn't in sight. I figured he was probably ringing the police. I took off my black pullover and threw it away. I jogged for about a mile before catching a taxi into town where I went to a hotel and counted the money in the toilet. About £90. Not as much as I had thought but a nice Christmas present. I had a pang of conscience as to how the ticket collector would account for the loss, but I quickly dispelled it. From the day Mum had died I resolved to stand by my friends and not give a damn about anyone else. I mailed £30 to St Vincent's Hospital. I included a note explaining that it was part payment of my debt. At least the old nun would be pleased. No need for her to know I was a thief.

During the Christmas period Jutta and her parents went to Apollo Bay for a week. On my own, I became depressed and homesick. On Christmas Day I watched some guys playing tennis on the courts opposite my place. They were good players. After a while I walked away, more depressed than ever. If it hadn't been for Jutta I would have caught a train to Sydney that day. I did catch a train the next day: to the races. I didn't back a winner. That night I couldn't afford a meal. A few books of raffle tickets would solve my problem but after robbing the railway I had thrown away the toy printing set. Jutta had loaned me her record player and six LPs, but the pawnshops were closed for the holidays. My best bet was to sell a few of the records, buy the printing set, sell some tickets and buy some new records. I went to a local hotel where I soon found a buyer for a couple of Elvis LPs. A few hours later I was in the Caulfield area selling raffle tickets for the 'Caulfield Judo Club.' By the time I had sold the last ticket it was getting dark.

I had a nice meal in a café in Albert Park. After leaving the café I was walking past a hotel when I heard someone shout: "That's him!"

There, in the doorway of the hotel, stood the ticket collector. He was pointing towards me. I figured it had to be fate playing a hand in my destiny. I started running up the street. Taking a quick glance over my shoulder I saw the ticket collector and four or five of his mates running in my direction. Concerned that I might not be fit enough to elude them I ran as fast as I could. After a few blocks, gasping for breath, I looked around, they had all given up and I was on the verge of collapse. I immediately decided to return to Sydney. It was a safe bet that from that point on the ticket collector and his mates would be watching out for me in the Albert Park area. The next morning I left Jutta's record player and few remaining LPs with one of her neighbours. I asked the neighbour to tell her that I had returned to Sydney for an emergency and would send her a letter when I arrived. On the train to Sydney I became friends with two girls who invited me to a New Year's Eve party at Strathfield. I assured them that I would be there.

Booking into the People's Palace in Pitt Street I spent the last two days of the year selling raffle tickets for the 'Croydon Judo Club.'

Although I went to the New Year's Eve party, I soon became bored with it. I had a strong sense of urgency to go to Dad's place and see the New Year in with him and David. I rushed out and ran to Strathfield Station. I had to wait a while before I caught a train, arriving at Fairfield at ten to twelve. I ran the mile to Dad's place; the lights were still on. I knocked on the door; Dad opened it.

It was a minute to midnight. "Hi, Dad. I wanted to see in the New Year with you and David."

He shook my hand. He wasn't drunk. "Blood's thicker than water," he said. "Come in and have a drink with your family."

David came up and gave me a hug. As we toasted the New Year in, Dad and I had tears in our eyes. Although Mum had only been dead for six months, so much had happened that none of us would ever be the same again. Some years are more important in our lives than others, and for the three of us, 1959 had been a momentous year. Mum had died, I nearly died and I had left home and became a criminal. Looking back, the overpowering urge that caused me to rush home proved to be uncanny. It was to be the last time the three of us would spend a New Year's Eve together.

14

ARMED ROBBERY
(January 1960)

In 1960, the world population passed three billion. John F. Kennedy was elected President of the United States. In January, the mighty *Tulloch* made his long-awaited return to racing. The memory of that race still stirs my blood. *Tulloch* hadn't raced for nearly two years due to a severe attack of colic that nearly killed him.

His comeback race was the Queen's Plate at Flemington, a 10-furlong (2000 metres) weight-for-age contest between the best horses in Australia. The favourite was the Melbourne champion, *Lord*.

"*Tulloch* can't win," said experts. He started at the incredible odds of 4/1.

The two champions drew clear of the field at the top of the long, gruelling, straight that had broken the spirit of many Melbourne Cup aspirants. *Tulloch* … *Lord* … locked together, stride for stride all the way down the straight. Surely *Tulloch*'s condition would give out? *Lord* put his head in front but the smaller *Tulloch* somehow came again. They went over the line locked together. "*Tulloch* by a head!" screamed the course announcer and Flemington erupted as it had in 1930 when the great *Phar Lap* won the Melbourne Cup.

For the first few weeks of the year I sold raffle tickets every day, averaging about £50 a week. Tax free, it was good money in 1960. Renting a room in Parramatta, I stocked up on new clothes and shoes. Enclosing £5 I sent an apologetic letter to Jutta, assuring her she was still my favourite Austrian girl. But she returned the money, explaining that her father insisted on it. She didn't want to see me again, adding that she couldn't love anyone who could steal someone else's Elvis records. About mid January, fate again played a hand in my life; I ran into Jim at

Town Hall. He was unshaven and looked haggard. He was broke but he had a surprise for me: he showed me a small, black automatic pistol he'd had concealed inside his jacket. "It's only a replica," he said. "But it's hard to tell the difference."

I was impressed. "Where did you get it?"

He grinned. "I knew you'd want one. It's not far from here, but it'll cost you four quid."

"That's not a problem."

I went with him to a gun shop in George Street and bought a brand new replica, identical to the one Jim had. The salesman took my money, wrapped up the replica and handed it to me without a word.

"You'll have to wear a sports coat or a suit when you carry it," Jim said as we walked outside. "I was thinking of getting a shoulder holster."

"We could rob a bank with these," I said, only half joking.

"No way," Jim said. "They've got real guns in banks."

I shrugged. "They'd never know these weren't real."

"Why risk getting shot when we can stick up drunks in the park without any risk?"

"Because banks have got more money than drunks," I said.

"Well little fish are sweet, as far as I'm concerned. I need the money, so tonight I'm going to rob a drunk." He paused. "Why don't you come along for laughs?"

I went with him. It was Friday and Jim figured that there would be plenty of drunks who had been paid that day. His reason for robbing a drunk instead of just anyone who came along was that, in his opinion, the drunk wouldn't be capable of giving the police an accurate description of his robbers. Because I knew the area well, we went to Fairfield Park. Apart from the football field, it consisted of a huge area of tracks and trees stretching to Carramar. After about an hour, I became tired of waiting. Although four or five people had walked through the park, they had all appeared to be sober. I was about to suggest to Jim that we give it away when I heard someone whistling.

"Sshh. Someone's coming," I said.

Then we saw the drunk. He was staggering along the main path towards us, whistling *Singing the Blues*.

"Let's get him!" Jim said.

Pulling out our pistols, we rushed over to confront him.

"Okay, Pop," Jim said, "just hand over your money if you don't want to get shot."

The drunk, who was about forty and of medium build, stopped in his tracks. For a few moments he just stared at us, his befuddled brain unable to react to the shock.

"Come on, Pop! Give us the money!" Jim shouted.

I was nervous and constantly looking around to see if anyone was coming.

"Give me a break, lads," the drunk said. "I need the money to pay the rent." He didn't sound too drunk to me, and I wondered if the shock of being held up had sobered him some.

"Fuck your rent!" Jim said. "Give me the money or I'll shoot you."

The drunk held up a placating hand. "Okay, take it easy, lad. You can have it." He began to fumble inside his coat for his wallet. "You boys are putting me in a bit of a spot, though, you know. You don't know my landlady like I do. She's liable to throw me out if I don't pay the rent." He handed Jim his wallet.

Jim went through it. "Sixteen quid," he said, disappointed. He took the money and handed the wallet to the drunk.

I couldn't help feeling sorry for the drunk. "How much is your rent?" I asked.

"Seven quid. I get full board."

"Wait there a minute," I said.

I pulled Jim aside. "Let's give him the money back," I said. "I don't feel right about this. He's just a working man, it could be my father walking through here."

"Mate, I need the money."

"What, sixteen quid split two ways? It's nothing. We can make that tomorrow selling raffle tickets."

"Fuck the raffle tickets, we've got bloody guns! Anyway, I haven't got two bob to bless myself with."

"I'll lend you a few quid," I said. "I've been thinking we could rob a railway station Sunday night. All the money from the weekly tickets would be there. We could get a thousand quid out of it."

Jim started at me. "A thousand quid. Are you sure?"

I nodded. "Hundreds of people come and buy their ticket on Sunday to beat the Monday rush. And if we give him all his money back he probably won't go to the police."

We walked back to where the drunk was standing.

"I thought you'd forgotten all about me," he said.

"We've decided to give you the money back," I said.

He stared at us as Jim went to hand him the £16. Then he shook his head. "I can't do it. You boys must have needed the money or you wouldn't have done it in the first place. I'll just take the money for rent and you can rob me of the rest."

It was turning into a French farce. "No, we don't want to rob you," I said. "You worked hard for the money, you keep it."

"I insist, boys. You lads risked going to gaol for this money. You take it."

"Take the fuckin' money," Jim said, "before we change our minds and keep the lot."

The drunk took the money. "All right – and thanks, boys. You've given me new faith in human nature. You two lads are two of the nicest boys I've met."

I felt embarrassed. I wished he hadn't have been such a nice guy. "We're sorry about what happened," I said.

He held up a hand. "Think nothing of it. I understand why you boys do these things." He winked. "I was a bit of a knockabout myself when I was your age." He shook my hand. "I have to go. It's been nice meeting you boys."

Jim shook his hand. "Might pay to catch a taxi home next time, Pop."

"She'll be right, mate," the drunk said as he walked away. As he disappeared from sight I could hear him whistling *There's a Pawnshop on the Corner*.

"Well, which station do we stick up?" Jim said as we began walking to Fairfield railway station.

"Canley Vale would be a good one," I said. "Only one guy works there, and it's pretty deserted on Sunday nights."

I had often seen the pick up train arrive at Fairfield, which was the station after Canley Vale on the way to Sydney. One of the railway attendants would come out of his office holding a leather cash bag and hand it to a guard on the train. The guard would then slip the bag through a small trap door into a large steel safe. It would be extremely risky to try and rob the railway attendant as he came out of the office with the cash bag, apart from the train guard, there could be passengers who might try to intervene. I figured that the best way to do the robbery at Canley Vale would be to wait for the arrival of the train preceding the pick up train. When the railway attendant came out to collect the tickets we could be hiding in the toilet. Then, as he walked back towards his office, we could put stockings over our faces and run out and force him to let us in to the office where we could get the cash bag. The main risk would be if there was someone waiting for a train on the opposite platform. But, at that time of night on Sunday at Canley Vale, the chances of someone waiting for a Liverpool-bound train were slim.

We arrived at Canley Vale a bit before 7.30 pm Sunday. The pick up train was due at 8.30 pm. We sat at the far end of the station on the opposite platform, waiting to see what the railway attendant would do when the 7.30 train arrived. As soon as we heard it coming, the railway attendant came out of his office, closed the door and walked down towards the exit. Only one passenger got off. The railway attendant took his ticket and walked back inside, slamming the door behind him.

"It looks simple enough," I said.

"I don't know," Jim said. "He's a bloody giant."

"It doesn't matter how big he is, we've got the guns."

"Except they don't work. What do we do if he comes at us?"

I shrugged. "We run. But he won't come at us, no one argues with guns."

Jim had lost his nerve. "He looks big enough and fit enough to catch us. It's all right for you, you're a good runner."

"You're not going to back out of it now are you, Jim?"

"I'm not backing out. We'll look for a station where some old guy is on."

"Stuff it! I'll do it myself."

"It's risky, mate." He avoided my eyes. "I'll be just across the street."

Five minutes before the 8.00 pm train was due I went into the toilet. Although I was nervous I psyched myself to the point where I was confident of success as long as I kept my cool. I opened the small overnight bag, which contained the stockings, gloves and pistol. As I reached into the bag for the gloves the door to the toilet cubicle opened and an immaculately dressed middle-aged man stepped out.

He looked me up and down, and then gave me a nervous smile. "You'll never guess what just happened," he said.

Instinct told me he wasn't a cop. "What?" I said, deciding to cancel the robbery, this guy would be able to give the cops an accurate description of me.

He wet his lips with his tongue. "Ten minutes ago a bloke just sucked a young boy off in here. He gave the boy a pound."

I shrugged, inwardly cursing my luck. "That's their business." I hadn't seen anyone come in or go out of the toilet in the past hour.

His face was flushed as he stared at me. "Would you have let him suck you off for a pound?"

With deceptive calm I said: "I don't think so."

He edged closer. "What about the two pounds?" His eyes were unnaturally bright.

I pulled the pistol out of the bag and pointed it at him. "How would you like to suck this for nothing!"

He backed away; the excited look replaced by one of fear. "Don't hurt me, please. I was only joking."

Moving towards him I was tempted to hit him. Controlling myself, I said: "I want all your money. If you try to hide some on you and I find it, I'm going to pistol whip you."

He was terrified. "All right, you can have it all."

I could hear the train coming. "Get in the toilet!"

He stared at me. "What for?"

I shoved him backwards. "Just do it!"

The toilet was one of the type in which you had to put a penny in the slot to open the door. But he had left the door slightly ajar. He backed into the cubicle. I followed him in and closed the door. I put the point of the pistol against his chest. "If someone comes in, don't make a sound."

He was shaking. "Could you point the gun away from me? Please. It might go off."

"You shouldn't hang around in toilets trying to corrupt young boys, should you?"

I heard someone come in. I peeked through the crack in the door. It was the railway attendant. As he stood there urinating I lamented at my lost opportunity. After he had gone I gave the deviate another poke with the pistol. "Now give me your money. And remember what I said about hiding any."

He handed me his wallet. "That's all I've got."

Going through it I could only find £8. He was wearing an expensive suit, hand-stitched lapels and a silk shirt. Surely he'd carry more than £8.

"I think you're holding out. I'm going to search you. If I find any more money you're in trouble."

For a moment he hesitated, then he capitulated completely. "I do have some more. This has all been such a shock, I forgot about it."

He undid his tie, then, his hands trembling, unbuttoned the top button of his shirt. Folded inside his collar were five £10 notes. I'd never have thought of looking there.

"You had enough for 50 boys," I said, pocketing the money. "If you go to the police about this, I'll deny it. I'll tell them you tried to molest me. I've got a feeling they know all about you."

His eyes registered shock; I'd hit a nerve. "I have no intention of going to the police. I'm an important person."

"Sure you are." I opened the door. "Don't come after me."

I ran out and across the street to where Jim was waiting.

He ran alongside me. "Did you get it, mate?"

"No. There was another guy there. A bloody poof! He got nosey so I stuck him up instead. But he only had eight quid on him." Damned if I was going to share my hard-earned £50 with Jim.

"Yeah, they don't carry much," Jim said. "They're always getting bashed and robbed."

I vowed to myself that never again would I embark on an armed robbery with Jim. Rolling drunks and shoplifting were his limit.

15

ALBERT AND ATHOL MULLEY
(January 1960)

About a week after the Canley Vale incident Jim introduced me to a fool named Albert. Although boyish-faced he had the build of a front row forward. He was from Blayney, a little town situated between Bathurst and Orange.

Jim told me that Albert had come to Sydney to work for the PMG, now Australia Post, until he had been sacked for putting letters in the wrong boxes.

"But", Jim said triumphantly, "he found out where Athol Mulley lives."

Albert looked as though he were bursting with pride. "I delivered a letter to his place."

Athol Mulley was one of Australia's leading jockeys. He was famous for having ridden the immortal *Bernborough* to 15 consecutive wins in the mid-1940s.

I was puzzled. "So what?"

"We can rob him," Jim said.

"Leave me out. I'm finished with armed robberies."

"I'm not talking about sticking him up. We can break into his house and find his snook."

"His what?"

"His money," Jim said impatiently. "All the top jockeys back their own horses and it's illegal, so they can't bank the money. I'll bet he's got thousands hidden away at his place."

The idea appealed to me. If Mulley did have illegal money at his place he wouldn't be able to go to the police if it was stolen.

"All right," I said. "I'm in."

According to Albert, Mulley lived in a two-storey house in a quiet street in Burwood. When we arrived there at about 8.00 pm the place was in darkness. The doors and windows on ground level were locked, but climbing on to the top of the adjoining garage I was able to reach one of the side windows on the second level. It was unlocked. Climbing inside, I switched on the lights and went downstairs and let the others in. As soon as we began searching the place it was obvious that Albert had again got it wrong. The trousers in the wardrobe would have gone close to fitting a jockey inside each leg.

"No wonder *Bernborough* got beaten in the Caulfield Cup," I said, "having to carry a jockey this big."

"I can't work it out," Albert said, scratching his head.

"Tell you what, he's got some snazzy clothes," Jim said. "We can hock them, say that our rich uncle died and left them to us."

"You have to be kidding," I said.

"We have to get something mate," Jim said. "There's no money, jewellery, not even a trannie. We can't carry the TV."

"They're probably on holidays and took it all with them," I said. "We should go. The clothes are useless."

"I'll sell them," Albert offered. "It's easy money."

We could find only two suitcases and, after cramming each one full with the man's suits, sports jackets, pullovers and cardigans, we had to leave a lot behind. For me, it highlighted the disparity in lifestyles between the affluent and the poor. In my 17 years, my father had owned just one suit. The three of us walked to Burwood railway station taking turns carrying the suitcases. Three idiots. But it was a different era. No one seemed suspicions of us.

Albert was staying at Jim's place so we parted at Burwood.

"See you at the Town Hall Hotel at one o'clock," Jim said.

"I'll get us a good price for these," Albert boasted.

The next morning the police came to my place and arrested me for breaking and entering. When they searched my room they found the replica pistol. But it wasn't illegal. Neither the drunk nor the deviate had gone to the police so I was in the clear unless Jim confessed. Thankfully, he had sold his replica a few days previously. I was taken to Sydney CIB in Campbell Street. Jim and Albert were there drinking coffee at a table in the interrogation room.

Albert smiled at me. "I got caught trying to pawn the clothes," he said. "The bloke didn't believe my uncle left them to me."

I stared at him. "Why did you put us in?"

"I didn't want to go to gaol on my own, John."

The cops laughed. One of them, tall and thin with a wart on his nose, said: "Albert's only a country boy and I think you two misled him."

He patted Albert on the head, like he would a dog. "We're going to let him go. Now, how about chipping in for his fare to Blayney?"

I was glad to co-operate, anything to see the last of Albert. I'd have hated having to share a cell with him. Jim complained that it wasn't fair, why should Albert go free when the whole thing had been his idea?

But Wartnose was adamant. "He's going home. Are you going to help with his fare or not?"

We gave Albert his fare. He thanked us and promised to write.

"Where will they be, sir?"

Wartnose gave a grim smile. "My bet is Long Bay Penitentiary."

After Albert had gone, Wartnose got nasty. He grabbed me by the hair. "What were you going to do with that pistol?"

"Nothing. It's only a toy."

His face was contorted with rage. His mood change shocked me. "Do you think we're stupid?" Letting go of my hair he shoved his fist close to my face. "I'll ask you again, why did you have the pistol? Were you going to rob a bank?"

"Come off it!" I yelled.

He slapped my face, hard, then walked over to a table where the pistol was, and picked it up. I glanced at Jim. He was white.

"This might be a toy," Wartnose said, "but if you pointed it at an old lady she could die of a heart attack." He pointed the gun at me. "Do you want to finish up like Darcy Dugan?" Darcy Dugan, who began his criminal career at eleven, was probably the most notorious Australian bank robber to that time in the 20th century. He was serving a life sentence after his accomplice, Mears, shot and wounded the manager during a bank hold-up in Ultimo in the early '50s. At the time Dugan and Mears were prison escapees. When he died in 1991, he had spent 44 of his previous 60 years locked up.

"No I don't," I said.

"Well, don't touch guns," Wartnose warned.

It was good advice. I heeded it for six years.

Jim and I were taken to Central Police Station where we were fingerprinted and photographed. We were then put in a small cell where the police took our belts and our shoelaces to prevent us hanging ourselves. The walls were covered in graffiti, most of it short, obscene diatribes against the cops or other criminals. Some of it was written in excrement, some in blood. There were no beds, just a solitary wooden plank attached to a wall. There were a few filthy blankets that looked and smelled as though they had never been washed and a steel toilet bowl that was emitting an irritating gurgle. I tried to turn it off, the flush button didn't work.

"Nice place," Jim said.

"Why did you tell the cops where I lived?"

"It wasn't me, it was Albert."

"Albert didn't know where I lived."

"I told him the other night, in case we got separated or something."

I stared at him. He tried to meet my gaze, and then averted his eyes. I knew he was lying. Albert had proven he couldn't remember addresses. I would never again trust Jim.

"I'm starving," I said, changing the subject without giving him the reassurance I knew he wanted.

"Yeah, me too," he said.

Neither of us mentioned the matter again.

In those dingy cells at Central Police Station where you can't see if it's night or day, you soon lose all sense of time. We had been walking up and down for hours, wondering if we would ever be fed and then a cop brought us a few soggy sandwiches and a lukewarm cup of tea without milk or sugar.

"What time do they switch off the lights?" I asked.

"They stay on all night," the cop said. "That way, you can't get into any mischief."

Eventually I curled up on the bench. Jim had to settle for the floor. Being January, it wasn't cold and I used a blanket as a pillow. Although I managed to drift off to sleep, I was woken many times during the night by drunks screaming abuse at the cops. They ignored them. Lying there in that filthy, depressing cell, it occurred to me that you could be dying and no one would take any notice of your cries for help. Even though Jim was short on principles, it was comforting to know that at least I was with someone I knew.

I remembered Albert's words: "I didn't want to go to gaol on my own."

Now I knew what he meant.

16

Long Bay
(January/April 1960)

After a restless night in the cell, we were taken before a magistrate at Central Court and remanded for a week. Although bail was set, neither of us had any hope of raising it. Technically, because I was 17, I should have been in a children's court and taken to Albion Street, but because I was within a month of my birthday, the authorities sensibly decided I could be classed as an adult. Ironically it would be another 14 years before the voting age was lowered from 21 to 18.

That afternoon we were handcuffed and, with about 20 other prisoners, herded into the back of a large police van. The rear of the van was sectioned off into two compartments with half of us in one part and the remainder in the other. Although there was a metal bench to sit on, a few of us had to stand and there was nothing to hold on to. Every time the van came to an abrupt halt, which was often, we were thrown from one end to the other. Despite there being no air conditioning, some of the men were smoking. By the time we arrived at the gaol, I was sweating profusely and close to vomiting. When we stepped out of the van, an old, red-faced guard with a protruding gut shouted at us to stand in a line and to empty the contents of our pockets on to the ground. Although the police had taken our money, wallets and valuables, some of the men had cigarettes, matches and papers.

The guards then began to search us for contraband. This was the era when drugs weren't a problem in Australian gaols. I looked around. The wall behind us was at least six metres high. Standing on a catwalk attached to a tower, a guard, rifle on his shoulder, watched us. About 30 metres ahead of me was a block of about eight small yards with steel bars and gates at the front.

"They're the front yards," one of the guards said as he began to search me. "That's where you go if you play up."

I noticed that the old, red-faced guard had three stripes on his shoulder. I later learned that the three-stripers were high up on the pecking order. Next step was a crown, then the Deputy Governor and finally the boss, the Governor.

After we had been frisked we went to a room behind us that was known as the reception room. In 1949 Darcy Dugan, waiting to be processed, cut a hole in the roof and climbed out, walking away to freedom in his civilian clothing. Inside, we had to lower our pants while a male nurse gave each of us a short arm inspection for VD and other diseases. Because we were remand prisoners, Jim and I were permitted to wear our civilian clothing, a procedure that was abolished in the '70s.

The sentenced prisoners were issued navy blue pants and jackets. The shirts consisted of a coarse material with red, white and blue vertical stripes. Each sentenced prisoner was allocated a number that was stamped on to white patches, which were then sewn on to his jacket and shirt, one on the middle of the back and the other just above the heart. I was later told by an old crim that these patches were targets for the guards to shoot at if someone was trying to escape. The final ignominy for the sentenced prisoners was that they had to wear army green canvas hats. Dressed in their uniforms and wearing these hats made it difficult for the guards to distinguish one prisoner from another so they addressed them by their number. It's probable that a lot of prisoners served years in gaol without some of the guards even knowing their names.

It's easy to imagine a scene in a hotel. An ex-prisoner approaches a prison officer: "Hello Mr Mugabe, remember me?"

The prison officer stares at him, then recognition sinks in. "Number 362! Of course I remember you. You shared a cell with number 426. When did you get out?"

After everyone had been processed, those of us on remand were taken to a building named A Wing. It was one of the six large cellblocks in the complex. In the centre of the complex was a large building containing the cookhouse and the Governor's office. At the rear of the cookhouse was a block of showers. Each of the six cellblocks contained first and second levels. Prisoners awaiting trial or appeal, as well as those confined to the front yards, were housed in the B Wing. Appeal prisoners were dressed in brown. Two of the cellblocks, 1 Range and 2 Range, were for sentenced boys, that is, prisoners under 23. Both 3 Range and 4 Range were for sentenced men. The anomalous thing about this arrangement of separating the boys from the men once they were sentenced, was that they were all housed together while on remand, trial and appeal. Jim and I had to share a cell with a little guy, Ted, who wore glasses and was about 50. He was a friendly guy who was on remand for forgery. He had been in gaol before and was able to advise us on a lot of the do's and don'ts of a prison society.

At the time, conditions at Long Bay Penitentiary, as it was known then, were appalling. The cells were, and still are, about two metres wide and four metres in length; the only furniture was a small metal cupboard and a wooden stool. There were no toilets or taps and a tin bucket with a bit of disinfectant in it sufficed as a toilet for three men. Two thick iron bars impeded a small window. There was no glass in the windows; sometimes the rain came into the cell. A tin jug holding about two litres of water was the only water we had access to in the cell. Most of the cells had triple-decker bunks. Sheets and pillowslips were non-existent in the remand section. There were no radios or TVs and the only newspapers permitted were the Sunday editions. Although there was a good library, remand prisoners had no access to it; we were locked in our cells for 19 hours a day, and the lights were switched off at 9.00 pm.

The meals were atrocious. For breakfast they served up a plate of crushed corn that they called porridge, the old crims called it mush. A small portion of watered down milk was issued with the mush. Hot meals were served for lunch and dinner. Dinner was given at 3.00 pm every day, just before we were locked up for the night. Most days one of the meals was a thick, greyish stew, nicknamed the grey death. The other meals usually consisted of boiled, tasteless mutton with mashed potatoes and piles of boiled cabbage. Fruit was never on the menu. Three times a day one of the prisoners known as a sweeper, the trustees who watered down the milk, poured black tea into each prisoner's tin mug before we came in for our meals. By the time we got to our cells the tea was, at best, lukewarm. It was rumoured to be dosed with bromide to reduce our sex drive.

The one redeeming feature about the meals was the bread. Each prisoner was given a freshly baked half loaf of bread made by the inmates in the bakehouse behind 3 Range. For many years it won prizes at the Royal Easter Show. It was supplied to many hospitals and public institutions. We all looked forward to the bread. Remand prisoners who had money in their accounts were able to spend about five shillings each week on margarine, honey, jam, biscuits or tobacco but no sweets, chocolates or tailor-mades.

We were limited to writing a single regulation one-page letter per week. Pen and ink were issued for the occasion. Before the letter was posted one of the guards would read it. If there was any mention in the letter about the gaol or the conditions, or anything the guards didn't approve of, the letter would be destroyed. Letters received had the used stamp removed because no image of the Queen was permitted inside the goal.

Until the '70s there were no female guards in men's prisons, so it was rare to see a woman. Although, until 1969 when they were transferred to Mulawa at Silverwater, women prisoners were held at Long Bay, we never got to see them. Sentenced prisoners were permitted one 20 minute non-contact visit per month. With these types of archaic, oppressive conditions, most prisoners found it difficult to maintain any kind of relationship with their wives, children and sweethearts. Even in today's era of contact weekly visits, phone calls and generally uncensored mail, gaol is a great destroyer of relationships. In the '60s a gaol sentence was a virtual death sentence to most man/woman relationships.

Jim, Ted and I spent the time out of our cell in a large, concrete yard with about 70 other prisoners. It was one of two such yards for remand prisoners. Half of one side of the yard had a tin shelter containing a few wooden benches. At the rear of the yard were a urinal and two flush toilets. Men using the toilets were in full view of everyone in the yard. The only recreations available were a couple of chess sets and a few decks of cards, which were constantly in use. Showers were twice a week. Ted warned Jim and I to be alert while we were in the shower room.

"There've been a few boys bashed and raped in the shower," he said.

Although Jim and I had no problems, about a week after we arrived, a young blonde guy was knocked out and raped in the shower room. The two guards who were standing by the entrance door neither saw nor heard anything suspicious. The victim said he hadn't seen his attacker. While I was on remand there were a couple of stabbings in the Ranges. No one was killed. In those days prisoners were issued with steel utensils some of which were used as weapons or to cut the iron bars in escape attempts. Now prisoners are provided with throwaway plastic utensils. One of the main topics of conversation among the prisoners was the pending trial of Kevin Simmonds and Les Newcombe. Simmonds, who had been serving a sentence for a 1958 Rose Bay bank robbery, had escaped with Newcombe from Long Bay in late 1959. They had removed an air vent from the chapel during the showing of a James Cagney movie. Squeezing through the vent, they had climbed over a part of the wall that had a blind spot from the nearest tower.

While on the run they had broken into a storeroom at Emu Plains Prison Farm with the intention of stocking up with food, rifles and ammunition. When a prison officer had tried to stop them they battered him to death thus ensuring one of the largest manhunts in Australian history. Although Newcombe was later arrested at Woollahra, Simmonds made his way to Kuringai National Park. While he was digging a hideout in the side of a hill two forest rangers challenged him. Holding them at gunpoint, Simmonds escaped in their car and headed north. After being sighted near Wyong, he dumped the car and ran off into the bushes. Hot on his trail, the police brought in specially trained tracker dogs from Adelaide. There was huge media interest in the manhunt until, after 39 days on the run, Simmonds was captured near Kurri Kurri.

"They've got them in OBS," Ted told us. OBS was a small wing containing padded cells with no furniture in them where unstable and uncontrollable prisoners were held and observed.

"Why are they in there?" I asked.

"They committed the unforgivable crime, they killed a screw. And they'll pay for it for the rest of their lives."

"They're lucky we don't have the death penalty in this state," Jim said.

Ted shook his head sadly. "They'd be better off dead. After they've been sentenced to life for murder they'll go to Grafton and I doubt if either of them will walk out alive."

I stared at him. "What's Grafton?"

"That's the punishment gaol," Ted said. "They've got it up at Grafton out of the way. That way they can do what they want to without anybody interfering. Even the toughest crims in the state fear it because they know they are helpless up there. As soon as you get there you're met by a reception committee of six or seven screws who flog you with batons until you're unconscious. After that you're bashed every day for weeks until you're a nervous wreck. Then they might leave you alone for a few weeks and you start to think you're over the worst, and they'll rush into your cell at midnight and bash you senseless. And that's only if you're up there for belting a screw or trying to escape. So you can imagine how it'll be for Simmonds and Newcombe after what they've done."

I shuddered thinking about it.

"We all have to learn to be responsible for our actions," Ted said.

It's probably the best advice I had even been given. And I couldn't have had a better example than Simmonds and Newcombe. Both were sentenced to life imprisonment, although Newcombe, on appeal, had his sentence reduced to 15 years. Simmonds, the bank robber, had the appeal against his life sentence dismissed. In 1966 he was found hanged in his cell in Grafton.

A few weeks after arriving at Long Bay I was involved in a fight. An arrogant young German boasted he could beat anyone in the gaol at chess. One of my tennis teammates, a Russian, had taught me to play chess and I found I had a natural talent for it. I had watched the German play and I was confident I could beat him. I challenged him to a game, wagering a jar of honey on the outcome. When I beat him he picked up the board and hit me on the head with it. Instinctively, I jumped up and threw a punch at him, but I was off-balance and missed. He rushed at me, grabbing hold of me and we fell to the ground, rolling around and wrestling. He managed to grasp me by the hair and thump my head on the concrete. I caught him with a wild punch that split his lip. Breaking free from each other we scrambled to our feet. Everyone stepped back to allow us space to fight. When he came at me with his head down, throwing roundhouse punches, I knew that he had no idea how to fight. I easily blocked his punches and danced around him, jabbing him in the face with my left. Although he was off-balance, he came at me wildly. I hit him flush on the jaw with a right hand that Dad would have been proud of. He went down and stayed there. Amazingly, the guards hadn't noticed anything unusual. Ted later told me that they usually allowed the inmates to fight among themselves, as long as it was one on one, with no weapons involved. Although I shook hands with the German, I insisted on collecting the jar of honey.

Ted said that having the fight and winning was a positive thing. "Now that you've proved you can handle yourself and will have a go, most of the bullies will leave you alone." He looked at me and smiled. "But don't let it go to your head. There are a few blokes in here that could beat you and that wog together with one hand tied behind their backs. And when they share a cell with a good-looking boy, it's not for the conversation. Be careful who you get friendly with."

In later years I realised how fortunate I had been to share a cell with Ted during my first few months in gaol. He taught me to be gaol-wise about matters, which, otherwise, I might have had to learn the hard way.

17

Bye Bye Barbara
(April/July 1960)

After three months on remand Jim and I were taken before a judge at Darlinghurst Quarters Sessions. For me, appearing before a judge proved to be much more intimidating than going before a magistrate. The judge, wearing a greyish-white horsehair wig and black robes, looked quite old. From his elevated position he stared down with hooded eyes at Jim and I standing in the dock, his expression impassive but nevertheless disquieting. It was obvious the lawyers held him in awe. The atmosphere was one of pompous solemnity, increasing my nervousness and anxiety; I was at the total mercy of this judge.

A Public Defender pleaded for both Jim and I. He said that the offences had been more of a boyish escapade than a premeditated crime. A probation officer stunned me when he told the judge that he had interviewed my father and that Dad felt he hadn't been a good father. The probation officer said that this factor undoubtedly contributed towards my delinquency.

To my surprise Jim also had a record. He was on a 12 months bond for theft. The judge commented that both Jim and I were becoming a problem. After warning us that this would be our last chance, he gave each of us a three year good behaviour bond. After we had signed the bond papers Jim was allowed to go, but, despite my protests, I was taken back to the cells that were situated underneath the courtrooms. Shortly afterwards two plain clothes cops handcuffed me and drove me to Liverpool Police Station where I was charged with three counts of false pretences concerning goods I had purchased on credit under false names.

That afternoon I was taken to court and remanded. Because I had been given a bond by the judge the magistrate gave me self-surety bail. "I hope those three months you spent on remand taught you a lesson," he said.

Catching the train to Fairfield I went to Dad's favourite hotel opposite the station. Sure enough, Dad was standing at the bar, a middy of beer in his hand.

"Hi, Dad."

I had caught him off guard. For a moment he didn't say anything, then he held out his hand. "When did you get out?"

"A few hours ago. I want to thank you for what you told the probation officer. It helped."

He looked embarrassed. "Forget it, Johnny. We all make mistakes. Have a beer with your old man."

We had a few drinks while he lectured me on the foolishness of my ways. "You're the son of a working man," he said. "It's in your blood. If you try to be something you're not, you'll finish back in gaol."

I didn't have the heart to remind him that I didn't know whose blood runs through my veins. When I returned home with him, David was there. He told me that my name was now mud throughout Fairfield tennis circles.

"Forget tennis," Dad said. "You're out of chances and playing tennis won't save you. You'll get a job in a factory, that's an order."

"Fuck the factory," I said and walked out.

I felt sorry for him. From the time I had been arrested and taken to Albion Street he had made efforts to help me get back on track but it was too late. I had no respect for him or his beliefs. I booked into the People's Palace and began selling raffle tickets again, this time for the 'East Hills Judo Club'. Two weeks later I went to the Liverpool Magistrates Court for sentencing. The magistrate was scathing in his assessment of me.

"If you appear before me again on any matter," he said, "I'll have no hesitation in sending you to gaol."

He gave me a 12 months suspended sentence. I knew that if I were caught selling worthless tickets my booby prize would be a one-way ticket to Long Bay Penitentiary. I was lonely and depressed with no idea of what to do. I felt that if I took a job in a factory I'd be capitulating totally to Dad's will. For me gaol was preferable. A few days later I caught a train to Orange. One of the conditions of Jim's bond had been that he had to live in Orange. As I walked down the main street of Orange I felt the same exhilaration at being in a new city as I had experienced in Melbourne. This time I didn't have to worry about deviates. When I went to the address Jim had given me, his mother told me he was sharing a flat in town with a young guy named Warren. The flat was at the top of a renovated two-storey house near the park. He was pleased to see me.

"We get a few days work at the abattoir," he said. "If you come with us tomorrow you should get a start."

I was a staunch animal lover; working in a slaughterhouse was beyond my capabilities. "I'm okay for money at the moment, Jim. I'll look around for something that suits me."

He shrugged. "You won't find much work in Orange." He paused. "Could you lend us ten quid?"

Still the same old Jim. "Sure. But get it back to me, I'm going to need it."

A week later Jim and Warren were arrested for stealing a car at Bathurst. Jim had broken two bonds and was certain to remain in gaol. Warren was remanded in custody. I took over the flat rental. In 1960, if you were staying in Orange for only a few weeks it was a nice little town. Then it became a bore. I could understand why most of the young guys headed for the big smoke. I was there during the winter months and it took a while before my body adapted to the excessive cold temperatures. Sometimes it snowed. It was the first time I had seen snow. I began to date a girl named Barbara. She was a pretty brunette who loved to talk. She brought me up to date on all the local gossip. Sometimes we would go to the little milk bar/café across from the park and she would play her favourite songs on the jukebox while we drank coffee and ate raisin toast. Often, while we were there, her ex-boyfriend, Bruce, a short, thickset guy with rugged good looks, would saunter in, order a bowl of vegetable soup and sit and glare at us.

"Just ignore him," Barbara said. "He's still in love with me."

Although we didn't speak to each other during my stay at Orange, I must have seen him 50 times. Barbara said that even at the best of times he didn't have much to say. She was a fun girl and we had some good times together. Sometimes she would stay with me until well after midnight. Her parents liked me and didn't hassle her about staying out late. I was 18, she was 19. Her father and brother worked for a farmer, digging potatoes. I often went with them. It was a physically exhausting job but it helped pay the bills. I wrote to Dad and told him I was getting my hands dirty digging potatoes. He wrote back saying he was proud of me.

Barbara worked at a grocery store. She earned more than I did and she often paid for our outings. On Saturday afternoons, we would go to a hotel and I'd bet on the races with an SP bookie who openly took bets in the pub. Winter is a bad time to punt. Inferior horses go around while the good ones are in the spelling paddocks and the tracks are often rain-affected. During my stay in Orange I usually lost on the punt. After one disastrous Saturday with the bookie, I stole a flash bicycle on the Monday and rode it to Bathurst where I sold it at a bicycle shop. Prior to hitching a ride to Orange I went for a walk around the city. Walking into The Western Stores, reputedly the largest department store in the West, I noticed that the skylights appeared to have no alarm system. Nor did the jewellery cases.

A few days later I mentioned it to Barbara's brother, Barry. Although I didn't know the details, I knew he had been in trouble with the law and had spent time in a boys' home. He agreed that robbing it would be a piece of cake. We didn't pursue it any further and a week later he went to Sydney to try to find a better job.

Life in Orange carried on as usual until one night a few weeks later Barry returned. Barbara and I were sitting in the milk bar/café listening to Roy Orbison singing *Only the Lonely* when Barry walked in. I could see he was excited about something.

His narrow face had a weak chin, thin lips and a beak nose; it was hard to think of him as Barbara's brother. "I've got a couple of mates outside," he said. "We're going to do The Western Stores."

For a few seconds I was at a loss for words. "Are you serious?"

He gave me an impatient look. "We only came here to pick you up."

Barbara either hadn't heard, or else hadn't comprehended our conversation. She gave Barry a sisterly smile then put another coin in the jukebox and played Elvis's latest hit *Stuck on You*. Telling her I'd be back, I went outside with Barry to meet his friends. The driver, whose name was Taffy, was a solidly built guy with slicked down hair, who looked to be in his late thirties. The other guy, Les, was tall, dark and stick thin. He looked to be about 18 or 19.

Barry and I got into the car, a late model Holden. "This is a bit unexpected," I said, my mind racing.

"Look, man," Taffy said, "we've come a long way for this. If you don't want to be in it, just say so." Although he later claimed to be a Welshman, he had an American accent.

"Come on, John," Barry said. "It was your idea."

There would never be a better chance to rob the place.

"Whose car is it?" I asked.

"It's mine," Taffy said.

"All right. Give me five minutes to explain things to Barbara."

I returned to the café. Barbara must have become sentimental. Jim Reeves was singing *He'll Have To Go*. Bruce was sitting a few tables away eating his vegetable soup and giving me the hard stare. It must have been killing him wondering what was going on. Maybe he had played the Jim Reeves' number.

Sitting down I took Barbara's hand. "Barry and I are going away for a few days."

"Where to?"

"We're going to knock over The Western Stores at Bathurst tonight. We'll take the stuff to Sydney, sell it and come back."

An idiotic look came to her face as her mind tried to cope with the news. "But … but what if you get caught?"

I laughed. "I won't get caught."

For a moment she looked as though she was going to cry, but realising Bruce was watching closely, she managed to control herself. "Please don't go, honey."

"I have to. This is our big chance. Just think, no more digging potatoes. We'll never look back from here."

"I'm scared. Something will go wrong, I can feel it."

I gave a reassuring smile. "Nothing will go wrong. I'm a professional." I gave her a kiss, then stood up, gave Bruce a wink and walked out.

She ran after me, grabbing my arm as I went to get into the car. "Be careful, honey, I love you so much."

I hugged her. "I love you too." At that moment I meant it. Impending danger heightens your emotions.

As we drove off, I waved to her from the window. I never saw her again.

On the drive to Bathurst, Taffy made it clear that he was running the show. "I've got a friend at the Cross who's one of the biggest fences in Sydney," he said. "I've already spoken to him and he said he'll take whatever we get."

"Do we get a third?" I asked.

"We get a quarter."

"Stuff that," I said. "Everyone knows you get a third for new gear. As it is we've got to split it four ways."

"So you keep your share and sell it for a third," Taffy said. "And don't blame me if you get pinched doing it, half the fences in Sydney will give you up if they don't know you."

"It's better to take a quarter, John," Barry said.

"We haven't got anything yet," I said. "Let's discuss it then."

I asked Les about himself. He told me that he was a pickpocket and shoplifter. He had only come along on this job because Barry had told him how easy it would be. His nickname was The Sparrow. Years later he gained notoriety as one of the best pickpockets in Australia, eventually being banned from every racecourse in the country. I was intrigued as to how Barry had met up with these guys. I later learned that he and Sparrow had served time together at Mittagong Boys' Home. Taffy was a friend of Sparrow.

We arrived at Bathurst at about 11.00 pm. There weren't many people or vehicles in sight. We drove behind The Western Stores and parked. Because I knew the layout, I agreed to be the one to have a rope tied around my waist, and be lowered down through the skylight, a drop of about 15 metres to the floor. We had no difficulty getting on to the lower part of the roof, but the skylights were situated at the highest point of the building, we had to crawl up the incline with extreme care. Taffy smashed one of the skylights with a jemmy. Tying the rope securely around my waist I looked down. There were small lights in some of the showcases. Suddenly I was scared. The distance from the roof to the floor seemed to be a lot further when you looked down from the skylight instead of up from the floor.

"Are you sure you can hold my weight?"

"Of course we can," Taffy said. "The only way you can fall is if you pull the three of us through with you and that's impossible."

I knew he was right. Bracing myself, I gripped the rope with both hands. "All right, fellows, take the weight. I'm going down."

Easing myself feet first through the skylight I slid down into the darkness as the others took up the slack and steadied the rope. I heard them grunting with the strain. Slowly they began to lower me down. It was an eerie feeling gradually descending in the darkness towards the display cases.

Suddenly I began to descend too fast. "Stop", I screamed.

I stopped with a jolt, about a metre above the display cases. The abrupt halt causing me to sway from side to side like a pendulum. Slowly I was lowered to the floor.

Unfastening the rope, I went to the back door that had no alarm system. Unlocking it, I slid back the bolt waiting for the others to join me.

As soon as they arrived Taffy said: "Sorry about the slip, man, it was burning my bloody hands and it nearly got away from me." He glared at Sparrow. "Bloody Les was useless."

"We had it under control, mate," Barry said. "Come on. Let's clean this place out."

"We'll get the jewellery first," Taffy said.

He began to jemmy open the jewellery display cases while the rest of us grabbed some overnight bags and started filling them with jewellery, mainly rings and watches. After we had emptied the jewellery cases we went to the far wall, which was lined with hundreds of suits. We filled six suitcases then decided to go. Leaving via the back door we reached the car without incident. We had five overnight bags and six suitcases. After we loaded them into the car, Sparrow had to sit on Barry's lap.

Driving out of Bathurst all of us were in high spirits.

"That's how professionals work," Taffy said. I had to agree.

We estimated about £5,000 worth of property. By today's standards, that's well over $200,000.

About five miles from Lithgow, Taffy said: "We're nearly out of gas."

I was stunned. "Why didn't you fill up before we did the job?"

"We didn't have the money, man."

"I don't believe this, we've got a car full of hot gear and we're out of petrol in the middle of nowhere. You should have asked me for petrol money," I said.

"We're in a hot car, man. If the jug-head filling it up notices I'm driving without the keys he might call the coppers." In those days self-service stations were rare.

I hadn't noticed he was driving without keys. "If I'd have known it was hot I wouldn't have come. You said it was your car."

"You're worrying about nothing, man. We can siphon petrol any time we want it. I've got a piece of hose and an empty drum in the boot."

On the outskirts of Lithgow he turned into a side street. "This'll do," he said. "Barry, you can help me."

After getting the empty drum and piece of hose they walked about 20 metres to a car parked outside a house. Unscrewing the petrol cap, Taffy pushed the hose into the petrol tank and told Barry to suck the petrol up. After a few tries Barry succeeded, spluttering petrol everywhere. Taffy grabbed the hose and shoved it into the drum. At that moment a police car turned into the street. Taffy saw it immediately. Dropping the hose he jumped over a small picket fence of the nearest house and ran down the side path as the police car, its siren blaring, rushed towards Barry who stood there wondering what to do. A cop jumped out of the car with a pistol pointed at him. While all this had been happening, Sparrow and I each grabbed a bag of jewellery and began running down the street. The cop, who was in the process of handcuffing Barry, shouted for us to stop. He had to be kidding! I knew he was on his own otherwise the driver would have come after us. But I knew he would radio for help. Running around a corner, I saw a school.

"Quick, in there!" I shouted. We ran into the school. "We have to find somewhere to hide the bags."

The girls' toilet block was unlocked. "Put your bag on top of one of the cisterns," I said, going into one of the cubicles and placing my bag on top of the cistern.

Sparrow did the same in the next cubicle. Both of us were gasping for breath. "They'll probably look for us in here," Sparrow said.

I nodded. "We'll go somewhere else and hide. We can return before school starts and pick up the bags."

We ran out of the school and down another street, then down a lane. Halfway down the lane a police car came screeching up behind us. Two cops with guns withdrawn jumped out. "Stop or you're dead!" one of them shouted.

We stopped. As they handcuffed us I cursed myself for getting involved in something that had gone so terribly wrong.

"Where are the bags you had?" one of them asked.

I gave him a puzzled look. "Bags? What bags?"

The other cop hit me in the guts as hard as he could. I hadn't been expecting it and doubled over, gasping in pain.

He grabbed Sparrow by the hair. "We know you had the bags, where are they?"

Sparrow told him. They would have found them anyway.

Another police car drove up. Barry was in the back. We were taken to Lithgow Police Station. On arrival we were un-cuffed and told to strip off. About six cops stood around us as Barry and I stripped naked. Sparrow stood there in his socks.

"Take your bloody socks off, you look ridiculous," the desk sergeant said. "Don't be embarrassed if your feet smell, we're used to it here."

Flushing, Sparrow took off his socks. Six or seven diamond rings fell on to the floor. One of the cops burst out laughing.

Barry stared at Sparrow. "You cheating bastard!" he shouted. He turned to me. "He ripped us off!"

I shrugged. The fact that the three of us were standing shivering naked in the middle of winter on the cold floor of a police station, facing a certain prison sentence, was all that mattered to me. The cops were upset that Taffy managed to escape. They used the old ploy of taking us to separate rooms. I was threatened with a bashing if I didn't tell them who he was. But after a while they realised I knew nothing about him. Maybe Barry or Sparrow gave them a clue as to where Taffy might go. The next day he was arrested in Sydney.

It was about 4.00 am when the cops put us into a cell. I covered myself with three grimy blankets and, although deeply depressed, I was soon asleep.

18
A FOWL ESCAPE
(July/August 1960)

Later in the morning we were taken before a magistrate who remanded us to Bathurst Court. He set bail for each of us at £500. It might as well have been five million.

That afternoon we were taken to Bathurst Gaol. In those days Bathurst held only recidivist prisoners. There were four wings, holding a total of about 400 prisoners. The three of us were allocated the same cell in D Wing. Although it was about the same size as the cells in Long Bay, it had a flush toilet and, attached to the wall, a radio receiver box. The guards controlled the radio from the front office; it was switched off every night at 9.30. The only station we received was the local 2BS, but it was good to be able to listen to music and the news. Another bonus was that each week we received clean pyjamas and bed linen. But there were no proper facilities for remand prisoners. During the day, remands were held in the front yards, which were carbon copies of the punishment yards at Long Bay. The days in the yard dragged. There was nothing to do all day except walk up and down in the small, cramped area and try to avoid bumping into someone. If you didn't walk, you stood huddling in a corner shivering. Most of the time I paced up and down. The exercise usually made me ravenous. I couldn't wait to get into the cell and eat the meal and my loaf of bread.

It was particularly wretched when it rained. We had to huddle under the small tin shelter at the rear of the yard next to the toilet until it was time to go to our cells.

Sparrow summed it up: "If they treated animals like this, the RSPCA would be screaming blue murder."

During our third day there, Taffy was brought in. He had a black eye.

As soon as he entered the yard he demanded to know which one of us betrayed him. We all pleaded not guilty.

He stood there, hands on his hips, staring at us. "One day I'll find out who it was, and God help you when I do!"

My opinion of Taffy was that he was all bluff but I could understand how he felt. I doubted he understood how I felt about being lied to about the stolen car and then being arrested because we ran out of petrol. I wrote to Dad explaining why I wasn't digging potatoes anymore. With nothing to lose, I asked him if there was any chance of him raising the bail money. He wrote back and told me he had bought a lottery ticket and for me to keep my fingers crossed.

Barbara visited Barry. She asked him to tell me that she didn't love me anymore. She had gone back to Bruce. Although I didn't love her, it hurt my pride. After Barry gave me the news I had to fight back the tears as I imagined her and Bruce sitting in our favourite café, listening to the jukebox and having vegetable soup. For a few days I was depressed until I admitted to myself that before my arrest I had been bored out of my brain and on the verge of leaving Orange and Barbara. Barbara eventually married Bruce but soon afterwards he was killed in a car accident.

After a few court appearances the four of us pleaded guilty and were remanded for sentences. I had appraised the situation and decided that an escape would be easy. In those days country cops weren't as suspicious as city cops. When we went to court they didn't handcuff us. There were usually only two of them who escorted us across a small lane from the police cells to the courthouse. I calculated that if the four of us took off at the same time and split into four different directions when we reached the end of the lane, at least two of us were certain to get away, if not all of us. I mentioned it to the other three. After a great deal of discussion we all agreed to make a bid for freedom. Once we split into different directions, it would be every man for himself.

In mid August, we were taken to court. We were escorted from the cells to the courtroom by a fat detective and an old uniformed cop who looked to be close to retiring age. The judge told the four of us that we committed a very serious crime. And although Taffy was old enough to be our father and should have known better, we were all equally involved. All of us had been in trouble before and obviously we hadn't learned our lesson. There were no extenuating circumstances. He remanded all of us for sentence at a later date. He then later sentenced me to 12 months hard labour for stealing a bicycle and radio.

We were led from the court by the old cop with the fat detective behind us. I felt the now familiar rush of adrenalin as my body prepared for the task ahead. The moment we stepped into the lane I shoved the old cop in the back, causing him to stumble forward and almost fall over. Expecting the others to follow me, I began running as fast as I could down the lane.

"Good luck, Johnny!" Taffy shouted.

I was on my own! The gutless bastards. At the end of the lane I ran across a street to a park. I glanced over my shoulder. About 30 metres behind, Fatso was chasing me. Running through the park I heard a bang. He was trying to shoot me! At the end of the park was the main street. Recklessly I dashed across the road, forcing vehicles to a screeching halt. One driver screamed abuse at me. I ran past some shops and turned left into another street. I looked around; Fatso had given up the chase. Aware that the cops would soon be out in force to search for me I climbed over the side fence of a house and crept into a chook pen. As I entered the enclosure the chooks began squawking. I spoke soothingly to them and they quietened down. After about five minutes I began to think I was safe when I suddenly heard loud voices. Looking through a small crack in the shed I saw two uniformed cops talking to an old lady. She was pointing to the chook pen! Scrambling out, I ran down the backyard as my chook friends squawked their goodbyes.

The cops immediately saw me. "Stop, or I'll shoot!" one of them shouted.

A wire fence partitioned off the yard; they would have to open a gate before they could come after me. I ran to the back fence, which was about three metres high with barbed wire at the top. Leaping up I

Shot fired as youth breaks from police

BATHURST, Mon.—A policeman fired a shot today to try to stop a youth escaping from custody.

Daily Telegraph, 16 August 1960

grasped the top of the fence and heaved myself up. Although the wire cut into my hands I was in such a state I didn't feel it. A rotund cop was trying unsuccessfully to climb over the fence of the neighbouring house. He also shouted for me to stop. If it hadn't have been such a serious situation, I would have laughed. I flung myself over the fence; one of my fingers caught in the barbed wire and was ripped open as I forced it free. I was in a narrow side street. A police car, siren blaring, came rushing towards me. I ran across the street and down the path of a house.

Another cop, a gun in his hand, was running after me. "Stop, or I'll shoot!"

As I reached the back fence I glanced around. He was pointing the gun at me. "Put your hands in the air!"

Turning around, I shrugged. "You've got me." Cops came from everywhere. As I was being handcuffed I said: "I've cut my hand badly." Blood was oozing from it.

"You're lucky you weren't shot," one of them said.

I was driven to the police station where Fatso was waiting. He and a couple of uniforms took me to a cell. As one of the cops took my handcuffs off I looked at Fatso. "Don't worry, you didn't do it to me, I cut my hand on a fence."

He punched me on the side of the head. "You little bastard!"

The force of the blow knocked me down. He lashed out at me with his boot, I tried to twist away but the kick caught me on the elbow, causing it to go numb. I grunted with pain.

"I should have shot you, you little bastard!" he said.

They went out and locked the door. I got up and began walking up and down, nursing my elbow. My ear was ringing from the punch and my finger was aching. The bleeding had ebbed to a trickle but it looked a mess with pieces of skin and gristle hanging from it. The cut was about three centimetres long. I had to re-evaluate my situation. Things hadn't gone as planned. In less than half an hour I had been sentenced to 12 months gaol, escaped, had been shot at, ripped my finger open, been recaptured, punched and kicked. I still had to be sentenced for the Western Stores' robbery and now I would get extra time for escaping. There was definitely a flaw in my thinking mechanism.

After a while Taffy, in a nearby cell with Barry and Sparrow, yelled out to me: "Hey, Johnny! Are you okay, man?"

"No, I'm not! What happened to you guys? I had no chance on my own. There were cops everywhere."

"You moved too fast for us, Johnny!" Barry yelled.

"Bullshit! You're all a pack of weak bastards," I said, finishing the conversation.

A few hours later we were returned to Bathurst Gaol. On arrival I was escorted to A Wing and placed in a cell on my own. I noticed it didn't have a radio in it. I had been expecting harsh treatment and didn't ask questions. The next morning I was taken before the Governor, an old fat guy who was dressed in a country suit. He told me that by escaping I had ruined any chance I had of going to an easy gaol or Emu Plains Prison Farm.

"You'll be branded as an escapee for the rest of your life," he said with a gravity that implied I had committed one of the worst crimes imaginable. "I'm sending you to the pound for a few days so you can ponder on the implications of your stupidity."

I was escorted to B Wing and taken to a steel door on the ground floor. One of the guards unlocked it. There was a small area inside leading to another steel door. The guards unlocked the second door. Inside was a small, darkened cell. He told me to step inside, strip off and hand him my clothing. Silently, I did as I was told. As I handed him my clothes he searched them, then dropped them on the floor outside the cell.

I stared at him. His face softened. "It's not as bad as it looks, son. No one's going to hurt you. If you remember that, you'll be okay."

He closed the door and locked it, leaving me in an almost total darkness. There was a tiny shaft of light coming from an air vent. After my eyes had adjusted to the darkness, I noticed a roll of toilet paper and a small rubber bowl, obviously to be used as a toilet. The only other item in the cell was a *Bible*. The idea was that while you were in solitary you could read the *Bible* and repent. The trick was, of course, finding a way to read it in the dark.

Even under normal conditions, winter in Bathurst is cold. Being naked in a concrete cell in total darkness was close to torture. I began to jog up and down until I had raised a sweat. Then I slowed to a walk. After a while I began to sing. The acoustics were good and I soon became convinced I was in the same class as Elvis. I spent most of the day pacing the cell singing. I had lost all track of time when two guards came in with what was called dinner. It consisted of a half loaf of bread and a jug of water. I was also given some blankets and a coir mattress.

After wolfing down the bread I was still hungry. Aware that my next meal was 24 hours away, I decided to make up what was called a bed and tried to sleep. I was soon asleep. At about six o'clock the next morning they came again and took the mat and blankets.

"When am I getting out?" I asked.

"Tomorrow morning at ten," one of the guards said.

"Any chance of a bowl of porridge?" It was a long shot, but I was ravenous and had nothing to lose by asking.

"Sure, I'll fix it up right away. What would you prefer, Uncle Toby's or Quick Oats?"

The other guard was laughing.

In gaol, you soon learned how to repress your emotions. It was important to me that they couldn't see the dejection and humiliation I felt. "Unless you've got semolina, forget it," I said casually.

For a few seconds they stared at me, and then they walked out and slammed the door. My second day in the pound was much the same as the first. Walking up and down either singing or daydreaming. The forced confinement within that small, cold, darkened cell made even the most mundane happenings in my life on the outside seem like highlights. It was easy for me to romanticise and imagine how things might have been if I'd have played my hand a little differently. Always the optimist, I promised myself that one day I would transform some of those daydreams into reality. The next morning I was taken to the clothing store. I was given two sets of prison clothing, including two pairs of woollen underwear, and allocated a number that was sewn onto my jackets and shirts.

The guard addressed me as "Three sixty two."

The overall effect of the past few days impressed indelibly upon my mind the fact that, at 18, I was already a convict. A despised outcast of society. After a while you learn to accept it. The way I looked at it I deserved everything I got for being a fool. After putting my extra clothing in my cell I was taken to the front yards where I was placed in a yard on my own. I was told that as further punishment I had to spend a few months in the yard.

19

Sin City
(July/December 1960)

After about six weeks of isolation in those miserable yards at Bathurst, I thought my luck had changed when I was unexpectedly escorted by two guards to Bathurst railway station. A warrant had been issued for my appearance at Darlinghurst Quarter Sessions to be sentenced for breaking my bond. Despite being handcuffed, I enjoyed the scenic trip by train to Central railway station. Today the Department of Corrective Services has a fleet of prison vans and wouldn't consider transferring a prisoner by train, especially an escapee.

At Central railway station, we were met by another guard who drove us to Long Bay. The next day I was taken to the Darlinghurst Quarter Sessions. The trip was a waste of public money. When the judge realised I still had to be sentenced on the escape he postponed the matter until December. At Long Bay, I expected to be housed in one of the boys' wings but I was told I was still on punishment and had to be confined in B Wing.

I was put in a cell with two guys who were both in their early twenties. The cell was similar to the one I had shared with Jim and Ted, except there were no beds. Three coir mats on the floor with a few blankets had to suffice as beds.

"Welcome to Sin City," one of them said. He was short, thickset with black, crew cut hair. He held out his hand. "Max." He indicated the other guy. "That's Karl."

Karl, who was redheaded and freckled, was taller but not as solidly built as Max. He was reading a paperback western. He nodded, and then carried on reading.

"I take it we're in the front yards," I said.

"Yeah. We call it Sin City," Max said. "Nothing to do but have sex."

I knew I was in for trouble. "A few boys in the yard are into that sort of thing are they?" I said casually, my mind racing. I could tell by the way he was staring at me that he would make a move on me. Would Karl back him? If he did I was lost.

"Not as good-looking as you," Max said.

I met his gaze. "I'm not that way inclined," I said trying to psyche myself for a violent battle of survival.

"Well, they shouldn't put good-looking boys in our cell," he said and stepped towards me. "Just give it a try, kid. You might like it."

I hit him with a flurry of wild, mostly ineffectual punches. Surprised, he tried to fight back, catching me with a right hook to the side of the head as he stumbled back, off balance. His defence was wide open. I moved in and hit him with a straight left to the face and crossed with a powerful right flush on the nose. It was the first decent punch I landed and he crumpled to the floor. I jumped on him and hit him again.

Karl grabbed me. "He's had enough, mate!"

Breaking free, I went into a fighting stance. "Come on!" I yelled. "You want to try it, too?"

"No, I don't. Calm down, mate."

"Why do you share a cell with a deviate?"

He shrugged. "He's never tried it with me."

Max staggered to his feet. "Sorry, mate. This is what gaol does to you."

Karl gave him a towel. "You blokes made a hell of a racket. Better clean yourself up in case the screws come." He looked at me. "You too, mate. Your eye is cut."

There was blood on the floor and blankets. Before we could finish tidying up, the door opened. A big, solid three-striper with greying hair, stepped inside. Four guards stood outside. The three-striper stared at Max whose nose was still trickling blood. "What happened to you?"

"I fell over," Max said.

"Don't give me that bullshit," the three-striper retorted. He turned to me. "Who hit him?"

"No one," I said.

He stepped towards me. "What happened to your eye? You fall over as well?"

"We had a bit of a blue," Max said. "It was my fault. I started it."

The three-striper smiled. "You must be a piss weak fighter. Both of you are charged with fighting." He paused. "Does one of you want to move to another cell?"

No one answered. He nodded. "All right then." He walked to the door, then stopped and turned to look at me. "I'm not a fool, son. I know exactly what happened." He slammed the door.

Although I had been charged with fighting, I felt a sense of satisfaction. I had no doubt that this little episode would become common knowledge among the prisoners. They would realise that I was no easy mark. The next morning, after breakfast, we were taken to the front yards. They were overcrowded and the three of us were put in a yard with three others who were on punishment. With six of us in the small yard, even walking up and down was difficult. Some of the other yards held prisoners on protection if they were known to be homosexual. Those of us in the yards for punishment were not permitted to have tobacco, buy-ups or even books from the library. Most of the guys were smokers and found it tedious having nothing to do all day and not having a smoke. Tempers became frayed and fights in the front yards were regular occurrences.

Tobacco was the gaol currency. You could exchange it for extra food and small luxuries such as decent soap, toothpaste, tea, extra jam, bread and sugar. Coffee was unavailable at that time in NSW prisons. All prisoners were issued with small packets of crushed chalk to be used as toothpaste and a cake of harsh washing soap had to suffice for showering, shampooing and washing clothes. In gaol, being a non-smoker was a big advantage.

Later in the morning Max and I were taken before the Governor. We pleaded guilty to fighting, claiming we had argued about whose turn it had been to empty the toilet bucket. He sentenced us to two days in the pound. He explained that because he had dealt with the matter we wouldn't lose remissions. If we had been sentenced by a VJ, a Visiting Justice, usually a magistrate, we would have lost four days remission for every day spent in the pound.

The solitary confinement block consisted of dungeon-type cells situated at the rear of One Range. I was put in a cell identical to the one at Bathurst. This time I was permitted to wear my clothing, minus shoes, socks and belt. Forty-eight hours in solitary can seem like a week. The darkness, loneliness and boredom combined with the gnawing hunger, will inexorably weaken the strongest of spirits.

Probably it would influence some people to resolve never to return to gaol. But it simply hardened me, enabling me to adequately cope with the dehumanising effects of gaol. I began to learn how to switch off, to suppress emotions until they were gone. At 18 I was already tough but I didn't know it. After spending two days in the pound I returned to the front yards. I was also allocated to another cell. My new cell mates gave me no problems.

It was the year of the Centenary Melbourne Cup. On Cup day I was still confined to the yards. Although I hadn't seen a newspaper or listened to the radio for months I knew that the great *Tulloch* would be running in the Cup. One of the guys who had recently come into our yard told us that *Tulloch* had won the Cox Plate in record time and that, although he'd have to carry a crushing weight, he was favourite for the Cup. If they had allowed me to listen to the race I'd have willingly spent another day in the pound. I considered *Tulloch* to be a greater horse than even *Phar Lap*.

When the guards on yard duty disappeared for about five minutes we knew they had gone to listen to the race. Although the guard on the tower was watching us, I could see a transistor in his hand.

As soon as one of the guards returned, someone yelled: "Who won it, boss?"

"*Hi Jinx*."

Who? I'd never heard of it! "Where did *Tulloch* run?" I asked.

The guard laughed. "Nowhere. So much for *Tulloch*. He had too much weight."

I walked away in a state of shock. *Tulloch* unplaced! I couldn't believe it. It was to be the only time in 53 races that *Tulloch* finished out of a place. What an anti-climax. I was depressed for days. That same week John F Kennedy won the US Presidential election. Those of us in the yards knew nothing about it or any other important happening in the world outside Long Bay. But at least we knew that bloody *Hi Jinx* had won the Melbourne Cup.

A few days later I was put on an escort van to Bathurst. We stopped off at Parramatta Gaol to pick up extra prisoners and the trip took about four and a half hours. I always dreaded those long van trips. Car sickness was always my companion and I usually had to fight against vomiting on the floor.

In mid November I was sentenced to an extra 18 months hard labour for the Western Stores' robbery with another three months cumulative for the escape. A month later I was back in Sydney to be sentenced for the broken bond. The judge remarked that I was well on my way to becoming an habitual criminal. He sentenced me to two years hard labour, to start from that day. The five months I had spent in punishment yards at Bathurst and Long Bay was dead time. The next day I was taken off punishment and allocated to Two Range. I had access to the library and was eligible for work. All the prisoners in Two Range were under 23 and classed as remedial, prisoners who hadn't previously served time in gaol. The boys in One Range were repeat offenders. They were classed as recidivists.

Most of the boys worked in one of the workshops doing menial chores such as folding NRMA magazines or sorting pages and stapling school magazines. The average wage was one shilling per week plus a two-ounce packet of tobacco with matches and papers. The tobacco was of very poor quality and known as boob weed; anyone who had a packet of Drum or White OX, which was nicknamed grouse tobacco, could swap it for four or five packets of boob. Three times each year, Christmas, Easter and Queen's Birthday, sentenced prisoners could buy grouse tobacco and groceries on a special 35 shilling buy-up if they had the money or could get it sent in. Dad sent me the money.

I spent Christmas 1960 in a cell in Two Range with two Dutch boys. They had no money and no friends in Australia. I shared my buy-up with them. In 1960, 35 shillings bought a lot of groceries and sweets, but split three ways didn't last long.

20
GOULBURN TRAINING CENTRE
(1961)

In January 1961, I was transferred to Goulburn Training Centre (now Goulburn Correctional Centre). It was almost a replica of Bathurst Gaol, at least in structure. But whereas Bathurst had flush toilets and a tap and sink in the cells, Goulburn had the same systems as Long Bay: a bucket with disinfectant in it for a toilet and a tin jug containing drinking water. Everyone at Goulburn was a first-timer. Nevertheless in 1961, some of the most dangerous criminals in Australia were incarcerated in Goulburn. Some of the more infamous ones had had their cases dramatised on the popular radio show in the '50s, *Police File*. It had been one of my favourite programmes and I was familiar with the case histories of more than a few of the infamous criminals at Goulburn.

The Bega Bomber was there. I remember him as a short, tubby, balding man named Kelly who worked in the carpenter shop. In 1957, he blew up a house in Bega with gelignite, killing a policeman, his wife and child. A stepson miraculously survived. He was released after serving more than 30 years in gaol. He died in 2007, aged 89.

An Aboriginal named Allan Arnold was there. He was nicknamed the Black Prince and was notoriously gay. He was in gaol for carnal knowledge of a young white girl. He told me in 1961, "I've spent 14 years in gaol, I'm getting out next year." It was another 18 years before they released him.

The man I disliked the most in Goulburn was Stephen 'The Pig' Bradley. On 7 July 1960, Stephen Leslie Bradley had kidnapped eight-year-old Graeme Thorne. A week earlier the boy's father had won the £100,000 ($200,000) Opera House lottery. Bradley, a Hungarian migrant, rang Mr Thorne and demanded £25,000 for the safe return of his son.

Thorne agreed to pay the ransom but he also contacted the police. Bradley didn't follow up on his ransom demand. Five weeks later the body of Graeme Thorne was found wrapped in a rug on a vacant lot in Seaforth. He had been strangled. Bradley was connected to the crime through an anonymous phone call and forensic evidence taken from the rug. But before police could arrest him, he had fled the country. He was arrested in Ceylon (now Sri Lanka) and extradited back to Australia. In March 1961, he was found guilty of murder and sentenced to life imprisonment.

The kidnapping had been the first of its kind in Australia. The case received worldwide media coverage. Reacting to the public outrage, some of the media demanded the return of the death penalty in NSW but in 1954 the State Labor government had abolished capital punishment. In late 1961 Bradley arrived at Goulburn. He was the most despised man in the prison, by both prisoners and guards. Not only had he perpetrated an abhorrent crime, but also he was an arrogant pig of a man with an aggressive nature. In October 1968, at the age of 48, the overweight Bradley died of a heart attack after a game of tennis with the Governor. There were some who said he was poisoned.

Eric Thomas Turner was also there. He had served thirteen years of a life sentence for strangling his girlfriend and then killing her father with an axe in 1948. Although he was released in 1970, he was back again in 1973 for killing his mother-in-law and his 11-year-old stepson. All the killings had been committed while he was heavily intoxicated. He died in 2008, aged 80, entering the record books as having spent 57 years of the past 60 years in prison, the longest amount of time served in any Australian prison.

At the time there were others at Goulburn whose crimes were as heinous as any in Australian history. One of these men, John 'Ratty Jack' Leach, was a thin, grey-haired man of about 50 who wore the number '1' on his jacket and shirts. The story was that he had raped and murdered two seven-year-old boys, leaving bite marks all over their bodies, then led a search party to a cave where he discovered the bodies, crying out: "I found them! The rats have been at them!"

It's the most horrific story I had ever heard. People with no criminal history often commit murder. So, although Bathurst was the recidivist gaol, Goulburn held most of the murderers. Looking back, the amazing thing was that men like Ratty Jack were able to walk around Goulburn Gaol without fear of being bashed or killed by other prisoners. It wouldn't happen today in any maximum-security gaol in Australia. They would be on strict protection. In the early '60s it was rare for prisoners to be on protection at Goulburn. The few who did go on protection while I was there, were confined to the front yards, the same as those on punishment. Today, half the Goulburn prison population are on protection.

When I arrived at Goulburn I had to work on the wood heap, chopping and sawing wood. Notorious murderers and thugs worked alongside each other using axes and saws while a couple of bored prison guards looked on, supervising. That type of trust and complacency could only occur in a minimum security prison camp today.

I was given a cell of my own and, after a few weeks of hard work on the woodheap, I was given a job in the tailor shop making pyjamas. The guy seated beside me was Dave Scanlon, the Kingsgrove Slasher. I knew his case well. Until his arrest in April 1959, for about 18 months he terrorised residents in the Kingsgrove area by sneaking into bedrooms and slashing with a razor blade the nightclothes of sleeping females. As soon as one of them screamed, he would rush out of the house and run away. He had been a top class cross-country runner and got his thrills by easily eluding his pursuers. For a long time he had police baffled as to his method of escape as there had been no reported sightings or even sounds of a getaway vehicle. Being a distance runner he had the perfect excuse to be out at night running. Although he didn't physically harm anyone, his escapades received so much publicity that the judge decided to make an example of him by sentencing him to 18 years imprisonment. With remissions he did eleven years.

He taught me how to proficiently use a sewing machine. Eventually we became friends. He had brown hair, parted on the side, a Roman nose and, despite shaving every day, a permanent five o'clock shadow. One day he was called to the front office and given his divorce papers.

He returned to the shop, sat down and cried. He told me that he still loved his wife but she could never forgive him for what he had done. I realised then that when you strip away all the media hype about high profile criminals, they were human beings, who bled, hurt and cried like everyone else.

Four times a year at Goulburn they held sports events and gave out prizes to the winners. I told Dave I was a good runner and he advised me to do a bit of training by running on the spot in the cell.

The boys in gaol always caused more trouble than the men. A lot of the young guys try to establish themselves as heavies. The respect of the other prisoners is often measured by how well you can fight. This was especially so in the '60s. At Goulburn, there were two ways of having a fight. You could fight illegally, usually during recess, in one of the cells on the top landing. Other prisoners would keep watch and give the signal if a guard started to come upstairs. Anyone caught fighting in this manner would be automatically charged with fighting. This usually resulted in at least a couple of days in the pound as well as a loss of four days remission and a week in the front yards for each day spent in solitary.

The other choice was a fight legally. Every Saturday morning an old guard nicknamed Monkey Nuts would allow the men to settle their differences in what he termed a gentlemanly manner. This was achieved by locking the two combatants and himself in the yard of the education centre and telling them to sort it out. His only stipulations were that it had to be a fair fight and the fight was over immediately if either one said enough.

Within two months of my arrival I had been in two illegal fights. I won both encounters, acquiring without trying, something of a reputation. The acknowledged best fighter in the gaol was nicknamed Big Bruce. He was a fitness fanatic who boasted that every day he did 1,000 push-ups. Everyone was wary of Big Bruce.

Taking Dave's advice, I trained rigorously for the coming sports event. Sit-ups, push-ups, squats and running on the spot. One night while I was running on the spot, the occupant of the cell underneath mine began banging on the wall.

"Cut that noise down, arsehole!" someone yelled. "What do you think you're doing up there?"

I didn't like his attitude. "Get fucked!" I shouted.

"We'll see who gets fucked in the morning, Killick!"

"Sweet! And who are you, big mouth?"

"Big Bruce! I'll see you in the morning, arsehole."

Damn! He must have changed cells. What was I going I do? Maybe if I stopped he'd forget about it. No, not Big Bruce. He was always looking for an excuse to bash someone. Oh well, what's done is done. I might as well carry on, as it wouldn't make any difference. I continued to run on the spot as hard as I could for half an hour. The next morning when they opened my door I came out warily. As I came downstairs, Big Bruce was waiting for me. There were guards everywhere; I knew he wouldn't start anything there.

"I'll see you at sports Saturday morning," he said.

Surprised, I nodded. I had expected him to want to fight me in a cell. On Saturday morning, Dave counselled me. He considered himself my mentor. My first self-appointed mentor, Joe, had been a crook who ripped off the social security and had tried to molest me. My second self-appointed mentor was the Kingsgrove Slasher whose favourite pastime was breaking into houses and slashing women's bedclothes while they were still wearing them.

"Move around him and keep jabbing him with your left," Dave said. "He might do a lot of push-ups, but he can't run. He'll soon get tired of chasing you. Then you move in for the kill."

I didn't tell him I was scared. Big Bruce outweighed me by at least 20 kilograms and was three years older. In desperation I tried, for the first time in four years, to summon Paleface, but to no avail. Despairing, I wondered if he had been nothing more than a childhood illusion. Later, I assumed it was because Monkey Nuts was there to ensure a fair fight. Paleface would have none of that. With him, it was win at any cost.

Big Bruce, who had taped his hands, was a southpaw. I hadn't known this until he jabbed me with two straight rights and then dropped me with a fast left. I'd never encountered a southpaw before. Getting up, I tried to use a bit of fancy footwork to move around him but I was dazed from the punches and he dropped me again with a powerful left. Jumping up, I grabbed him around the waist, but Monkey Nuts rushed in and separated us. Big Bruce hit me with another left and I went down again. As I staggered to my feet, my vision was blurred. Blood was gushing from both my nose and my mouth. All thoughts of caution or defence had gone. I rushed at him, wildly throwing punches at his head. I had taken him by surprise. One of my punches caught him on the mouth, splitting his lip and drawing blood. As he jumped back, I saw a flash of fear in his eyes. I sensed then that Big Bruce was a coward. He could give it but he couldn't take it. But I was unable to take advantage of my sudden insight. Still dazed and unsteady on my feet, I was easy pickings for him. He dropped me twice more before Monkey Nuts moved in and stopped the one-sided contest.

"That's enough," he said, helping me to my feet.

I didn't argue with him. I was well and truly beaten.

Big Bruce spread it around that he had knocked me down five times. I felt ashamed until I heard Dave say to a couple of guys: "If he got knocked down five times he must have kept getting back up again."

I deleted running on the spot from my training programme. The fight with Big Bruce had taught me a valuable lesson. You should never go into any contest, no matter how overwhelming the odds against you, believing you can't win. If you do, you'll lose for sure. You have to believe in your ability to come through as a winner. If you do that you've got a chance.

21

Leonard Keith Lawson and The Lone Avenger
(1961-1962)

When the Easter Sports carnival began, I entered the 440 yards (400 metres). The race was run around the inside perimeter of the gaol. Dave estimated it to be closer to 550.

There were about 60 entrants for the race. We were a motley lot from petty thieves, conmen and forgers, to arsonists, rapists and murderers.

I decided that I would drop out early and sprint home. It was the way I liked my horses to win. When the race began I merely jogged and soon found myself among the tail-enders. It was a mistake. Guys were pushing and jostling each other in a no holds barred contest. As I increased my pace and began passing runners a tiring rapist shoved me into a burly housebreaker who swore at me. By the halfway mark a lot of the unfit runners were tiring. There was a long, clear run at the back of the tailor and carpenter shops and I was able to sprint full speed. I was still full of running but five or six runners had a big lead on me. On the final corner I was fast closing the gap when a nasty-spirited murderer saw me coming and cut me off. I had to ease and go around him.

"Arsehole!" I yelled.

Straightening up, I saw three runners ahead of me. I gave it everything I had, passing two but unable to catch the winner, a conman from England.

I shook his hand. Dave came over. "Good run, John."

"It was a bit rough back there. Sixty runners are too many."

For the Queen's Birthday Sports Carnival they ran heats. This time

I won both my heat and the final. I was never beaten again in a race at Goulburn.

For me, 1961 went slowly. In February, the last trams to run in Sydney made their historic final trips to Maroubra and La Perouse and I felt a sense of loss. Memories of all the tram trips with Mum to visit her sister in Maroubra pervaded my thoughts and I became depressed. Mum and the trams were gone forever.

Although the Sunday newspapers were the only ones we had access to, I was able to keep abreast with important events by listening to the news and reading *Time* magazine. It didn't concern me that President Kennedy sent 5,000 US troops to Vietnam and called them military advisors. And while the West was outraged over the building of the Berlin Wall, I despaired of being trapped behind the Goulburn Wall. The Russians launched the first man, Yuri Gagarin, into space and orbiting Earth. President Kennedy's disastrous attempts to liberate Cuba resulted in 1,500 Cuban refugees being killed or captured during the Bay of Pigs fiasco. In July, Ernest 'Papa' Hemingway, one of America's greatest writers, killed himself with a shotgun blast to the head. He was 61. I was disappointed when the Menzies Government, which had held office throughout the '50s, continued its dominance by winning a close Federal Election. Although I was disinterested in politics I knew Dad, a staunch Labor man all his life, hated Menzies. The mighty *Tulloch* made his farewell appearance at Eagle Farm, winning the Brisbane Cup by two lengths carrying the crushing weight of nine stone 12 pounds (62.5 kg). When I heard about it on the radio, I had tears in my eyes. What a way to go out!

A few days after the 1961 Melbourne Cup, Leonard Keith Lawson raped and stabbed to death a 16-year-old girl in his Collaroy flat. The next day he took hostages at a Moss Vale girls' school and killed a 14-year-old girl. It created a huge media uproar because at the time when there was no parole system in NSW, Lawson had been released on special license only months before the killings. Lawson was another notorious criminal whose case I had been familiar with after hearing it on *Police Files*. He was a brilliant artist who created the comic book hero *The Lone Avenger*. I had read quite a few of them. In 1954, he had taken five models to a bushland area in Terrey Hills, tied them up at gunpoint and raped three of them. Although he had been sentenced to death, it was later commuted to 14 years of which he had served seven, most of them at Goulburn. When he died of a heart attack in his cell at Grafton in November 2003 he had spent 49.5 of his last 50 years in prison.

In December 1961, I was notified that I had passed my Leaving Certificate in English. I knew it wouldn't gain me anything but it gave me a sense of satisfaction, proving to myself that when I tried I could do it.

Dad and I corresponded every few months. In February 1962, he sent me a birthday card and a photo of a fibro house in Canley Heights. On the back he had written "Johnny, this will be your new home when you get out."

I knew that he was trying to salvage something between us, but it only saddened me. During the 19 months I had been in gaol he hadn't bothered to visit me once.

22
BIG BAD JOHN
(March 1962)

The day before I was released in early March, my mentor the Kingsgrove Slasher came to say goodbye. He wished me well and advised me to think twice before I did anything foolish.

He shook my hand. "If you can manage it, could you get me a penfriend? I'd prefer a pretty one."

"I'll try, Dave."

That night I was so excited I couldn't sleep. Most of the night I paced the floor. Tomorrow, after 20 months, I would be free again.

I walked through the gate at 11.00 am with nearly £12 and a train ticket to Sydney. After catching a taxi to the station, I found I had a few hours to wait before the train was due. For a while I walked along the streets and through the park, savouring freedom. My whole being was tingling with excitement that only a person who had been imprisoned for a long period of time can experience. No matter what I looked at, I felt an inner glow at the beauty of it all. To be alive and free, was a wonderful thing. I had read where some people, after being released from gaol, became depressed to the point where they longed to be back inside. I could never feel that way. During the trip to Sydney I sat beside a girl named Colleen. Although I hadn't spoken to a woman for 20 months, I didn't feel nervous or self-conscious talking to her. I told her I'd been in Goulburn visiting my aunty.

She smiled. "With a haircut like that I thought you must have just been released from Goulburn Gaol."

She had me. I shrugged "You're a clever girl. I suppose you don't want to talk to me now."

"On the contrary, I find you interesting. What were you in gaol for?"

"Robbing a bank." In those days, bank robbers were rare and highly regarded by other criminals.

She smiled again. "You don't look like a bank robber to me."

"That's because I'm not wearing my mask."

She laughed. "Really, you look more like a cheque forger or a burglar."

I didn't like her much. She had a smart arse attitude, freckles, and from what I could see, she was a bit on the plump side. We chatted for a while. Like most people who haven't been inside she was curious about gaol. I entertained her with gaol anecdotes and stories about some of the infamous prisoners. She told me she shared a flat in Bondi with two girlfriends. Although I wasn't overly attracted to her, she appeared to be ready to be propositioned.

"Would you like to have a few drinks with me before you go home?" I asked.

"Oh, I suppose it would be an experience to have a drink with an ex-bank robber," she mocked. "My girlfriends will be green with envy."

As we walked through the exit of the country platform at Central, I saw Dad. I hadn't seen him for two years and his appearance shocked me. He had aged noticeably.

We shook hands. "Hi, Dad. How did you know I'd be on this train?"

"Your old man could've been a detective, don't forget that."

"I could have got off at Strathfield."

He feinted with his left and threw a right, stopping it a few inches from my jaw. Colleen gave him a startled look.

He gave her a wink. "Johnny's always been open to a sucker punch." He turned to me, "Who's the young lady?"

I introduced them. "Perhaps your father would like a drink with us?" She smiled at Dad. "Do you drink, Mister Killick?"

"Don't answer that, Dad. You might incriminate yourself."

Colleen laughed. Dad glared at me. It was obvious that he had been drinking. "You're still a mug lair, Johnny."

The three of us went to a hotel in Haymarket. We were a peculiar combination. After we all had a few drinks, Colleen became anxious to leave. Dad held her by the hand. He stared at her, tears in his eyes. "Johnny's my son. My own flesh and blood. While he was in that place I felt helpless. Have you heard the song *Big bad John*?"

Colleen nodded. Dad continued, "Well, that was me and Johnny. Big Bad Johnny, trapped down the mine and I couldn't get him out."

Colleen gave me a desperate look. "John, I really do have to be going."

"Get your girl a taxi, Johnny! Never keep a lady waiting."

Stuff this! Father or not, I'd had enough. For two years he hadn't bothered to come and see me, now he was spoiling my night out. "Come on, Colleen," I said. "I'll take you home."

She stood up. "It's all right, I can get home okay. You stay with your father John, you haven't seen each other for a long time."

I shrugged. There were better looking girls around. I walked with her to the door. "Would you like a penfriend in Goulburn? He's a really nice guy."

She showed interest. "Who is he?"

"Dave Scanlon. He was my best friend."

She gave me a searching look. "Why is he in gaol?"

"He was the Kingsgrove Slasher."

She slapped my face, and then walked out. Some of the drinkers yelled their approval. Rushing after her I grabbed her by the arm. She tried to jerk free. I held her firmly. "Why did you slap me?"

"Your sick little joke didn't impress me," Colleen said. "What type of girl do you think I am that I'd write to a mass rapist?"

"He's not a rapist. All he did was slash night clothes and things."

"I don't care what he did. He's a bloody pervert. You are your father are unreal people. Now let me go!"

Dad came out. "Johnny! What's going on?"

I released my grip on her arm. "Don't worry about it, Dad. The lady's leaving."

She hurried away. Dad scratched his balding head. "Never trust a woman who's got a good right hook." He laughed. "What did you do to upset her?"

I stared at him. "You honestly don't know, do you, Dad?"

He put his arm around my shoulder. "Let's go and have another drink."

I pulled away from him. "I want to be alone for a while. I'll be home later."

We looked at each other, embarrassed, a million things left unsaid that never would be said. For a moment, I softened. I moved forward and hugged him. "Thanks for being there, Dad. I'll be home by twelve."

He nodded sadly. "Keep your guard up, Johnny."

I walked away. The euphoric feeling I'd experienced immediately after my release had well and truly gone, replaced by an awareness of loneliness and uncertainty. The episode with Colleen had shattered my confidence. Unreal people! Was I an unreal person? Seeing carefree couples walking hand in hand, I began to feel alienated from normal people. I had no one with whom I could share intimacy. Eventually I wandered up to Kings Cross. Walking down Palmer Street I debated whether or not I should pay £2 for a prostitute. I'd always sworn that I'd never hire a pro, but at that moment the idea was enticing. As I walked past the doors where the girls, dressed in short-shorts or flimsy dresses, were standing, I noticed one particularly pretty girl. I stopped and stared at her. She smiled at me. I was tempted. But I was young and proud. I wondered how many customers she'd had that night or that week and I walked away. I decided to have a good meal and then go home. I'd gone 20 months without a girl and I wanted my next girl to be someone special.

23

LOVE AT FIRST SIGHT
(1962)

The house at Canley Heights contained only one bedroom where Dad and David slept. Although I had to sleep on the couch it was more comfortable than the prison bunks I had become accustomed to. The three of us living together again was a novelty. For a while we managed to get along reasonably well. David, now 17, was slightly taller and heavier than me. Blonde-haired and blue eyed, he had developed into a good-looking youth. He was employed in a pharmacy at Wynyard.

Reluctantly, I took a job working in a factory at Yennora. Every morning it was a battle for me to get up and trudge off to do my menial, boring chores at the factory. David and I paid Dad board and he cooked our meals and did the washing and cleaning. David had a girlfriend and he spent a lot of time at her place. One Saturday afternoon, a few weeks after I had moved in, a girl who lived in the house behind called me to the back fence. Puzzled, I walked over. She looked to be about 15. She said something, but it was barely audible.

I looked at her: she had a pert little nose and a perfect complexion. "Pardon?"

She cleared her throat. "Did you get the invitation I put in your letterbox?" She was red with embarrassment.

"No, I'm sorry, I didn't. What was it for?"

She again cleared her throat. "It was an invitation to come to our church tomorrow."

I laughed. "No wonder I didn't get it. My father would have thrown it away. I'm afraid we're not very religious."

Biting her lip she looked away. "Oh, I'm sorry to have bothered you." She began to walk away. Her long, blonde hair almost reaching her shapely buttocks.

I felt sorry for her. It was obvious she had summoned up all her courage to approach me. "Excuse me," I called out.

She turned around. Although she wasn't pretty, she was one of those girls who attracted me.

I smiled. "I'd like to come to your church."

She gave me a flashing smile. Her teeth were flawless. "I'm pleased. I'm Irene."

That night I mentioned the missing invitation to Dad. He admitted that he had thrown it away. I told him of my intention to go to church with Irene.

He gave me a look that implied I was a cretin. "If you get mixed up with that mob down the back you're sillier than I thought. The mother's a religious nut."

Dad was totally anti-religion. Early in my life Mum had encouraged me to say my prayers every night. For a while I went to Sunday school. Dad consistently ridiculed God, priests, Sunday school, church – anything to do with religion. I was uncertain what to believe. As I grew older I found it hard to believe in an Almighty Being with angels in the sky and the Devil and demons beneath the Earth in a place called Hell. And what type of God would sacrifice his son under the most horrific circumstances imaginable? And if dinosaurs roamed the Earth hundreds of millions of years ago, why did it take so long for God to put human beings on Earth? What was he doing during those hundreds of millions of years? I had huge doubts about God.

I had agreed to go to church with Irene because she interested me. On the way to church she told me that, in 1952, she and her family had emigrated from Russia. When she was ten, her father had walked out leaving her mother to support her and her younger brother. Her mother had turned to God for help. Her church was the Russian Orthodox in Cabramatta. I was relieved that the minister spoke in English. After the service, Irene introduced me to some of the people, including her mother – a small, plain looking woman who did her hair up in a bun. I walked home with Irene, her mother and her brother, Peter, who was ten. Her mother asked if I was a Christian. I told her I was. She asked when I had been baptised.

"When I was a little boy."

She gave me a hard look. "If you wish to go to church with Irene you'll have to become baptised."

I wasn't sure what she was talking about.

Despite her mother's coolness towards me, Irene and I soon became romantically involved. A few weeks after meeting her I left my factory job. For an income, I used my old trick of selling raffle tickets. I was able to choose my working hours and I was often waiting for Irene when she came out of school. In many ways she was naïve. She didn't have a radio or television in her house and her mother forbade her to read the newspapers. All those things her mother said were tools of the Devil. One day I took Irene into a milk bar. Going to the jukebox I played an Elvis song *Can't Help Falling in Love*. After listening to it she said it was a beautiful song. She pointed to a photo on the jukebox of Ricky Nelson. "Is that Elvis Presley?"

I wondered how many people in Australia didn't know what Elvis looked like. It made me feel protective towards her. But occasionally she would surprise me by demonstrating that she could be hard-hearted, even cynical. One night I accompanied her and her mother to a church service in the city for homeless men. When an old guy asked me if I could lend him ten shillings, I gave it to him. Irene immediately came over.

"Don't give them money," she said angrily. "They only spend it on methylated spirits."

Sometimes she would point to someone in church declaring them hypocrites because, according to her, it was common knowledge that they were committing adultery. Dad hadn't been far off the mark with his summation of the mother. She lived for the church. She told me that she wasn't happy about Irene and I becoming serious because I wasn't a true Christian and my father often came home drunk. The young minister,

Nickolai, liked Irene and wanted to marry her. The only problem was, Irene didn't fancy him. One night Irene and I went for a walk. We strolled into a nearby school and I took off my jacket for her to sit on. When we returned to her place the police were there. Certain that we had eloped, her mother had rung them.

She pointed to the back of my jacket. "Look at his coat! They've been rolling around in the dirt fornicating. He's ruined my daughter!"

Irene ran inside crying. I protested her innocence. The old sergeant took me aside. "Look, son, I think you'd be wise to give that girl a miss. If the mother's like that, the daughter will turn out to be the same, I know what I'm taking about."

"The power of the flesh!" the mother screamed. "It's the work of the Devil!"

"Let's get out of here," the cop said.

After that, Irene's mother placed her under a curfew. She was forbidden to talk to me again. But we continued to meet. Irene was concerned that I had stopped going to church. I confessed that I had doubts about God and religion.

"Maybe Nickolai is the right guy for you," I said, meaning it.

She began to cry. "I love you. But you've lost your way. You have to come back to the church."

I hugged her. "Don't worry, things will work out. I think I'll get a place of my own."

"I think you should." She cleared her throat. "I don't wish to be disrespectful, but your father is a bad influence on you."

Dad and I had been arguing a lot. No matter how hard we tried, after a while we couldn't live in the same house together.

I rented a room from an old couple, less than half a mile from Dad's. The next day the couple's two granddaughters called in. Both girls were extremely attractive. Joyce, who was 20, was married; she was the prettier of the two. Maureen, although only 16, had a figure to rival Sophia Loren's.

One Saturday afternoon, not long after I had met them I walked to the shops at Canley Heights with her. She was wearing a pair of red shorts that looked as though they were going to burst at the seams. After she had bought some fruit and vegetables we went into a milk bar. As we sipped our drinks we stood by the door. I told her a joke and she laughed.

Remembering that Irene's mother worked on Saturday afternoons cleaning the hairdresser's across the street, I glanced over. Standing inside the hairdresser's window, a cleaning rag in her hand, was Irene. She was staring at me. I looked at Maureen. A girl like Irene might get the wrong impression. "Maureen, I'm going to duck around and see Dad. I'll see you later."

"Can't I come?"

"No, better not. He might be drunk."

I hurried across the street. Irene saw me coming and turned her back to me. I tapped on the window. Ignoring me, she rinsed out her cloth in a bucket of water. Shrugging, I walked away. I'd see her after she had cooled down. I had gone about ten metres when she ran out and tipped the grimy, soapy water over me. I spun around. She was running with the empty bucket as fast as her stocky little legs would carry her towards the door of the shop. I ran after her but she managed to get inside and slammed the door. I banged on the door. A short, fat guy came in from the rear of the shop. He was the owner's son. He said something to Irene, and then came to the door, peering at me through the glass. My clothes were saturated. "What do you want?"

"Open the door. I want to talk to Irene."

"She doesn't want to talk to you." He gave me a dismissive gesture. "Go away."

His attitude riled me. "Listen, Roley Poley, either you open that door or I'll fucking smash it!"

He glared at me. I made a bet with myself that he would threaten to call the police. "Irene, call the police!"

"If you call the cops on me, Irene," I shouted, "you and I are finished!"

She came to the door but didn't open it. She looked pretty when she was angry. "Just go away and leave me alone. I don't want to see you again." She started to cry.

Suddenly Maureen was by my side. "John, what happened?"

"Please, Maureen, go away. I'll explain later."

Irene was glaring at Maureen with undisguised loathing.

"Maureen and I are just friends!" I shouted.

"I hate you!" Irene yelled, tears streaming down her face.

"Come on, let's go," I said to Maureen. Maybe Irene would cool down in a few days, but I doubted it. Hate and love, due to the intensity of the feelings can often transpose.

That night I met Cathy.

Maureen had persuaded me to accompany her and her mother to a bingo game in Fairfield. "It'll help you forget what happened today," she said.

The church called the game housie and it was conducted in a large hall by the Catholic Church. The players were mostly women. It cost sixpence a ticket. A guy drew marbles from a box and called out the numbers. The first person to cross off all the numbers on their cards won £6. Cathy was one of the girls who sold the tickets and gave change.

I walked over to buy some tickets from her. "Hi. Could you give me a couple of lucky tickets?"

She gave me a beautiful smile. There was electricity between us. I could see she was affected as much as I was.

"I can't guarantee they are lucky," she said, her face flushed.

I stood there staring at her. Her pretty face was highlighted by big, brown eyes and dark brown hair done in a pageboy cut. I thought she was the most beautiful girl I had ever seen.

"What's your name?"

"Cathy."

"I'm John. I'm sitting at the third table. I won't buy tickets from any other girl."

I won with my first card. Excited, I jumped up. "I'm out!"

A few women gave me irritated looks. One of them pointed to her card. "I've been waiting for one number for five calls."

Cathy came over. "Congratulations."

I looked into her eyes. "This is just the start. Give me some more tickets. You're my lucky charm."

Before a halt was called to the proceedings, I had, much to the rancour of some of the ladies around me, won three more and tied one. Maureen's mother said she couldn't recall anyone winning five rounds on the one night.

Cathy was just as excited as I was. I tried to hand her £3. "That's your tip."

"Oh, I couldn't take that."

"Take it. It was because of you that I won."

"My parents wouldn't approve. They'll only tell me to give it back to you."

I shrugged. "Don't tell them." I held her gaze. "Do you tell your parents everything you do?"

She blushed. "Yes, I do."

"How old are you?"

"Nearly 16."

I was surprised. She looked older. "So you're 15. Do you realise that if I kissed you I could get into trouble." The blush deepened.

"If you take the money I won't kiss you. I'll be here next week. If your parents insist, you can return it then."

On Sunday I went for a long walk. Cathy was constantly in my thoughts. I now realised that Irene and I weren't suited to each other. I came to the tennis courts known as Premiers in Canley Vale. I had played on them many times. I stopped to watch the players, some of whom I knew. One of them, my old teammate, Val, gave me a wave. I returned the wave then walked away. My days with the old gang were gone.

On Monday I was waiting for Cathy when she came out of school. She looked younger in her Catholic school uniform. Although she had been walking with two other girls she said something to them, then, smiling, rushed towards me. I wanted to grab her and hug her, but I took her hand and we walked as though we had been going steady for years. As often as I could I met her after school. The walk to her place was about a mile and sometimes it took us an hour to get there. I'd often take her into a phone booth and kiss her and stand there looking into her eyes. She confided to me that she loved me, and didn't know what she would do if we parted. I told her we wouldn't part. I rang her every night. Sometimes, much to her father's chagrin, we were on the phone for hours. We were never stuck for something to talk about. It was young love and for me it was real.

Her parents were strict and she wasn't allowed to date until she was 18. But gradually they became accustomed to John ringing their daughter. Eventually they relented to the extent that they permitted me to come to their house to see Cathy. She told me that her father approved of the way my shoes were highly polished and that I had avoided the stovepipe, flecked pants which were popular at the time with young guys. But he wouldn't relent with regard to dating and even taking her to the movies was prohibited. She had two sisters. One sister, Patricia, was 19 and was already disillusioned with men. She had fallen in love with an American sailor who was ten years older and was married. After his ship sailed she didn't hear from him again. The younger sister, Mildred, was twelve. She was a delightful little miss who often teased Cathy about me. Although Cathy had been born in Australia, they were American citizens. The father, Roland, an American, had met Cathy's mother in Sydney during the war. He was a slightly built, good-looking man of forty who still spoke with an American accent.

During the days I became a professional seller of raffle tickets. Most days I sold two books of tickets. I was averaging £40 a week. Roland, a foreman for Cablemakers at Liverpool, was earning £29 a week. But I found it difficult to save. I spent freely on clothes, shoes, records and I often dined in restaurants, something I had promised myself while starving in the pound. Occasionally I went to the races or the trots; on most Saturdays I placed bets with the SP bookie at Canley Vale. Sometimes I won, more often I lost. I rarely had much money at one time.

At one stage I decided to become a professional gambler. Every night, at ten o'clock, I'd catch a train to Town Hall and walk to the baccarat game at Perc Galea's Victoria Club in Kings Cross. The second night I was there one of the gamblers said to Perc Galea: "Hey, Perc, I've had a bad night. Can you give me a winner for tomorrow?"

At the time Galea was the biggest punter in Australia. He gave the gambler a hard stare, and then rubbed the huge diamond ring on his finger. "Have you got a house?"

The gambler nodded. "Yes."

Galea shrugged. "Put it on *Indian Prince* tomorrow."

Galea owned *Indian Prince*. He had given the gambler what he'd believed was a certainty. *Indian Prince* started at 7 to 1 on and was beaten. The Sunday papers claimed that Galea had lost a fortune on it and he was known to bet up to £50,000 on horses that he fancied. I wondered if the gambler had lost his house. If I'd been smart, I would have realised then that betting on horses truly was a mug's game.

At the baccarat game, I tried the double up system. I'd bet one pound, if I lost I'd bet two, then four, eight, 16 and finally 32. To lose my bank of £63 I had to lose six consecutive bets. As soon as I won six times I'd leave. I considered £12 profit a night to be excellent wages. For three consecutive nights I won. On the fourth occasion I lost my bank. Stunned, I walked out.

The doorman enquired how I had fared.

I looked at him. It was hard to accept what had happened. "I lost six bets straight."

He gave me an incredulous look. "Gees, that's got to be a record."

As I walked away, I heard the bastard laughing.

The next day I was selling raffle tickets again. Each day I chose a different suburb to work in. Sometimes I travelled as far out as the migrant hostel at East Hills. I always did good business at the English hostels at East Hills, Cabramatta and Bunnerong. The English migrants were only too willing to risk a few shillings for the chance to win a transistor. But the other ethnic groups in the hostels such as the one at Villawood were frugal with their money. They rarely bought a ticket and after a while I avoided them.

In later years I experienced true remorse at having ripped off those people who were obviously battlers. To me it was worse than robbing a bank.

24

Mugged in the Park
(1962)

One night I was watching television with Cathy after the others had gone to bed. For the first time, I made a serious pass at her and she hit me in the eye.

I jumped up. "You're still a little girl, aren't you?"

"Yes, I am."

We stared at each other in the semi-darkness. "I must be crazy," I said, holding my eye.

She switched on the light. "Let me have a look at your eye."

"Don't worry about it. I've had worse."

"I guess it's time for you to go."

I gave her a hard look. "I might be going away for a while."

She shrugged, but I could see she was shaken up.

"I'll see you," I said and walked out.

For a week I didn't see her or call her. I met a beautiful Ukrainian girl named Stacey. I took her to a movie, most of the time I thought about Cathy. She was in my blood. I took Stacey home, kissed her goodbye and left her wondering what she had done wrong.

The following night, after selling raffle tickets in the Newtown area, I went to the Town Hall Hotel and drank too many Bacardis. Being drunk was a new experience for me. On my way home, instead of a Liverpool via Granville train, I caught a Liverpool via Regents Park, which didn't go to Canley Vale. Blissfully unaware that I was on the wrong train, I began a conversation with a plain looking girl named Pam. By the time we reached Lidcombe there was only one other passenger, a queer looking guy, in the carriage. As I chatted to Pam the guy moved to the seat across from us. I glanced at him. He was staring at us, a glazed look in his eyes. He had an erection and was rubbing himself through his trousers. I couldn't believe what I was seeing. He gave me a sickly smile and nodded. Pam looked over and gasped. He stopped rubbing himself but the erection remained. Instinct told me to attack him, but I controlled the impulse.

I whispered to Pam. "This guy should be taught a lesson."

She nodded. I could see she was outraged. I turned to the deviate who was eyeing us uneasily. He had an egg-shaped balding head and dribbling lips. He sickened me.

"Would you like to come and watch my girl and I do naughty things?"

He nodded excitedly. He couldn't believe his luck. "I'll pay you," he said.

"How much?"

He hesitated. "Two pounds."

That's what you think, skinflint.

The three of us got off at Carramar. The railway attendant didn't bother to come out and collect our tickets. Maybe he was scared of being robbed. It was an isolated area.

On the way to the park the deviate began to worry that he could be walking into a trap. I reassured him.

About 50 metres inside the park I stopped. "This will do."

His licentious nature overcame his fear. "Are you both going to take your clothes off first?"

I punched him in the mouth. He fell to his knees, clutching his mouth. Blood was dripping onto the grass. "What did you do that for?"

"Because you're a deviate. Now give me your money."

"No."

Grabbing hold of his shirtfront I heaved him to his feet. He grabbed me around the waist and started screaming. The touch of him repulsed me. I head-butted him in the face and he again fell down. His screaming had subsided to a low groaning.

Pam began to panic. "Leave him alone." She grabbed hold of me trying to drag me away. "Quick, we'd better go!"

I shoved her away. "Keep out of it."

The deviate began to whimper. "Please don't hit me any more. I haven't done anything to you."

"Don't you realise what you did, you deviate dog!"

"I'm sorry. I really am. Please let me go."

"Give me your money."

Pam began running away. She might go to the police. I'd have to hurry.

"I've only got a few pounds."

I remembered the deviate in the toilet at Canley Vale. "Undo your collar and tie." Did all deviates wear collars and ties?

Holding his face, he sat up. Blood was dripping onto his shirt. "No," he said defiantly. His money seemed to be more important to him than his personal safety. He probably had a hundred quid on him. I bent over and threw a punch at him but I was still a bit drunk and unsteady on my feet. I slipped over.

Jumping up he started running. Scrambling to my feet, I went after him.

Stopping, he picked up something and turned around. "Don't come near me!" he yelled, backing away. I stopped, trying to ascertain what he was holding. It was a beer bottle. I hated this guy. Irrespective of whether or not I got hurt, I was going to get him and his money. I rushed at him. He tried to hit me with the bottle but I had been prepared for it and took the blow on the arm. I hit him with a crunching right to the face. Dropping the bottle he fell backwards, hitting his head on the ground.

I grabbed the bottle. "You want to fight dirty, do you!"

He rolled over and scrambling to his hands and feet, began to scamper away on all fours. He was screaming again. It was a terrible sound. I went after him and belted him on the head with the bottle with such force that it smashed. Without a sound he collapsed on the ground.

My God! What had I done?

I dropped to my knees and shook him. "Hey, mate! Are you all right?"

He groaned. At least he was alive! "Take it easy, mate," I said. "I'll help you."

He began to whimper. "Please don't hit me anymore."

I felt ashamed. The poor bastard. How could I have done this?

"Don't worry, I'm not going to hit you." I helped him to sit up. His head was covered in blood.

"I'll have to go to the hospital," he said.

I took out my handkerchief and dabbed his head with it. Although the back of his head was cut, it wasn't deep. "You might have to wait for a few hours at the hospital." If we went to the hospital they would be certain to call the police. "I'll take you to my father's house. He's a male nurse."

He was too sick to argue. I piggybacked him for nearly half a mile to the Fairfield taxi rank. He told me his name was Arthur.

"Well, listen, Arthur. When we get to Dad's, I'll tell him we were attacked in the park by muggers."

There were a few vacant cabs on the rank. We got in the first one. I gave the driver an address a few streets from Dad's. He turned around and stared at Arthur. "What happened to you, mate?"

"We got mugged in the park," I said.

The driver shook his head and started the car. "It's a bad park for bashings and robberies. Hadn't you better go to the police?"

"We can't," I said. "We're homosexuals."

The driver gave me a filthy look in the rear vision mirror. He didn't say another word. When we arrived I paid the fare tipping him a shilling, then walked with Arthur to the gate. The cab sped away.

I turned around. "Dad lives a couple of streets away."

Arthur had become suspicious. "Why did we come here?"

"In case the driver calls the cops. All taxi drivers are frustrated cops." I paused. "Arthur, I want you to punch me as hard as you can in the mouth."

He stared at me as though I'd confirmed his suspicions that I was a lunatic. "I don't want to punch you."

"I have to be marked up a bit. Otherwise Dad will be suspicious with you being all cut up and me without a mark on me." I stood there with my hands by my sides. "Now come on, belt me one."

He backed away. "I can't do it, John."

"Of course you can do it. Just remember what I did to you. Remember you tried to hit me with the bottle."

"That was before I knew you. I couldn't do it now. Honestly."

I sighed. "All right, I'll have to say I ran away. Remember, whatever I tell Dad, you back me up."

A few minutes later I knocked on Dad's door. I was relieved to see the lights were on. David, in his pyjamas, opened the door. "Hi, Dave. Me and Arthur have just been mugged." I walked inside. "Come in, Arthur."

David was staring at us. "Gee, John, where did it happen?"

I walked into the lounge room. Dad, who had been watching TV, stood up. "Hi, Dad. Arthur and I were attacked by louts in Fairfield Park. They nearly killed him."

It wasn't often Dad was stuck for words. But this time I had him. He stared at Arthur with a dumbfounded look on his face.

"There were five of them," I continued. "I managed to run away. If I'd have tried to help Arthur I'd have been bashed too."

Arthur was nervous; he was dribbling. He gave Dad a sickly smile. "I was going to go to hospital but John said it was best to come here because you're a male nurse."

Dad, who, fortunately, was sober, continued to stare at this dribbling, queer-looking guy with the bald, egg-shaped head covered in blood. He turned to me. "What were you doing in the park?"

I'd been prepared for that one. "I got a bit drunk in town and caught the wrong train so I got off at Carramar. Arthur lives at Carramar and was on the same train. He was walking ahead of me through the park when the five louts attacked him."

Arthur nodded. "That's right, five of them."

"When they saw me three of them came after me," I said. I grinned. "Lucky, I'm a good runner."

I could see he didn't believe me. But he bathed and cleansed Arthur's wounds before using strips of towelling for a bandage. It was obvious that he didn't like Arthur. He probably figured out that Arthur was a deviate. But I knew that he had concluded that I was the one who had bashed Arthur; by tending to his wounds, Dad was doing his best to help me avoid being arrested. Thanking Dad for his assistance, I walked with Arthur to Canley Vale station. He was strange looking at the best of times, but with his clothing dishevelled and bloodstained and the towelling wrapped around his head like a turban, he looked like something out of a horror movie.

Before he got on the train I shook his hand. "We are what we are, Arthur. I'm sorry about what happened."

He gave me his sickly smile. "You're a nice young man, John. But you have to control that temper of yours."

I didn't know it then, but the episodes with Arthur were far from over.

25

A Rogue and a Vagabond
(1962-1963)

For the next few months life was good. Cathy and I were getting closer. A few times I persuaded her to take the day off from school and we would spend it together. Her father hinted that as soon as she turned 16 he would allow her to go out with me.

In October, I became convinced there would be a nuclear war. For two weeks most people lived in fear that the world would be blown to pieces. A US U2 spy plane took photos proving the Soviets were placing nuclear missiles in Cuba. The US placed a strict quarantine on all offensive military equipment being shipped to Cuba. Kennedy called on the Soviet leader, Khrushchev 'to move the world back from the abyss of destruction.'

When one of the two U2 pilots, who had discovered the missile sites, was shot down over Cuba, I met Cathy after school. "There's going to be a war," I said.

She gave me a concerned look. "Dad thinks the Russians will back down."

"I'm not so sure. Khrushchev is an old man. Maybe he doesn't care any more. Could you imagine Hitler backing down?"

"Hitler was a maniac."

"How do we know Khrushchev isn't a maniac? Or Kennedy for that matter? These two guys are playing a dangerous game and people like you and I are sitting back praying that they won't kill the lot of us. I can't see either of them backing down."

She gripped my hand. We stared at each other appalled at the thought that we might not have a future. "Cathy, I want you to come with me to Orange. If Sydney gets hit by a missile, Orange will be safe."

She gave me a sad smile. "I couldn't leave my family, John. We just have to hope that it won't happen."

I'd known that, short of kidnapping her, I wouldn't be able to persuade her to leave her family. She was that type of girl. "Well if you're not going I'm not going either."

Disregarding anyone walking past, we stopped and hugged each other. "Whatever happens," I said, "remember I love you as much as it's possible for a man to love a little imp."

She held me tight. "And I love you, John. I just know everything will be okay."

On 28 October, Khrushchev agreed to move, under UN supervision, all the missiles from Cuba if the US would remove the blockade and promise not to invade Cuba. There was also a secret agreement that within six months, the US would remove their missiles from Turkey. A promise that was honoured.

Nevertheless, the second half of October 1962 will always be remembered as the time when the world held its breath, terrified that mankind would destroy itself and every living creature on Earth.

Despite the missile crisis, the Caulfield Cup was run as usual. When the New Zealander *Even Stevens* won easily, I was convinced that only a missile attack would prevent him from winning the Melbourne Cup. On Cup eve I entered Cathy and I in a Cup sweep. I couldn't believe my good fortune when I drew *Even Stevens*, Cathy drew a 40 to 1 outsider, *Comicquita*. *Even Stevens* won from *Comicquita*.

I met Cathy after school. She gave me an impish grin. "Where's my money?"

I stared at her in mock disgust. "Is this the same girl I met at the housie game who wouldn't take a tip?"

"You've turned me into a gambler. One of the girls brought a transistor to school and the sisters let us listen to the race." She smiled. "Last night Dad said *Comicquita* didn't have a chance, so I didn't hold out much hope. When the guy said *Comicquita* was finishing fast I couldn't believe it! I started jumping up and down."

I laughed. "That's how it gets you."

Not long after the Melbourne Cup, I was in the St George area selling raffle tickets when my luck ran out. A middle aged woman with tinted hair and a nervous twitch that forced her head slightly sideways about every 20 seconds, became aggressive when I tried to sell her a ticket.

"Where are your credentials?" she demanded. Her head twisted sideways, gave three spasmodic jerks then pivoted back to its normal position.

I gave her my nicest smile. "I don't have any credentials, but the tickets are stamped." I handed her the book. "Here, have a look."

She examined the book of tickets. "Hmphh! Anyone could have stamped these. Why should I risk giving you a shilling when, for all I know, you could be pocketing the money?"

Occasionally, I'd encountered similar reactions. "Well, if you feel that way about it, madam, I don't expect you to buy a ticket. I'm sorry to have bothered you."

She gave another quick exhibition of head twitching, then said: "Before you go, I'd like to see some form of identification."

Why do some people go out of their way to cause trouble? I'd had enough. "Listen, Swivelhead, I don't have to give you anything. Goodbye!"

Instinct told me to leave the area. I headed towards the nearest railway station, which was about a kilometre away. A few minutes later a police car came up alongside me. The driver, who was on his own, yelled out to me that he wanted to talk to me.

Deciding to bluff it out, I walked over, frowning. "Yes, officer?"

He was a dark-haired guy aged about 25. "I've had a complaint about you from one of the residents." He gave me a hard look. "What have you got in the bag?"

"A transistor radio." I had bought a new transistor to show prospective ticket buyers what they could win.

"Who are you selling raffle tickets for?"

"Kogarah Judo Club."

"I've never heard of them. Do you have any form of identification?"

"Well, all the tickets are officially stamped."

"Hmm. I think the best thing we can do is for you to come with me and we'll check out your story. If it checks out okay there'll be no problems."

I felt adrenalin rush through me. He looked fit; this would be a good chase. I decided to confuse him first and gain a few seconds start. "Oh, there's my judo instructor."

He looked around. Dropping my bag, I began running. I ran past three houses then jumped the fence of the next one and ran down the path to the back yard. Scrambling over the fence, I glanced behind me. About 20 metres away the cop was coming after me. Trampling over the garden I had to unlatch a side gate before dashing up a path and out on to the street. Turning left, I ran down the street with the cop still after me. I ran about 300 metres before slowing down. Gasping for breath, I looked around: the cop, about 50 metres behind, was still coming. I continued to run but at slower pace. The cop had also slowed down. I ran into the yard of a nearby house and climbed over a few more fences before jumping down on to a railway track and climbing up the embankment to the other side. I saw the cop climbing over the fence; I gave him a wave and began jogging up the street. What a dumb cop! If he'd have been smart he would have stayed in his car and radioed for help.

I jogged along the street until Dumbo had climbed up the embankment and reached the street. Then I jumped down onto the track, scrambled up the other side and heaved myself over the nearest fence. This cop would rue the day he had chased me. After running through a few more yards and gardens I ran out to another street. A few times I heard people yelling out to me, but no one pursued me.

I began to jog in the direction from which I had come. No doubt the cop Dumbo had given up the chase. My plan now was to return to the police car and get my bag, if the police got hold of it they would be able to fingerprint the transistor. Anyway, the radio was too expensive to leave for the cops. I jogged most of the way to the police car. Four or five women were standing in a small group outside the house directly across the street. They were staring at me. I could sense the danger; they had called the police and were waiting for them.

Picking up my bag, I continued to jog along the footpath. Suddenly a police car turned into the street. Too exhausted to run faster, I continued jogging, studiously ignoring the car as it went past. Abruptly the car, its siren blaring, did a U-turn and came rushing towards me. Dropping the bag I leapt over the nearest fence. A cop jumped out of the car and came after me. It was almost a replay of the previous chase. I scrambled over a few fences and ran down a street. My lungs felt as though they were going to burst. This time the cop chasing me had his gun drawn.

"Stop, you bastard, or I'll shoot!" he shouted.

I kept on running. Stuff him! No cop would shoot me over a few raffle tickets. I ran across another lawn and down a path. Fear of arrest gave me enough adrenalin to keep going, but I knew I couldn't continue much farther. I ran into a back yard where a couple of little kids were playing. Rushing past them I leapt at the back fence and tried to heave myself over. The cop lunged at me and grabbed me by the back of my pullover. I felt it rip as I tried to jerk free.

He put a gun to my head. "Don't make me do it!" he screamed.

He sounded serious. I remembered Bathurst, talk about déjà vu!

"What are you chasing me for?" I gasped.

The two kids, a boy and a girl, were staring at us. Fancy a policeman catching a baddie in their own backyard. Wouldn't they have something to tell the other kids. I was taken to Kogarah Police Station where I was interviewed by two detectives. I had been expecting a bit of a thumping in reprisal for leading Dumbo up the railway track and leaving him there, but the detectives thought it was funny. One of them, a big guy who had false teeth that slipped when he laughed, nearly fell out of his chair laughing when I told him about Swivelhead.

"You're a funny bugger, John," he said, "so I'll tell you what we'll do.

We'll take you to court this afternoon, you plead guilty to imposition, and you'll get a 50 quid fine with time to pay."

I shrugged. "Sounds fair enough, will I need a solicitor?"

"What for? You're copping a plea on a misdemeanour," he said.

That afternoon I pleaded guilty to imposition. The magistrate regarded me with obvious contempt. "You're nothing but a rogue and a vagabond," he said.

I'd settle for that. Isn't that what they had called Errol Flynn?

"I sentence you to six months hard labour."

Six months in gaol for selling a few raffle tickets! I should have known you couldn't trust cops who laugh at the misfortune of others. Six months! What would Cathy say? I'd have to tell her I robbed a shop or something. I'd never live it down if she found out I went to gaol for selling raffle tickets. Later, before they put me in the van to go to Long Bay, I had to check my property. The transistor wasn't there. They said they hadn't found it. I'd expected that. But I was astonished when one of the cops said: "You've got some money here, two pounds."

I stared at him. "I had six pounds in my wallet."

His eyes narrowed. "You've got two pounds in your wallet."

I shrugged. What would be the point in arguing about it? I couldn't refrain from saying: "Did you keep it for yourself, or did you split it four ways?"

He looked away. "Put him in the van before I lose my temper."

As they shoved me, none too gently, into the van I wondered what the kids who had witnessed my arrest would think if they knew the policeman had robbed the baddie.

26

OUT AGAIN
(1962-1963)

Although nearly two years had passed since I'd been at Long Bay, it hadn't changed. After being processed in the Reception Room I was given a meal and taken to a three out cell in One Range. Still shocked at finding myself a convicted prisoner within hours of my arrest, I told my two cell mates what happened. Both of them advised me to appeal.

"It's only a shit charge," one of them said. "You'll get appeal bail and be out."

Bail would be useless to me because I had no chance of raising it. I knew guys who had waited nearly two years before their appeals had been decided. The possibility of languishing in the appeal yard for a longer period of time than my original sentence was a risk I wasn't prepared to take. I resolved to grin and bear it.

Usually, anyone serving less than 12 months would automatically be classified minimum security and sent to a prison farm. But because I had escaped from Bathurst Courthouse in 1960, I was classified maximum security and sent to Bathurst gaol. I decided not to write to Cathy. With remissions I'd be out in about 4.5 months and then I could see her and explain why I had disappeared. I knew she would be concerned, even distressed at my sudden, unexplained departure from her life, but an impersonal, censored gaol letter from me would probably do more harm than good, particularly if her parents read it.

At Bathurst I was assigned a job as a yard sweeper, which paid sixpence (five cents) a week. Each week all prisoners were permitted to spend two thirds of their earnings on groceries. There were six yard sweepers; every week each of us would order four pence worth of broken biscuits. Ironically, The Western Stores, which I had robbed 30 months earlier, supplied the groceries. At that time, biscuits were sold from large tins. The girls who packed the orders always sent those of us who bought the broken biscuits a large paper bag full of them. These good-hearted country girls probably felt it wasn't fair that some of us only had four pence to spend while others were spending ten shillings or more. Eventually, though, the broken biscuits were deleted from the buy-up lists. One of the crims who bought a pound of Chocolate Montes complained that the broken biscuit boys had received larger bags of biscuits than he had.

A few days later he was noticed walking around with a broken nose and two black eyes. He told the authorities that he had bumped into a door. In gaol a lot of people bump into doors, fall down stairs and slip over in the shower. It seems to be an institutional hazard.

Each day I usually spent about an hour sweeping and hosing down the yard and polishing the brass locks on the gates. For the remainder of the day I had nothing to do other than pace up and down the yard. Fortunately, it was summer and I didn't have to spend too many days huddled under the tin shed.

I spent my 21st birthday at Bathurst. It didn't bother me. I had reached the stage where, having spent four consecutive birthdays in gaol, birthdays were unimportant to me. Early in 1963, Queen Elizabeth visited Australia. For all the prisoners in NSW gaols this was good news. We all received Queen's remission. It brought my release date forward to the middle of March.

During my stay at Bathurst I became friendly with a tall, thin guy of 23, named Don. We spent many hours pacing the yards together discussing our plans for the future. Although I spoke vaguely about buying a coffee lounge, I had no idea how I would finance it. I had no intentions of taking a tedious, low paying job after I was released. Inevitably, Don and I agreed that we would team up after he was released. "If we pull one good job," he said, "you'll be able to buy your coffee lounge."

He was due for release two months after me. "It'll be best if you get a job until I get out," he said.

"Don't worry about me, Don. I'll be there when you get out." He looked dubious. I gave him a reassuring smile. "I won't be selling raffle tickets."

The morning I was released there was no feeling of euphoria rushing through me as it had the previous year on release. I knew that there was no certainly I would remain free.

This time Dad wasn't at Central to meet me. I rang Cathy. "Hi, Cathy."

I heard her catch her breath. After a few moments she said: "Oh, hi. I was wondering when you were going to ring."

I had to smile. She was a class act. "I had to go away for a while," I said.

"You could have written or rang long distance."

"Actually I couldn't. I'll tell you about it when I see you." I had decided that at the right moment I'd explain to her where I had been.

"I didn't think I'd ever see you again."

"That'll never happen. I love you."

There was silence for a few moments, then she said: "I love you, too. But I'm still mad at you."

I arranged to meet her after college the next day.

When I arrived at Dad's, David wasn't home. I sat down with Dad and we shared a bottle of beer. Neither of us could penetrate the invisible barrier that seemed to prevent both of us from expressing our true feelings. We talked about trivial matters, avoiding the main issues.

It was only after we had finished a second bottle that Dad said: "You're my son and you're welcome to stay here until you get on your feet, Johnny. But you and I are like two bull elephants, we can't live together without fighting."

It was one of the few things we agreed on.

The next morning I got up early and prepared breakfast for the three of us. David, who had come home after midnight, was glad to see me. As the three of us chatted amiably over breakfast we seemed like a normal family. But it was an illusion. We had never been a normal family. After David had left for work, I walked out the back to have a look around. Irene was in her backyard hanging out some clothes. I walked across to the back fence. At first she didn't notice me. Then, as she pegged the last piece of clothing she looked up and saw me. She looked good.

I smiled. "Hi, Irene. How are things with you?"

She turned around and ran inside. Girls ... how could you understand them?

Later that morning I called on the old couple from which, before my arrest, I had rented the room. I asked the old guy, Bill, for my belongings. "I've been away fruit picking," I said.

He gave me a hard stare. "I thought you might have been in gaol."

I nodded. "It was nothing serious, they gave me a job picking fruit on the farm." I paused. He continued to stare at me. His manner was close to hostile. I smiled. "How are the girls?"

"Why don't you go and ask them?"

Once they know that you have been in gaol a lot of people will turn against you. I respected this old guy. I wouldn't allow him to rile me and he was entitled to be antagonistic towards me. I'd probably shattered his illusion about nice young men.

"I'm sorry if I let you down, Bill. Thanks for everything anyway."

I walked away with my luggage feeling a proper bastard. Since Mum had died I'd done nothing but hurt people. It had been bad enough hurting people like old Bill and Dad, but I hadn't spared anyone. Not even Cathy. But what's done is done. I hadn't intentionally hurt anyone I told myself. But I knew that I had disregarded consequences to others when I had decided on certain courses of action.

I waited for Cathy outside Wynyard railway station. She was now enrolled in a nearby business college. When she saw me she ran to me and we hugged each other. Her girlish figure had filled out fractionally, her hair was longer, and the pageboy style was replaced by a more modish cut. Dressed in a white summer frock, she looked beautiful. When she had worn a school uniform I had always been self-conscious about walking hand in hand with her. But as we held hands on the way to our platform I was proud of the young beauty at my side. While walking home with her I told her I had been in gaol. Stopping, she turned to stare at me. I could see that it had never occurred to her that I might have been in gaol.

"Why would they put someone like you in gaol? I can't believe it."

There was no way I could find the courage to tell this girl that I had been in gaol for selling illegal raffle tickets, the smallest of small time crooks. Nor did I want her to know that I was a thief. I had prepared a story for her.

"I got into a fight with a guy, he was drunk and he got a bit vicious. I hit him in the eye and he lost the sight of the eye. They sentenced me to six months but I got out early for good behaviour."

"That's terrible, but it wasn't your fault." She paused. "I didn't know you could fight."

I shrugged. "It's not something to boast about."

She gave me an impish grin. "It was probably a lucky punch. But I'm glad you defended yourself."

I pulled her to me and kissed her. She had taken the news of me having been in gaol in her stride. "You're my type of girl."

She ran her hand lightly across the side of my face. "And you're my type of guy."

27

AMERICA OR BUST
(1963)

Less than a week after moving in with Dad and David, I moved out again, renting a room with a Russian family not far from Fairfield railway station. They didn't speak much English, which suited me, as they didn't ask many questions. I spent a lot of my evenings at Cathy's place; the irony of living with Russians and visiting Americans appealed to my sense of humour.

Rather than look for a job I returned to selling raffle tickets. I told myself that immediately anyone became suspicious I'd stop. As the weeks went by, Cathy and I became closer. I was becoming anxious and uncertain about our future. The only certainty was that I loved her more than I'd ever thought myself capable of loving a girl. The thought of losing her became unacceptable. I began to question my lifestyle and in particular the intended robbery with Don. What if we were caught? I would spend years in gaol. I would be certain to lose Cathy. And if I continued illegally to sell raffle tickets it would only be a matter of time before my luck ran out. I had reached a stage in my life where I thought of myself as a criminal. The attitudes of the police, judges, prison authorities and even citizens had reinforced this belief. Stealing and conning had become a convenient way of making a living. It didn't bother me that these things were deemed wrong by law-abiding citizens. My code of ethics was in direct contrast to that of normal people. Society had demonstrated that it held me in low esteem.

But Cathy and her family viewed me in a different light. I had been deceiving all of them. The 28 months I had spent in gaol had taught me to accept without question that I was on the other side. The values I accepted and lived by while in gaol had become my guidelines for living on the outside. I believed that as long as I abided by my own code of ethics, robbing, stealing and conning were permissible. But how could I explain to Cathy and her family that although they considered it wrong to steal, I admired a smart thief and, in particular, bank robbers? How could I explain that whereas they would consider it to be their duty to inform on someone who they knew had committed a crime, I would consider such an act as traitorous? How would they react to my telling them that, to me, the police force they admired was full of corrupt cops? Or that the Kingsgrove Slasher was a good guy? Would they understand my rationale that people who worked in factories and menial jobs for low wages were mugs? I couldn't tell them any of these things. I had to pretend to be something that I wasn't. Eventually, they would see through my facade. I had a choice: either to end the relationship with Cathy, or to become an honest citizen. After a lot of soul-searching I decided to try the latter. I knew it wouldn't be easy.

In a genuine attempt to change my ways, I took a job in a factory at Enfield. I had to catch a train to Strathfield from where I caught a bus to work. Apart from about a sixty per cent drop in my weekly income, I had to cope with a job I hated doing, which included carrying ladles of molten metal from a huge vat and pouring it into casts. Every day I told myself I was a mug but I persisted with it. I knew that while I put in an honest day of slavery, I would stay out of gaol.

A few weeks after I'd taken the job, Cathy told me that Roland had decided to return to the USA to live. Despite my efforts to try to simplify my lifestyle, I was again confronted with a complicated crisis. The moment she told me of Roland's intentions, I had a foreboding of doom. I was aware that the United States had a policy of refusing entry in to the country to anyone with a criminal record. If Cathy went to America the odds were I'd never see her again. Cathy's feelings were ambivalent. She had always wanted to live in America and the knowledge that her dream would soon become a reality excited her. But she didn't want to leave me. Her solution was simple: I would have to migrate with them. I didn't tell her that, in all probabilities, I would be barred from entering the USA. I decided I would first check out all the possibilities, perhaps only habitual or dangerous criminals were prohibited entry. I made an appointment with a solicitor in Parramatta. He was about 30, well dressed, well groomed and had a glib manner. I took an immediate dislike to him. After I had made him cognizant with all the facts, he shook my hand and promised to "try to find a legal alternative around the problem". He then asked me for £50. It had taken me nearly three weeks of ladling molten metal to earn that amount of money. I formed the opinion then that all lawyers were legal robbers.

A few days later the lawyer informed me that my chances of gaining legal entry into the USA, even for a visit, were nil.

I was furious. "You're telling me to forget about Cathy, is that it?"

"Not necessarily. You have two legal alternatives." He held up a finger. "One, if the girl loves you, she can wait until she is 18 and then return to Australia."

"Forget it. She's too loyal to leave her family. Anyway, that's two years away. I can't wait that long."

"Well, your other alternative is to apply for a work visa into Canada. After you've been there for a while you may be able to obtain a visa into the United States. Once there, you could marry the girl and apply to live there."

It seemed to be my best chance. If they turned me down for a visa I could sneak across the border. "If I married her, what chance would there be of my being allowed to stay there?"

"A slim chance, I would say. But if you were married you could both go to live in Canada and she could keep in touch with her family."

I was exasperated. "Neither of us have any inclination to live in Canada." He shook his head. "It's the only alternative I can offer."

I didn't tell Cathy about the difficulties we would have to overcome before we could even think about getting married. As far as she was concerned I would be going to America with them. Once, while we were alone, I silently gazed into her eyes for a long time, trying to imagine how I'd cope if I knew I would never see her again.

Eventually she lowered her eyes. "Why are you staring at me like that for, John?"

"Because you're so beautiful." I paused. "What would you do if I couldn't come to America?"

She looked at me. "I don't think about it. I know you'll come."

"But what if I come after you. You might meet some rich young American who will sweep you off your feet."

She gave me a delightful smile. "You're jealous." She gripped my hand. "There will never be anyone else for me, John."

Despite my feigned gaiety with Cathy, I was becoming depressed. As a boy I had dreamed of growing up, meeting a nice girl, marrying her and living happily ever after. Hardly grandiose dreams. But now, for me to realise those dreams, I had to overcome numerous obstacles. If I failed to clear just one of them I would lose out. My first obstacle was money. I would need a large sum. I considered it pointless to continue working at the factory and resigned. Don and I had corresponded regularly. He was due to be released in a few weeks. I had to find a place to rob where each of us would clear at least £1,000. To me, the simple answer was a bank robbery. At the time, in Australia, bank robberies were rare. The people working in banks would be complacent, particularly as they were armed. With the element of surprise in our favour, robbing a bank would be easy. I set out to find the right one.

The day after Don was released, I met him in town. We walked to Hyde Park to enable us to talk without being overheard. I told him I had chosen a bank in Burwood to rob.

Don paled. "A bank? No way, mate. It's too heavy."

I smiled. "That's what everyone says. I'm telling you the banks in Australia are wide open, they're begging to be robbed. If we're going to do a job, lets make it worthwhile. I've found a foolproof getaway route. That's the key to it, a good getaway route."

Don agreed to come and have a look at the bank and the getaway route. The way I had planned it, after robbing the bank we could run out and get into a stolen car and drive around a corner and down a street where we could jump out and enter Burwood railway station via the back entrance and catch a train. If we timed it right we could get on a train as soon as we entered the station. If something went wrong and we missed the train, we would still be relatively safe. Trains stopped at Burwood on an average of one every three or four minutes. Although Don liked the getaway route, he felt that it would be too risky to try to rob the bank. Eventually, we decided to rob a jewellery shop that was situated near the bank. Among the display of rings in the window were two pads containing diamond rings with a total value of more than £6,000.

"If we get those two pads I can get a third for them," Don said. "And if we do get caught we'll only get 12 or 18 months for a snatch and grab, whereas we could get 14 years for robbing a bank."

I had no intentions of being caught, therefore the bank appealed to me more. But if it had to be the jewellery shop, then at least I would clear £1,000 out of it, which would be more than sufficient to get me to Canada. It was late May. We decided to wait a few weeks before we put our plan into operation. This would give Don time to buy a motorcycle and regain his confidence as a driver. One day in early June I persuaded Cathy to take a day off from college. We spent the day at her place. That afternoon we heard on the radio that Pope John XXIII had died of a stomach tumour.

"Do you want me to go home?" I asked.

"Why?"

"Well, you're a strict Catholic. I guess this is now a day of mourning for you."

She gave me a sad smile. "I know I should feel upset but I don't. To me he was just an old man who lived on the other side of the world. I've never seen him." She studied her fingernails. "I don't feel anything."

I nodded. Her honesty touched me. "I can understand that. At least you're not a hypocrite. I guess that before we can feel deep emotion about someone, we have to know that person."

She moved closer to me and gazed into my eyes. "I'm growing up, John. I understand my emotions. If I lost you, I'd never get over it."

Her words tormented me. Soon I would be risking everything, including her trust. But I felt I had no choice.

The day of the robbery I kept watch while Don stole a car, something he was expert at. Driving up Burwood Road, we parked across the street from the jewellery shop. Getting out, I walked across the street carrying a shopping bag. The only disguise I wore was a pair of sunglasses. Trying to control my nervousness, I walked into the shop. There were no customers inside; the only staff was an attractive brunette who looked to be in her early thirties. I told her I was about to become engaged and that I was interested in looking at the two most expensive display pads in the window.

Smiling, she brought them to me and placed them on the counter. "There are some really beautiful rings there," she said. "Did you have any particular type in mind?"

I picked up one of the pads. "I like them all," I said, dropping it into my bag. I had expected her to be momentarily shocked to the point of inaction. But, although I had moved quickly, she reacted with surprising speed, grabbing the other pad and stepping back. There was nothing I could do other than run out of the shop. Don saw me running across the street and opened the back passenger side door. I jumped in and he eased into the traffic. "Did you get them?"

"I only got one pad," I said, slipping my pullover off.

"Damn it! I told the fence I'd have two of them. He's got the money waiting."

"There was nothing I could do about it."

He stopped the car near the rear entrance to the station. Leaving the bag and pullover with Don, I got out.

"See you tomorrow," he said, and drove off.

Hurrying through the entrance, I reached the platform in time to catch a city-bound train. Getting off at Town Hall, I went to a movie. I met Cathy after college and rode home on the train with her. That night I had dinner with Cathy and her family. While all of us were sitting in the lounge room watching the news, the announcer gave details of the robbery. The description of the robber, although fairly accurate, could have fitted thousands of guys. Then the announcer said something that made my stomach churn: "The robber had cut himself shaving and there was a small bloodstain on the collar of his white shirt."

Pat stared at me. "You've cut yourself, John. Look, there's a bloodstain on your collar."

My heart was thumping so hard I was concerned that someone would hear it. Somehow, I managed to smile. "I have to confess, it was me. I've got thousands of pounds worth of diamond rings in my back pocket."

Everyone laughed. "You had better bring them to the States with you, John," Roland said. "You'll get a better price over there."

Cathy smiled. "Save the best for me."

"You're a little mercenary," I said. I held her gaze. "Would you still be my girl if I robbed a bank?"

She nodded. "As long as you got away with it, I would be."

Everyone laughed again. I had managed to bluff my way through the crisis but later that night I noticed Pat watching me. I sensed that from that point on, I would have to be careful of what I said in her presence.

The following morning I met Don in Hyde Park. He handed me £300. "It's the best I could do, mate," he said.

I gave him a hard stare. "I was expecting at least five hundred."

"The fence was upset. I only delivered half of what I promised. We were lucky he took it."

"We weren't lucky at all. We risked out necks for those rings, if he wasn't prepared to give us the correct price you should have told him to get lost."

"I'm sorry, mate, but I don't know any other fences and neither do you. I thought you'd want me to take the money."

"Well, it's done now. There's nothing much we can do about it. But three hundred isn't enough for me; we'll have to do another one. And this time don't sell them unless we get the right price."

Don nodded. "Fair enough. Give it a few weeks to cool down. In the meantime I'll look around for another fence."

A few nights later there was a knock on my door. "John, there are some friends of yours here to see you," the landlady called through the door. Thinking it was probably Don, I wondered how he had ascertained my address. I opened the door. Two strangers, both in their twenties, stood at the door. Although they were dressed casually, I sensed that they were cops.

"Hi, Johnny," one of them said, pushing past me. He had a flattop haircut.

The other guy, bearded and thickset, came in and closed the door behind him.

I began to protest. "What are you..." I didn't finish. Flattop kicked me in the stomach hard. The pain caused me to double over. Before I could do much about it, they grabbed me and handcuffed me. "Sorry about the kick, mate," Flattop said. "But we checked your record and we found out that you were a bit of a runner. We couldn't risk you running off on us."

"Why do you run, anyway, John?" the other guy asked.

I managed to gasp a retort: "I'm in training for the Olympics."

They looked at each other. "Well, he hasn't lost his sense of humour," Flattop said. He gave me a hard look. "Where's the money, John?"

"I don't know what you're talking about." All I could think about was Cathy. I'd lost her; there were no doubts about that.

They began to search the room. It didn't take them long to find the £250 I had hidden inside a pair of shoes. I was taken to Campsie Police Station. On the way the cops told me they were members of the Shadow Squad. They said they had been following me all day, waiting to see if they could catch me doing another job.

I didn't believe them. Someone had put me in. But who? I immediately thought of Pat. The other night she had been suspicious but would she have gone to the police? Although I didn't want to believe it, I had to concede that it was a possibility. At the police station two detectives interviewed me. One was tall and fat with a ruddy complexion and a fleshy, hooked nose. The other one was also tall, but beanpole thin. They told me that the woman in the jewellery shop had identified me from the photos. I told them it must be a case of mistaken identity. They laughed.

"Look, John," Skinny said, "we know it was you who did it. If you want us to bring the woman down here now, we'll do it. She'll pick you out and we'll make it tough on your in court. If you co-operate, we'll see that you get a fair go in court. You'll be out in 18 months."

At the moment 18 months seemed like ten years. By the time I got out, Cathy would have been living in America for a year. But I knew they had me. Now that I was in custody, the woman from the jewellery shop would be bound to identify me. "All right," I said. "But I want bail."

He nodded. "That won't be a problem. Now what about the car? Did you do the job on your own, or did you have a mate to help you?"

My mind raced! I'd have to say I stole the car or else they would be bound to try to connect Don with the robbery. If I accepted responsibility for both, Don would be certain to do the right thing and bail me out. Once out, I could get a passport and immediately leave for Canada. It was my only chance.

"I did it all on my own," I said.

Both cops smiled. "We're not sure about that, John," Skinny said. "But we'll take your word for it. Now, we'll just get you to make a handwritten statement, explaining how you did it."

I wrote a statement, adhering as close to the facts as possible. I confessed to stealing the car and driving it to and from the job.

"What did you do with all the rings?" Fatty asked.

"I sold them to a fence in a pub."

"What was his name?"

"Bob."

"What pub?"

"One in Redfern. I don't know the name of it."

"How much did he give you?"

"Three hundred."

"You got ripped off."

"Where's my 250?"

"That will be used as evidence," Skinny said. He paused. "But because you've done the right thing, we'll let you keep the money you had in your wallet. That way you'll be able to buy a few luxuries at the Bay."

When I was taken to the cells, I received a shock. Don was in the cell next to mine. After the cops had gone, he said: "I can explain, mate."

I was confused. "What are you doing here?"

"I was arrested in a hotel for fighting and they found some rings on me. I didn't rob you, I kept them out of my half."

"Why did you keep them?"

"I wasn't happy about the price. I sold the others because I thought you needed the money."

I tried to contain my rage. "So what happened?"

"They brought me here, thinking I was the one who did the snatch. But when they brought the woman from the jeweller's in, she said it wasn't me. I think she picked your photo out."

"If you hadn't kept those rings this never would have happened."

"I'm sorry, mate." He paused. "What did you tell them?"

"I copped the rap on both of them. I told them I stole the car."

"I appreciate this, mate. I won't forget it, I tell you."

"They're going to give me bail. I'm counting on you bailing me out."

"Consider it done."

The next morning they released Don. I was charged with robbing the jewellery shop and larceny of a motor vehicle. Bail was set at £300. I was confident that Don would soon have me out. On my way to Long Bay in the back of the van, I wondered how the cops had ascertained my address so soon after the woman had picked out my photo? It was the missing link. Obviously, the cops had been lying when they told me that they had been following me all day; by all accounts the woman hadn't identified me until later that evening. And Don couldn't have told them where I lived, because he hadn't known.

It was a puzzle that bothered me.

28
Future Armed Robbers and Murderers
(1963-1988)

At Long Bay I spent a few anxious weeks pacing the yard by day and lying awake most nights, waiting for Don to bail me out. After two weeks without a letter or a visit from him, I concluded that he had no intention of helping me. Rather than become bitter, I accepted it as my just desserts for having been a fool. Resigned to the fact that I wouldn't be able to raise bail, I wrote to Cathy and her family, explaining what happened. I told Cathy to forget me, that I was sorry I had hurt her and deceived her family. It was a letter exuding self pity. But now, at least they knew the truth.

About a week later I was jolted out of my depression when I received three letters: one from Cathy, one from her mother and one from Mildred bless her little heart. Her mother wrote that the whole family supported me. While I was in gaol I should study accountancy or something else worthwhile. Roland added that he considered me to be too intelligent to make the same mistake twice and that he expected me to come good. Mildred wrote that when I got out, I should make certain that I came straight across to the States. Until I arrived she would keep an eye on Cathy for me, and report to me if Cathy dated anybody. Cathy wrote a sad letter. She was devastated. She wanted to come and see me, and asked me to write with details of what days and times would be suitable. She went on about love and told me that, "the darkest hours were before the dawn." She urged me to take care and to remember that she loved me and that there would always be a special place for me in her heart.

After reading the letters, I had tears in my eyes. I'd thrown everything away for £300. What a fool! I tried to convince myself that it wasn't my fault, that the bureaucratic bastards had forced my hand by refusing my entry into the United States. But I knew I was kidding myself, I should have tried a legal alternative instead of risking everything, as I always did.

Although I longed to see her again, I wrote to Cathy telling her that while I was in gaol I didn't want to see her. I wasn't permitted to explain to her the archaic conditions under which she would have to see me, looking at each other through metal grille partitions in small, box-like compartments, with a guard standing nearby listening to everything that was said during the 20-minute visit. I didn't want her to see me under those conditions. I promised her that no matter how long it took we would see each other again.

Cathy and her family, with the exception of Pat, continued to write. They were all excited as the day of their departure approached. They had booked a passage on the *Orsova*, which would be leaving in the first week of November. In one of her letters, Cathy mentioned that Don had rung her early the night I had been arrested and asked for my address. I had finally found the missing link. I promised myself that his day would come. Ten years later Don Maher was convicted of murder and served fourteen years of a life sentence at Boggo Road Gaol, Queensland.

Pleading guilty to the snatch and grab and theft of a motor vehicle, I received a total of three years hard labour. The £250 taken by police on the night of my arrest was never mentioned. In those days in NSW there was no parole system, even with remission for good behaviour, I would have to spend 27 months in gaol.

When I returned to Long Bay after court, the wing officer handed me a letter from Cathy. She urged me to reconsider my decision not to see her while I was in gaol. She reminded me that soon she would be gone and she longed to see me one more time before she left Australia. When I replied, I emphasised that I would not, under any circumstance, accept a visit from her. It was a harsh letter written in a state of depression. I even criticised the delay of two weeks between letters. She didn't reply, leaving Australia without contacting me again.

The week the *Orsova* set sail for the USA, I was banished to the front yards for being disrespectful to an officer. I was put in the same yard as Arthur 'Neddy' Smith, who was there as punishment for assaulting a prisoner. Tall and solidly built, with wavy, blonde hair, he was only 18, but he would have weighed close to 90 kilos. He was already well on the way to becoming a standover man. He walked up and down the yard as though it belonged to him and the crims got out of his way. But while we were in the same yard, I learned quite a bit about him. He told me that, a few years previously, he had been sent to Endeavour House at Tamworth, a punishment gaol for juveniles, where he had been starved, beaten and brutalised. This wasn't the first time I had been told about the atrocities committed on young offenders at Tamworth by officers who had virtual carte blanche to do as they pleased.

Guys who had spent time at both Tamworth and Grafton claimed that Tamworth was worse. At least at Grafton the prisoners were supplied with decent meals. Ned Smith told me that on numerous occasions while he had been at Tamworth he had been placed on starvation rations, resulting in him losing more than 20 kilos in weight. He went on to become one of Sydney's most notorious criminals having committed theft, rape, armed robbery and two murders. Surely places such as Endeavour House worked more towards creating rather than curing hardened criminals. On December 1989, Endeavour House was finally closed down after a youth suicide.

After a few weeks in the front yards I was transferred to Bathurst Gaol. At Bathurst, I caught up on what had been happening in the outside world. The Beatles and The Rolling Stones had burst on the music scene with such impact that short-back-and-side haircuts soon became unfashionable, except in gaol where they were compulsory. In March, the notorious US island prison Alcatraz was closed down and later became a tourist attraction. In Great Britain, nearly £3 million had been stolen during the Great Train Robbery and a lot of crims talked about emulating Ronald Biggs and company, even though all but one of the robbers were eventually arrested. *Time* magazine and the Sunday papers were full of lurid details about the affair between Britain's War

Minister John Profumo and callgirl Christine Keeler. Keeler and her callgirl friend, Mandy Rice-Davies, came close to bringing down the Tory Government when details of sex orgies involving High Court judges and eminent politicians were revealed. High society osteopath Dr Stephen Ward was convicted of being the chief pimp and killed himself. In comparison to some of the hypocritical celebrities of the British Government and judiciary, the new breed of long-haired, rebellious youths didn't seem so bad.

Within a week of my arriving at Bathurst, John F. Kennedy was assassinated. Crims and screws walked around the gaol telling each other they couldn't believe it. How could the President of the United States, with all his security, be killed so easily? I thought of Cathy, she would hear the news on the passenger liner. What a terrible time to be arriving in the United States. I suppose everyone who was old enough to comprehend it would remember what he or she was doing on 22 November 1963. For example, I was making woollen socks on a special machine in the sock shop at Bathurst Gaol.

On most weekends I played bat-tennis, a game similar to tennis, except instead of tennis racquets, wooden bats are used. One of my regular and toughest opponents was James Finch. A fitness fanatic, Jim, a good-looking guy with a flashing smile, had a fierce will to win. While he was there we had some memorable battles on the concrete tennis court. At the time, Jim was a yard sweeper, earning sixpence a week. It is, perhaps, significant that James Finch, Don Maher and myself all had to endure the counter-productive task of sweeping yards and cleaning locks for sixpence a week. If this was the authorities' way of trying to rehabilitate young prisoners, it failed dismally. I became a bank robber; both Don Maher and James Finch became murderers. Maher was released from Boggo Road Gaol in 1987 after having served fourteen years of a life sentence for murder. James Finch, after being released from Bathurst, was later convicted for having fired a shot at the notorious hit man, John Regan. He served seven years of a 16 year sentence. Not long after his release, he was arrested and charged with the fire bombing of Brisbane's Whisky Au Go Go nightclub. Fifteen people died in the early hours of 3 March 1973, when drums of petrol were ignited near a stairwell leading into the nightclub. Both Finch and the notorious John Andrew Stuart were convicted of the crime. Stuart was found dead in his cell on 1 January 1979.

In February 1988, Finch, after having served almost 15 years of a life sentence, was released on parole from Boggo Road and immediately deported to Britain. James Finch, Don Maher and myself had, between us by 1988, spent more than 60 years in prisons, all of which were maximum security. You can clean a lot of locks and play a lot of bat tennis in 60 years.

29

Lucky Larry
(1964)

For me, 1964 was a year of strife. Bitter about the direction my life had taken, I often looked for trouble. On numerous occasions I was put on report by guards claiming I was disrespectful and had an aggressive nature. This usually resulted in at least a few weeks loss of privileges. In 10 months I was involved in eight fights. On a few occasions the guards caught me fighting, this always resulted in my spending more days in the pound, loss of remissions and many weeks spent languishing in the front yards.

During the latter part of 1964 I was classed as incorrigible and given a job as a permanent yard sweeper. The mundane existence of prison life, particularly being a yard sweeper, began to wear me down. I had nothing to look forward to, every morning I hated getting out of bed, I knew who I was going to see, what I was going to do, what time I'd be eating my humdrum meals and even what I'd be eating. I received no visits and very few letters. If something unexpected did occur, it inevitably would be some form of adversity. Nevertheless, I often found myself perversely hoping for something to happen, anything, to temporarily alleviate the soul-destroying boredom. Then along came Larry. At the time I was housed in a three-out cell. When one of my cell mates was released, Larry was his replacement. The previous day, my other cell mate Ray and I had received our special 35 shillings buy-ups. When Larry, who was a big, slow-moving, slow-thinking country boy who had been transferred from Broken Hill, saw all the groceries, he asked if he could have some.

"Take what you want," I said, looking at Ray who gave me a questioning stare. I turned to Larry. "If you ask the wing officer in the morning, he'll probably let you put in for a supplementary buy-up. Do you have any money?"

Shoving one of my chocolate biscuits in his mouth, Larry said: "Yes, my Mum put £5 in my property before I left Broken Hill."

Three days later he received his buy-up. Neither Ray nor I had much remaining from our buy-ups. Larry had demolished most of them. After we were locked in our cell for the night, Larry placed a bag of plain biscuits and a tin of plum jam on the table and said, "This is for you blokes for letting me have some of yours."

He placed the box with the remainder of the groceries in it under his bed. Later that night we heard him munching on goodies that he had surreptitiously extracted from his box. The next day Ray, a chubby, boyish-faced guy who had a quick temper, and I decided we would try to win Larry's buy-up from him by enticing him into a game of poker. Larry thought playing poker was a great idea. We began by playing for cigarettes, gradually increasing the stakes until Larry owed us his buy-up and a month's supply of tobacco. He then declared that he had been only playing for fun.

Picking up his box of groceries and placing it on the table, I opened a block of chocolate. "There's no playing for fun here, Larry," I said, putting some chocolate in my mouth. "But don't worry, we'll share it with you. Here, have a piece of chocolate."

Although he took the chocolate, I could see he was close to tears. Soon afterwards, he went to bed without talking to either of us again. Immediately the door was opened the next morning, he went to the wing officer and told him what had happened. The wing officer came to our cell and admonished Ray and I. He told us to return the buy-up to the lad, and if we took so much as one biscuit from it, we would spend a couple of months in the front yards. As Ray handed him the box of groceries, Larry gave him a big grin. Ray and I were furious. That afternoon while we were pacing the yard, Ray said: "He's not getting away with this. He ate all our buy-ups and then, when we won his fair and square, he gave us up."

"But if we bash him," I said, "he'll give us up again."

"He won't be giving anyone up again," Ray said. "I'm going to kill him."

I nodded. In gaol you often hear this type of talk. "He deserves it."

"Yeah. What I'll do, I'll wait until he's asleep, and then I'll cave his head in with that tin of jam he gave us. I'll go for his temple, that'll stuff him. The dog'll never know what hit him." He paused, and looked at me. "We can tell the screws he fell off the top bunk and hit his head on the jam tin."

"It'll be the perfect murder," I said, smiling. I didn't believe there was one chance in a thousand that Ray would go ahead with the plan.

That night, about an hour after lights out, Ray climbed down from his bunk and tiptoed over to the cupboard. Picking up the unopened tin of jam he turned around and crept towards the bottom bunk where Larry was sleeping.

Realising that Ray was serious, I shouted: "Ray, don't!"

It was too late. Clutching the tin of jam in his right hand, Ray struck it as hard as he could against Larry's forehead. Without uttering a sound, Larry leapt out of bed, landing on all fours. Then he shouted: "What happened!"

"You fell out of bed, mate," Ray said.

I jumped down from my bed. "You hit your head, Larry. Let's have a look at it."

There was enough light coming from the security light near our window to enable me to see the blood streaming from a gash in his forehead. He began to shout: "Ooohh, I've been attacked! Help! Officer! I'm being killed!" He moved on all fours towards the locked door. I grabbed him and tried to put my hand over his mouth. If the screws heard him, Ray and I would be in big trouble. "Stop yelling out, Larry! No one's going to hurt you."

Ray came to my assistance. Although we managed to calm him down, it was obvious he was terrified. I soaked a towel in water and tried to stop the flow of blood. After a while the bleeding stopped. I spoke to him as I would a small child, trying to reassure him that neither of us would hurt him. After he had a little cry, he promised that if the screws asked him about the cut on his forehead, he would say he fell out of bed and hit his head on the stool. Eventually, we all returned to our beds. The moment they opened the doors the next morning he went to the wing officer and told him that we had tried to kill him. The wing officer, whose name was Mutton, was one of the few screws who never hassled me.

He called Ray and me into his office and said: "You two boys get a bit horny last night, did you?"

I shook my head. "No sir. I don't know what Larry told you, but he had a nightmare and fell out of bed."

Mutton grinned. "He had a bloody nightmare all right. One of you bashed him on the head with the intentions of knocking him out and fucking him."

I gave him a shocked look. "That's not true, Mr Mutton."

"We're not into that sort of thing, sir," Ray said, stiffly.

Mutton nodded. "Well, that's what it looks like to me. But he's a bloody nuisance, this bloke; they should have left him at Broken Hill. I'm moving him to another wing and, as far as I'm concerned, that's the end of it. If either of you touch him again or go stirring any shit, you'll spend that long in the front yards you'll think you're a bloody troglodyte."

Unable to believe our good luck, Ray and I avoided Larry until, a few months later, he was released. Occasionally, I look back on the incident and shudder at the thought of what would have happened if Ray hadn't missed Larry's temple with the tin of jam.

30

It Must Be love
(1965)

As 1965 approached, I counted down the days. Although both the lights and the radio were switched off by 9.30 pm, I sat up to welcome in the New Year. I had turned into the home straight. Now I could say, "I get out this year." The finish was in sight. In May, after 24 years in office, Labor narrowly lost the State Election. Throughout the gaol rumours ran rife that the Liberals would re-introduce the death penalty. But the new Premier, Robin Askin, soon quashed the rumours. At the time I couldn't have cared less.

Early in September, after 27 months in gaol, I was released. This time there was no feeling of euphoria. I was a man with a goal of which the realisation would prove to be extremely difficult, if not impossible. But I had to try. I had to find out where Cathy was. I refused to accept that she might be married or no longer interested in me. I was still in love with her and, regardless of what the circumstances were, I intended to have her. This time I wouldn't bother trying to gain legal entry into the United States. An old safe-cracker had told me of a place at Kings Cross where, if I mentioned his name, I would be able to buy a false passport.

As I walked through the main street of Bathurst, waiting for the train to Sydney, I crossed through the park. Memories of running from the cops as one of them fired shots at me came rushing back. It only seemed like a few years ago, yet nearly five years had passed since I'd made that reckless attempt for freedom. Although it was a warm spring day, a chill ran through me.

Where had those five years gone?

After arriving at Central I caught a taxi to Dad's place. He had moved to a Housing Commission flat in Waterloo. He was pleased to see me.

He now had a pronounced beer gut, but although he hadn't done any hard physical work for more than six years, his large arms and shoulders still gave the impression of exceptional strength, which he confirmed by almost crushing my hand when he greeted me.

Predictably, he opened a bottle of beer. After a few drinks we walked to the local Chinese restaurant. The proprietors knew Dad well and gave us the VIP treatment. I asked him for a loan so I could move into a boarding house somewhere. Although David was living with a friend at Belmore, and Dad was on his own, he agreed it would be best if I found somewhere else to live. I soon obtained full board with a family at Croydon. The family consisted of Harry, a nice old guy aged 55, his wife, a small, pleasant lady who we all called Mum, and their two attractive, dark-haired daughters, Carol, who was 19 and Kaye who was 18.

Harry was almost bald and looked much older than 55. He told me that five or six other guys had enquired about the room, but he had chosen me because I looked to be "the type of young man who could be trusted with my daughters." In that respect he was right. I stayed with the family for nearly five months without even making a suggestive remark to either girl.

A few days after moving in I caught a train to Fairfield. Trudging from door to door along Hamilton Road where Cathy used to live I asked people if they remembered the family. A lot of people remembered them but no one could give me their address. Then I hit the jackpot. A talkative red-haired woman not only remembered the family, she corresponded with the mother. Casually, I asked her if Cathy was married. She gave me a smile that implied I hadn't fooled her. "No, not yet. But she's going with a young man whose family is extremely rich."

"Good for her," I said, trying to mask my feelings. "Could you give me their address?"

"Of course I will. But you'll have to get a move on, won't you?"

I managed to grin. "Lady, that's an understatement."

That night I wrote Cathy a long letter. But I wasn't overly optimistic about her replying. How could I, a criminal, barred from entering

America, compete for her affections with a rich young American who could offer her everything? Desperate to give her something about me to believe in, I wrote that while I had been in gaol, I had taken her mother's advice and enrolled in an accountancy course, I was now in my third year. Instinct told me that if I could see her and talk to her, the old magic would return.

Harry, a retired carpenter, had worked hard all his life. He persuaded me to try for a job as a storeman with Franklins at Bankstown. Surprisingly, despite my lack of references, I got the job. A few days after starting work I received a letter from Cathy. As I tore open the envelope my hands shook:

> Dear John,
>
> I can't describe how I felt when I received your letter. I was so overjoyed after reading it that I just burst into tears. Of course I still love you, but I couldn't bring myself to write after you refused to see me and some of the things you said in that angry letter. I sailed to the US with a heavy heart. But that's in the past. I always knew that you would contact me again. I didn't know when or how, but I prayed to God that you would, and so I didn't worry about it after that, as I knew he would arrange it.
>
> I must tell you that I'm going with a guy, but it isn't serious, although he would like it to be.
>
> I'm proud of you studying to be an accountant. We all knew you could do it. Mum said to tell you that now you are out to make sure you finished it. Everybody says "Hi," especially Millie who wants to know why you took so long to write?
>
> At the moment it is snowing. Believe me, winter in Chicago is cold, but after a while you acclimatise. When you arrive we will have to make sure that you will not freeze.
>
> We have a lovely two-storey house in a beautiful suburb. I have my own bedroom with my own pink phone.

I'm working as a receptionist with Prudential. It's a good job with great prospects. And I get on well with my boss, which is a big plus.

John, I have thought about you so often. I can't wait for your next letter. Please send a recent photo! Maybe soon we can arrange a phone call. Chicago is 15 hours behind Sydney so we will need to book the call and go through an operator. But it would be so nice to hear your voice again.

I love you, John, and I know things will work out for us.

Cathy, xxxx

Suddenly all my negative thoughts were gone. Despite everything, this wonderful, beautiful girl loved me and a rich young American was about to find himself relegated to a second string. This was true love all right. I immediately wrote her a 20-page letter and asked for her phone number. To hell with the expense.

In her next letter she included her number, advising me to ring on Sunday, as it was cheaper. When I rang her on Sunday morning it was Saturday night there. At least she wasn't out with her number two. Both of us were excited and the 15 minutes seemed like five. She was surprised that I still sounded the same. I joked about her ridiculous American accent and she immediately began talking like the Cathy of old, which made both of us laugh. When you consider that we hadn't spoken to or corresponded with each other for more than two years, the rapport between us was something special.

Every day we wrote long letters to each other. She never seemed to be short of things to write about; sometimes she would tell me about a dress she had bought, or how she had to take her dog to the vet to have its paw fixed. But she always spent a few pages describing how much she loved me and how good it would be when I came to Chicago. She found some cosy, inexpensive restaurants where we could go. Occasionally, I wrote about my adventures in gaol. I often laughed to myself as I imagined her blushing at some of the incidents I described.

I also had a letter from Mildred. The little imp wrote that David, a nice-looking guy who owned a Porsche, and whose parents owned a bubble gum factory, was crazy about Cathy, but Cathy had ended the relationship. Mildred concluded that Cathy must have lost her marbles.

31

HIGH NOON AT HARRY'S
(1965)

About a month after I'd moved into Croydon, Dad rang me. He was drunk and insisted that I come home to live. I told him that I didn't want to.

He became aggressive. "It's that Harry, isn't it? Tell the bastard I'll be over tonight to settle it. I'll fight him in a phone box."

"Come off it Dad. You can't blame Harry for anything. You know damn well that you and I can't live in the same house together."

"I'm coming over, Johnny. We'll see who's the better man."

He hadn't changed one little bit. "Listen, Dad. I'll tell you what I'll do. I'll come over, and we'll have a Chinese meal together."

"Johnny! Don't try and put one over on your old man. I'm a cripple, ain't I? A fuckin' cripple with a heart of a lion and the punch of a mule."

Sometimes, I wished I'd never met him. "You're not a cripple. And your fighting days are over."

"Don't tell your old man he can't fight any more! I'll tear this Harry apart with my bare hands. I can beat any man my age."

"Harry's not a fighting man."

"I've spoken to him on the phone and he thinks your old man is a fuckin' mug. Well, we'll see who the mug is!"

"Take it easy, Dad. I'm coming straight over. We'll talk about it then." I slammed the receiver down.

I caught a train to Redfern, but when I arrived at Dad's, he wasn't there. Fearing the worst, I ran and caught a taxi to Croydon.

As the taxi approached the house I could see Dad and Harry shaping up to each other on the front lawn. Mum was standing close by pleading with Harry to come inside.

Telling the driver to wait, I ran over and stepped between them. "Come on, fellas, this has gone far enough."

"Let it be, John," Harry gasped. He had his hands held high in the classical old bare-knuckle stance.

Dad, crouching like Rocky Marciano, was also gasping for breath. "He fights like a sheila, Johnny. Just give me another two minutes with him."

"Come on, Dad. Let's go home." Surprisingly, he allowed me to lead him away.

"Go and pack your bags, Johnny. You're not staying with this old fool any more."

"You should take a look at yourself," Harry said.

I gave Mum an apologetic look. "I'm sorry about this. I'll be back to get my things."

"You only have to leave if you want to, John," Harry said. "You're welcome to stay as long as you like."

Dad turned and began to move towards Harry. "He's my son."

I gripped him by the arm. "Let's go, Dad. We'll talk about this at home."

He stared at me. "Get your things now. That's an order!"

"I don't take orders from anyone. Come on, let's go."

I finally managed to get him in the taxi. On the way home he told the taxi driver and I about the way Harry had danced around the lawn like a big sheila.

"If I could've caught him, I would have killed him."

I spent the night at Dad's flat.

The next morning he woke me up. "Good day, Johnny. What are you doing here?"

"Don't you remember, Dad?"

He shook his head. "I can't remember a bloody thing. I think I must have had a few too many last night."

I told him what had happened.

He shook his head in disbelief. "I'll have to give up the booze."

A few hours later, I returned to Croydon with Dad's blessings.

32

OFF TO SEE THE CUP
(1965)

Although, on the surface, my relationship with Cathy was going well, I was becoming depressed about the impossible situation I was in. Despite the numerous letters I had sent her and the now weekly phone calls, I hadn't explained to her that, legally, I couldn't get to the US. She also believed that I was continuing with my studies in the non-existent accountancy course. And although I wasn't gambling very much at this stage, I was finding it difficult to save. Rent, food, fares and the phone calls to Chicago took up most of my wages from Franklins. To complicate matters, Cathy's elder sister Pat had a boyfriend, Chris, who would soon be travelling to the US to marry her. She had met him just after I'd been arrested.

Chris called around to see me a few times at Croydon and asked me some pertinent question about my accountancy course. I sensed he was, at Pat's instigation, trying to trap me. She had never liked me. On the second occasion when he called, I was curt and sometimes abrasive in my replies to his questions. He didn't return.

That night I went to the address in Kings Cross that the old safe-cracker had given me. "For a hundred quid this bloke will get you a false passport. Make sure you mention my name," he told me.

But the contact, a hard-looking guy in his 50s, quoted me £400. For that amount he would supply me with a false passport and a visa. He told me to take it or leave it.

I told him I'd be back.

The next day I gave a week's notice at Franklin's. The manager asked me why.

"All I do is unload trucks, stack shelves and stamp prices on groceries," I said. "You don't need a storeman, you need a slave."

He gave me a shocked look. "If that's the way you feel, you can leave now if you like."

"Good. Have the girl make my pay up. Don't forget holiday pay."

I knew that I was close to breaking point. Cathy was there for the taking and I couldn't get to her. I needed about £1,000 to cover the false passport, fare and expenses. Then, at best, I'd arrive in Chicago illegally and penniless. Chris had worked and saved for two years to do it legally. I couldn't wait another two years and even if I did the bubble gum guy would probably get Cathy.

I scraped together enough money to buy an old Holden panel van. A few nights later I broke into a coin dealer's place. Although most of the valuables were probably locked away in the large safe on the premises, I emptied the display case that contained nearly £500 worth of coins. The next day I sold the coins to a suburban dealer for about half their value. If he suspected they were stolen, he gave no indication of it.

During dinner that night, I told Harry and the others that I had left my job and that I would be going to Melbourne for a week.

Harry was nonplussed. "Why, John?"

"I want to see the Melbourne Cup, I've never seen one."

"You can't just throw a good job aside because you want to go to Melbourne and watch a horse race."

I shrugged. "That job's not important. You know I'm going to America soon. It's my last chance to see a Melbourne Cup."

Although Harry did his best to dissuade me from what he called a bad decision, I had made up my mind.

Before leaving for Melbourne I hired a tape recorder and did three three-hour tapes for Cathy. I had no trouble speaking to her on tape for nine hours. On each tape I sang a couple of songs. I concluded the last tape by telling her: "When you get lonely, and tempted to go out with the bubble gum guy, play one of these tapes and it'll be nearly as good as me being by your side."

I knew how to keep my girl on side.

33

ROBBING THE RAILWAY
(1965)

For me, the Melbourne Cup proved to be an anti-climax. The course was cluttered with people who wouldn't know a gelding from an entire. Trying to push past them to place a bet was often impossible. Women dressed in ludicrous outfits, paraded around the course as though they were queens. Imbecilic males, some dressed like tramps, others in top hats and tails, walked around playing guitars and uttering unintelligible sounds. The mini-skirt was still a few years away from being the in thing. Due to the much publicised appearance of English model Jean Shrimpton, who wore an above the knee dress at the 1965 Melbourne Cup, she attracted more of the not-really-interested-in-racing types than usual. The meaning of what the Melbourne Cup is all about is lost on these people. To them it's a social event. It's a good day for the professionals to stay at home.

As usual I walked onto the course full of confidence. I had spent ten hours studying the form for all the races. Maybe I could win enough to get to America. I was confident the champion stayer *Craftsman* would win the Cup. I couldn't imagine him missing a place. The race provided one of the closest finishes in the 105-year history of the Cup. The great little mare *Light Fingers* beat her stablemate *Ziema* by a few centimetres to give trainer Bart Cummings not only his first Melbourne Cup, but also his first Cup quinella. To my dismay, *Craftsman* finished in the middle of the field. It was a disastrous day for me. I lost more than £200. It was by far my largest gambling loss. During the excitement of placing the bets and watching the races the money seemed like Monopoly money to me. It was only as I despondently walked from the racecourse that the realisation of what I had done began to sink in. America and Cathy seemed a million miles away.

My situation was just about hopeless. Depression gripped me, my confidence was gone. I was desperately lonely and nearly broke. The next day I bought a black water pistol and a novelty mask with the intention of robbing a bank. But when the time came for me to go ahead with it, I told myself: "The tellers have real guns, I don't have a getaway car and there will be too many people to control with a water pistol."

With the toy gun and the mask in an overnight bag, I went to town and spent four or five hours in a hotel drinking Bacardi and Cokes, wondering what I was going to do. Later that night, more drunk than sober, I caught a train to a suburb that I can't recall. The station was deserted. Going into the toilet, I waited. When a train came I stood near the doorway of the toilet and looked outside. A few passengers alighted and walked towards the exit. The railway attendant took their tickets then opened the barrier, allowing them to walk through.

Putting on the mask, I waited until the attendant, a thin-faced guy in his twenties, approached his office, then I ran out and pointed the toy gun at him. "This is a hold-up! Get inside!"

I think he was too shocked to argue. Following him inside, I closed the door. "Now open the safe," I said, scooping up the money from the cash drawer.

"The safe is open," he said. "The day's takings have been collected."

My run of bad luck was continuing. My liquor-befuddled brain wasn't sure what to do next. I considered taking his wallet, but decided against it. I had come to rob the railway, not the ticket collector.

"Better take your pants off," I said.

"Pardon?"

"Take your fucking pants off. I don't want you chasing me."

"I won't chase you, you don't have to humiliate me like this."

I stared at him, thinking of all the times I had been forced to strip naked. "Take your pants off and get under the table or I'll shoot you."

Blushing, he undid his belt and slowly stepped out of his pants. He stood staring at the floor.

"Get under the table and face the other way. And stay that way for three minutes or I'll come back and shoot you."

Facing away from me he crawled under the table. Going to the door I took off my mask and put it and the water pistol in the bag, then slamming the door behind me, I walked out. I ran along the platform, passing an elderly lady who was probably on her way to buy a ticket. Even as I ran, I couldn't help smiling as I imagined her reaction if she looked through the window and the ticket collector was still under the table in his underpants. After jogging for a while, I saw a bus coming and signalled for it to stop. I counted the proceeds from the robbery, about £20. Not much of a score for a would-be bank robber.

34

OUT ON BAIL
(1965-1966)

A few days after the railway robbery fiasco I returned to Sydney by train. On arrival I called in to see Dad.

I was surprised when a solidly built, olive-skinned woman, who looked to be in her mid-thirties, opened the door.

"You must be Johnny," she said. "Come in."

Dad introduced me to May. She lived in the flat directly above. Although they had been friends since he had moved in, he had never mentioned her to me. When she walked over and put her arm around his shoulder I couldn't help smiling. The sly old fox had found himself a girlfriend.

"I told May the truth, you're an ex-crim. But you've done your time and you're going straight."

"You won't be able to go to Vietnam," May said. "My friend's son has already been drafted."

The US had started bombing North Vietnam. The Australian government had brought back conscription by ballot and troops had already been sent to Vietnam. But my criminal record exempted me.

"I wouldn't want to go to Vietnam," I said. "I'm off to America soon."

"You're still chasing that American girl," Dad said. "She dumped you when you were in trouble and now you're running after her again. Wake up to yourself."

"She didn't dump me," I said.

"You won't listen to your old man, will you?"

"I'm going to America, end of discussion."

"Johnny's the big tough boy. Can't be told anything."

"I have to go. It was nice to meet you, May." I walked out.

When I arrived at Croydon everyone was pleased to see me.

"*Light Fingers* any good for you, John?" Harry asked.

I grinned. "Only for the pickpockets. I was on *Craftsman*."

He handed me a thick envelope. "This will cheer you up. She writing a book?"

"No, but I might one day."

The letter was one of Cathy's best. After reading it I was overcome with guilt. What a sham I was! I had no idea of how to resolve this situation. I decided not to reply immediately. She would soon have the tapes and I'd ring her soon. I figured the best way to finance my trip to America would be to concentrate on doing break-and-enters on houses in wealthy areas. One good score would solve everything.

I had no difficulty breaking into houses. But there were no big scores. I was an amateur. Probably some of the houses had hidden safes. A few times I had run off when I set off the alarms. I stole a fair amount of jewellery but had difficulty selling it. I knew enough to stay away from pawnshops. Instead of banking my profits I deviated by gambling heavily, hoping to win large amounts with a few good winners. As Christmas drew near I had saved less than £200.

On New Year's Eve the police come to the house at Croydon. The girls were ordered to go to their rooms. A shocked Harry and Mum watched as police thoroughly searched my room, finding enough items to connect me with at least three break-and-enters. To this day it remains a mystery as to who or what initiated their coming to search the place. I was taken to the Burwood Police Station where I was charged with a number of break-and-enters. I spent a sleepless night in a small cell with two drunks. Both of them loudly protested about having to spend New Year's Eve in gaol. I didn't tell them that it was my sixth consecutive New Year's Eve in a cell. Arrest, it's the ultimate shock, particularly when you are aware that it will result in a long term of imprisonment.

Later that morning, I was in for another shock. Harry came to bail me out. When the cops brought me to the front desk to sign the bail papers, Harry gave me a sad smile. "I'm going to take a chance on you, John. I'm putting up my property at Woy Woy as bail for you." Pausing, he gave me a searching look. "If you run out on me, I'll lose faith in human nature."

I held his gaze, trying to reassure him. "Don't worry, Harry, you won't lose your property."

On the way home he asked me if I had committed the robberies. I admitted that I had. "You know that you'll have to go to gaol eventually, don't you, John?"

I nodded. "I know." I couldn't tell him that I had no intention of going to gaol.

"Well, me and Mum and the girls think you've got a lot of good qualities, John. You won't be alone in there, we'll stand by you."

When we arrived home, Mum and the girls gave me a warm reception. Embarrassed, I thanked them all and went to my room. I had to reassess the situation. Although my being bailed out was an unexpected bonus, it placed me in a dilemma. If I absconded, Harry would lose his property as well as his faith in human nature. My code of ethics wouldn't allow that to happen. But if I didn't abscond I'd be certain to go to gaol for three or four years. I could think of only one solution. I would have to rob a bank and give Harry enough to cover the bail money. If I played it right I could still get to America and persuade Cathy to go away with me. It was irrational thinking, but while I still had a chance, even if it was a minimal one, I had to go for all or nothing.

35

WHY JERRY NEEDED A SCOTCH
(January 1966)

For me January was a historical month. I was out on bail, knowing that it was only a matter of time before I would be sent to gaol for a number of years. On 5 January 1966, Ronald Ryan and Peter Walker who had escaped from Pentridge Prison in Victoria on 19 December 1965, were recaptured in Sydney. During the escape a prison officer had been shot dead, generating the biggest manhunt in Australian history. On New Year's Day, the Great Train Robber Ronald Biggs, who had flown into Australia the night before, went to Randwick Races, where he lost a sizeable amount of money. Harry and I had also planned a trip to Randwick that day, but we cancelled it after my arrest the previous day. Looking at the results later, we both agreed we saved our money. Later that month Sir Robert Menzies retired after a record 16 years as Prime Minister, replaced by Harold Holt who was to meet a tragic end the following year. On Australia Day in South Australia, the three Beaumont children disappeared from Glenelg Beach. They have never been found. This horrific crime is one of Australia's most infamous. To top it off Prince Charles arrived in Australia on 30 January to spend six months at Geelong Grammar's Timbertop School.

But for me, the most memorable day in January 1966 was the day I robbed my first bank.

I had no doubts that if I returned to gaol, Cathy would dump me. She would marry the rich guy whose father owned the bubble gum factory in Chicago. Stuff that! Somehow I had to save the situation. First, I had to get thousands of pounds in a hurry to repay Harry the bail money, buy a false passport, get to the US and somehow convince Cathy to leave her family and go to Canada with me. A big ask. But if I could get to Chicago

I knew I could persuade her. She loved me, not the bubble gum guy, of that I was certain.

I made a momentous decision. I would rob a bank. Which bank? The Commonwealth Bank at Canley Heights picked itself:

1. I knew every side street and dead end in the area.
2. The nearest police station was a few miles away at Cabramatta.
3. It was school holidays. I'd be able to run from the bank to a nearby school and out to another street where I could casually walk to my car without attracting attention.

My main problem would be going into the vault to grab the money. What if some quick-thinking hero slammed the door while I was inside? I needed an accomplice. Where would I find someone willing to rob a bank? The only Australian bank robbers I knew about were infamous and either in gaol or dead: Ned Kelly, Darcy Dugan, Kevin Simmonds and recently Ryan and Walker. They were already talking about hanging Ryan. Why didn't ordinary criminals rob banks in 1966? I figured it was because some of the tellers had guns under the counter. A bank robber could get shot. I had to find a young criminal, not too bright, with plenty of go in him.

At a gun shop in the city I bought a .22 calibre rifle and ammunition. The salesman didn't ask for ID. I also bought two clown masks from a novelty store. Now all I needed was another clown. The next morning I caught a train to Town Hall and went to nearby Playland, a large amusement centre in Pitt Street. After looking around for a while I approached a tough-looking youth who was vigorously playing a pinball machine. Judging by his scruffy appearance he was down on his luck.

I waited until the machine had beaten him. "Hi," I said. "You interested in making a lot of money?"

He gave me a suspicious look. "Are you a queer?"

I noticed a couple of his front teeth were decaying. Hardly a come on for a queer. I grinned. "Can't stand 'em."

He relaxed. "Me neither."

"It's too crowded in here", I said. "Let's take a walk."

We walked to Hyde Park. On the way he told me his name was Jerry, he was 19 and out of work.

"Have you ever been in gaol or a boys' home?" I asked.

He hesitated, and then nodded. "I've been to Mount Penang Boys' Home and last year I did three months at the Bay."

I had found my young criminal. Anyone who referred to Long Bay as the Bay had probably been inside. We walked through the park, sounding each other out. I revealed scant information about myself. Finally he asked me what I wanted him to do. I stopped and stared at him. "I'm going to rob a bank."

He didn't back off. "Wow! I've always wanted to rob a bank."

"Well, that's where the money is. But the tellers have got guns. Does that bother you?"

He hesitated, but only for a few seconds. "Doesn't bother me, we'll have guns too, won't we?"

"I will. Your job will be to jump the counter and take their guns and the money while I cover you."

He paled a bit before displaying the rotten teeth again. "You can count on me." He shook his head. "Wow!"

I wasn't 100 per cent sure about this guy but I needed an accomplice and I was short on time.

"You know we'll get a lot of years if we get caught," I said.

He shrugged. "We won't get caught. It's worth the risk."

"All right," I said. "You've got a guernsey." I handed him £2. "Book into the People's Palace. Clean up, have a meal and a good sleep. Meet me tomorrow outside Strathfield Station at ten, on the shopping centre side."

"What bank are we hitting?"

"You'll find out tomorrow."

As we shook hands I pulled him close and stared at him. "Don't let me down, or I'll find you."

He paled. "I'm solid, mate."

I nodded. Time would tell.

When I arrived at Strathfield the next morning Jerry was there. I was pleased to see he was wearing fresh, clean clothes.

I had chosen Strathfield because of the numerous amount of cars parked in the area by people who commute by rail to the city.

It didn't take long to find an FJ Holden parked within a few hundred metres of the station. During my stay at Bathurst Gaol, a car thief had described to me how the early model Holdens could be started by pushing some rolled up silver paper under the ignition switch behind the dashboard.

While Jerry kept watch I forced the side panel window open, unlocked the door and got in. At the first attempt with the silver paper I started the car.

On the way to Canley Heights, Jerry began to show signs of stress. He was sweating profusely and was as pale as a corpse. He asked me to stop and buy him a scotch to clear his head.

Inwardly cursing, I stopped at a hotel and drank a lemon squash while he downed a scotch. When he asked for another I gave him a look that I knew would intimidate him. "Let's go," I said, grabbing him by the arm.

We drove to the bank in silence. Our jovial camaraderie had dissipated. Talk was easy, action was harder. I guessed he was wondering how he could pull out of the venture without incurring my wrath. As far as I was concerned he was coming with me into the bank even if I had to drag him in. Otherwise he might decide to dob me in.

I knew that once I stepped inside the bank with a loaded weapon I would become not just a criminal on bail waiting to go to gaol, but a true outlaw: well and truly beyond the boundaries of the law. It would be the point of no return. Every breed of animal produces individuals that will not or cannot conform to the accepted pattern of behaviour. It seemed that I had evolved into the human equivalent of these animal pariahs. The logical part of me, the thinker, the chess player, was screaming silently to me that bank robbery was too extreme, even insane, but to no avail. Paleface had taken control.

36

WANTED FOR BANK ROBBERY
(January 1966)

When we arrived at the street behind the Canley Heights School, I looked at Jerry. "How do you feel?"

"I'm a bit worried about the tellers. And what about the manager? Where will he be?"

I had been expecting this reaction. I had a contingency plan. "Okay," I said. "I'll tell you what we'll do. Leave your mask here. You go ahead of me and pretend to be a customer. Ask to see the manager. I'll give you 30 seconds, then I'll rush in shouting orders and I'll pick on you to grab the money. If something goes wrong and we get caught, you can say you were a customer."

His relief was visible. "A good idea. But we won't get caught."

I nodded. His confidence had returned. I loaded the single shot rifle. "Okay, let's get the money!"

Leaving the car doors unlocked we walked through the deserted school towards the shopping centre. I carried a large overnight bag containing the rifle and one of the clown masks. Both of us were wearing gloves.

As we approached the bank there was tightness in my chest that I'd never experienced before. Apart from the fact that I was about to commit the most monumental criminal act of my life, I was concerned that someone who knew me might see me.

There was a small, cloistered passageway at the side entrance to the bank. I told Jerry to go inside and ask for the manager.

"Don't be long," he said.

I gave him 30 seconds, and then slipping the mask on I took out the rifle and rushed inside. "Don't move, anyone! This is a hold-up!"

There were about four staff and six customers. For a few moments they were all immobilised by shock. Then some of them raised their hands in the air. I noticed that Jerry had been talking to a guy aged about forty, probably the manager. At the rear of the bank the big vault was closed.

I pointed the rifle at the guy I assumed to be the manger. "You! Open the vault!"

He grimaced. "I can't. I only have half the combination. The head accountant has the other half and he's on lunch."

He looked scared. I doubted he was lying. I didn't have the time to find out. I pointed the rifle at Jerry. "All right, you! Take the bag and get all the money from the drawers."

Taking the bag Jerry jumped over the counter and began emptying the tellers' drawers. One of the tellers began to reach below the counter.

I fired a shot into the floor. "If anyone goes for a gun I'll shoot them! Put your hands in the air. Everyone!"

Everyone, including the teller with the wandering hands, did as ordered. Only Jerry continued with his task of scooping up the cash from the drawers.

Pretending to reload the rifle I turned to the manager. "Give me your pistol. Hold it by the barrel."

" I don't have a pistol," he said.

"Well, give me one of the tellers' guns."

As he reached under the counter I aimed the rifle at his head. "Don't do anything foolish."

He handed me an automatic pistol. It had Commonwealth Bank engraved on it. Dropping the rifle to the floor, I pointed the pistol at Jerry. "Come on you, hurry up!"

I wondered if anyone considered it odd that he was wearing gloves on this hot summer's day, gloves identical to mine. Jerry jumped over the counter and gave me the bag. "I've got it all," he said.

"You can come with me," I said. Turning, I rushed out to the empty passageway, pulled off the mask and began to run down the street, with Jerry just behind me.

We turned into another street and ran up to the school and through to the street where we had parked the car. It was a lengthy run. No one followed us. I started the car with the silver paper and, without speeding, drove the back streets towards Cabramatta. I figured that although the police would come from that direction they would take the main route and they didn't know what they were looking for.

After a few minutes I stopped in a side street. "It's time to split up."

Opening the bag I roughly divided the money into two bundles. "There's not much here for a bank robbery," I said, stuffing my share into my suit coat pockets.

He stared at me. "What about all the new money I got? Where's that?"

"I've got it. I'm going to burn it. Decimal currency won't be released for another three weeks. If one of us gets caught with even a dollar, it'll be enough to convict us."

"How do I know you won't keep it?"

I could hear police sirens in the distance. "Because I'm not that fucking stupid," I said, struggling into my coat. "I'm going. If you're smart, you'll leave the car here."

I got out and jogged down the street. I heard Jerry start the car. He sped past me and turned left. Cursing, I ran to the corner and turned right. Glancing behind, I saw Jerry stop the car, get out and run in the opposite direction. A strange guy. I never saw him again.

I walked a few hundred metres to the highway, about a mile from Cabramatta railway station.

A woman, aged about 35, was clearing some weeds in her garden.

"Excuse me, madam, I wonder if I could use your phone? My car has broken down and I have to get a taxi."

She smiled, displaying perfect teeth. Despite my situation, I noticed she had a nice figure.

"Of course," she said. "Come inside."

I followed her into the hallway. She gave me the number of a taxi company and her address.

"Would you like a cup of tea?"

"I'd prefer coffee if you've got it."

She smiled again. "No problem. White with sugar?"

I nodded and dialled for a taxi.

She returned with the coffee. As I sipped it she gave me a thoughtful look. I was aware of the bulge in my pockets, and probable dishevelled appearance.

I grinned. "I have an appointment in Auburn. When I couldn't fix my car I tried to run to the railway station, but I'm afraid I'm not very fit."

"You look fit enough to me. Where do you live?"

"Melbourne. I'm only visiting. I don't know this area very well."

She stared at me. I could see she was bursting to ask what I had stuffed in my pockets. I wondered what she would do if I told her my pockets were stuffed with stolen money and a bank pistol.

The taxi arrived and beeped its horn. I gulped down the coffee. "He was quick." I handed her a ten shilling note. "This is for the phone call and the coffee. Thanks very much."

She began to protest. I walked to the door. "Forget it," I said. "You've been very kind."

She walked me to the gate. "Next time you're in the area drop in for a cup of coffee."

A police car suddenly drove up alongside the taxi and stopped. The cop in the passenger side stared at me.

My mind was racing. The bulge in my suit wouldn't be so noticeable from a distance, especially a front on view. Turning my head towards the lady I grinned. "I might bring some rum to put with the coffee."

She laughed. The police car drove on. I walked to the taxi, the tightness in my chest had returned. I doubted bank robbers lived to an old age.

The taxi took me to Cabramatta Station. After he drove off, I went to the taxi rank and caught another cab to Croydon Station. From there I walked home.

Mum was the only one there. I went to my room and counted the money, nearly £600 and $100 in decimal currency. I had hoped for a lot more.

After packing my bags I told a shocked Mum that I was leaving. I handed her £500. "Give this to Harry to cover the bail money. There's an extra hundred there to cover court costs and expenses."

"John, don't be a fool."

"It's too late for that." I kissed her on the cheek. "Tell Harry not to mention the money to anyone. Tell the judge the truth, that when he bailed me he believed that I'd appear in court. The judge may be sympathetic and not impose a penalty. If that happens you'll be five hundred quid better off."

She gave me a sad look. "Where did you get the money?"

I grinned. "I backed a good winner."

That afternoon I rented a room in a small rooming house at Meadowbank. There were only four other lodgers, plus the woman-in-charge and her 10-year-old son, Casper.

I had robbed a bank and had less than £100. But giving Mum the money to cover the bail had had a cathartic effect on me. I could disappear and not have to worry about Harry losing his savings. A gaol sentence was not inevitable. They had to catch me first. But if I wanted to get to America I would have to rob another bank. At least I had proven it could be done. You didn't have to be Ned Kelly or Ryan and Walker to rob a bank. But I had to admit that my effort had been far from professional. Fired my only shot into the floor leaving me defenceless. One of the tellers could have shot me dead. And Jerry, who had been a handicap, cost me half my takings. The getaway route had been fine but leaving myself stranded after ditching the car had nearly brought me undone. If that cop had called me over to the car I'd have taken off and might have been shot.

Next time I must do better.

I knew that when I failed to report on bail that night a warrant would be issued for my immediate arrest. But it would have been too risky to remain at Croydon. Someone might have recognised me before I entered the bank. I was well known in the area. And the lady who allowed me to ring for a taxi might become suspicious when she heard about the bank robbery. She could give the cops an accurate description of me. Harry, also, was a concern. He would realise that I had stolen the money to cover the bail surety. But common sense should dictate to him to say nothing to police.

The reporting of the bank robbery was on the front pages of the morning newspapers. One of them reported that we had escaped with £8,000. My first shocked reaction was to conclude that Jerry had somehow managed to rip me off for nearly £7,000. But how? Had he surreptitiously extracted the money from the bag while I had been driving? Is that why he had driven the car a short distance? Or was it a diabolical plot by the cops to set the two of us against each other? I figured that was it. No way had there been £8,000 in that bag.

After reading the newspaper I rang Harry's. Mum answered. In a hushed voice she told me the police had been there asking about me.

"That's because I didn't report for bail."

"No, I think it's more serious than that," she said. "I think the police have tapped the phone."

Thanking her I hung up. Somehow, they were on to me already. But they didn't have a clue as to where I might be. I had a loaded automatic pistol and banks weren't difficult to rob. With money and a false passport I could still get to Chicago.

The interesting bit would be what Cathy had to say when I arrived.

37

AUSTRALIA'S FIRST C-DAY BANDIT
(January/February 1966)

Two days after the robbery I was scheduled to ring Cathy. I had decided to tell her the truth; that I was on the run but with a bit of luck I'd soon be in Chicago where we could discuss it all and decide what to do. It was vital that I talk to her first and allow a bit of time to assuage the shock before I arrived. In retrospect it was the reasoning of a madman but at the time I still believed I could salvage the situation.

Cathy's mother answered the phone. She calmly told me that the Chicago police had been to see them and that Interpol was looking for me. She refused to allow Cathy to speak to me and warned that if I tried to contact her again she would notify the police.

Well, that was that. The seriousness of my situation was emphasised by the speed with which Chicago police and Interpol had been notified. My heart went out to Cathy. She would be shattered and disillusioned. I had done all I could to hold on to her but fate had intervened. From the time she and her family had decided to return to the US, the odds had been stacked against me.

I figured it was the final chapter in a disastrous love story. At least I didn't have to worry about getting a false passport and risk trying to get to America where Interpol would be watching for me.

My priority now was to try and stay ahead of the Australian police.

I became ultra cautious. During the days I remained in my room reading. In the evenings I would go to a small café in West Ryde for dinner. Occasionally after dinner, I'd catch a train and go to a suburban theatre to watch a movie.

Helen, the woman-in-charge of the rooming house, was an attractive brunette in her mid-thirties who seemed intrigued by my lifestyle. Often, after the other tenants had gone to work, she came to my room with coffee and sandwiches and started up a conversation. I was lonely and didn't discourage her. Eventually we became lovers.

A few weeks after moving into Meadowbank I set out to find another bank to rob. I chose the ANZ at Cabramatta. I reasoned that the Cabramatta police had probably ascertained that after dumping the car I caught a taxi to the station. They would have assumed that from there I had taken a train. I figured it was probable that they would expect me to use the same modus operandi. This time I would use a different getaway route, going in the opposite direction, which should give me plenty of leeway.

I chose C-Day, 14 February 1966, Valentine's Day, the day when Australia would change to decimal currency, as the ideal day for a bank robbery. The banks would be certain to do a booming trade.

C-Day was a Monday, the day after my 24th birthday. Using the same method as I had used at Strathfield, I stole an early model Holden from Parramatta and drove to Cabramatta. Parking it on the opposite side of the street to the bank and about 30 metres farther down, I left the engine running and began walking across the street.

An old lady hurried up behind me and tapped me on the shoulder. "Excuse me, young man, you've left your motor running."

Inwardly cursing, I thanked her and returned to the car. She followed me. As I reached inside and under the dashboard searching for the silver paper between the ignition switch, she stood close by, watching. I wondered if she had been alert enough to notice that there were no keys in the ignition. I switched off the engine and turned towards her.

She smiled. "It's best to be on the safe side," she said. "Lots of cars are stolen around here."

"Madam, if I could afford it, I'd buy you some roses for Valentine's Day."

"Oh, how sweet. I hope you have a nice day, young man."

"Thank you, ma'am."

I started walking towards the bank. Although my chances of being caught or even shot had been increased by not having a car waiting with the engine running, I wasn't nervous. I was a fast runner and I had a loaded automatic. I didn't bother with a disguise. In 1966 banks in Australia didn't have security cameras. During the last robbery I had worn a mask and within 48 hours Interpol was looking for me. This time I was content with wearing sunglasses.

Striding into the bank, which was twice as large in area as the Commonwealth at Canley Heights, I pointed the pistol in the direction of the tellers and ordered everyone to put their hands in the air. There were about a dozen people in the bank. A customer, who was wearing a butcher's apron, had emptied some money from a calico bag on the counter.

"I'll take that," I said, picking up the money and putting it in my bag. The butcher's face flushed with rage, but he didn't say anything. He probably didn't know it, but he was covered by the bank's insurance.

Included with the money was a bank book with a picture of Donald Duck on the cover. It had two £10 notes enclosed. I pushed it aside. Even bank robbers draw the line.

The tellers had raised their hands and were staring at me. I tapped my pistol. "In case you're wondering, this is real. Now get all the money from the drawers and put it on the counter."

They placed an assortment of dollars and pounds in various denominations on the counter. I scooped it into the bag. I doubted that it would have totalled $2,000.

I pointed the pistol at one of the tellers. "I said all the money!"

He shrugged. He seemed unperturbed. "You've got it. They've cleaned us out today."

I didn't believe him, but there wasn't much I could do about it. I was concerned that they might have pressed a silent alarm alerting the police. Although I had the situation under control, instinct told me to leave with the money I had. Backing to the exit, I dropped the pistol in the bag, turned and ran, weaving along the footpath past startled shoppers. As I crossed the street I looked around, two guys were chasing me. I jumped into the car and cursing the old dear who caused me to switch off the ignition I fumbled with my left hand pushing the silver paper into the ignition switch while I held the pistol in my right hand ready for trouble. My two pursuers, no doubt aware I was armed, got into a car about four vehicles behind me. As I eased into the traffic I saw in the rear vision mirror that they were following me.

I wasn't concerned, I had planned a good getaway route and unless one of them was a champion athlete, they would never catch me.

I drove fast down a side street, then back onto the main road, then down another side street. By the time I came to the bottom of a no through street, I had lost them. I abandoned the car and ran through a large paddock. From there, I jogged along a couple of streets to Warwick Farm railway station. I had timed it to catch a Liverpool-bound train that arrived within two minutes of me buying a ticket. At Liverpool, I hired a taxi to Bankstown where I caught a train home.

The proceeds from the robbery totalled $2,600. Not much, when you considered the risks involved. The robbery was reported on the

C-Day hold-up man gets £ s d

The first C-Day hold-up man in Sydney robbed the A.N.Z. bank in John Street, Cabramatta, yesterday of about $2,600 (£1,300)—practically all in £ s d.

Sydney Morning Herald, 15 February 1966

front pages of the newspapers. It wasn't a nice way to make the history books.

I knew that if I were to survive, I would have to leave Sydney. First, though, I would have to see Dad, probably for the last time, and give him some money.

A few nights later I warily approached Dad's block of units. I circled the blocks a few times, trying to discern if the place was under surveillance. After a while, satisfied that the coast was clear, I went to Dad's second floor unit and knocked on the door.

When he saw me he visibly paled. "Johnny," he whispered. "What are you doing here? They've got the place staked out."

I walked in and closed the door. The radio was on. The Seekers were singing their latest hit *The Carnival is Over*. Appropriate, I thought.

"They've been looking for me for a month, Dad. They can't afford to put a 24 hour watch on every place where they think I might go."

"You're taking a big risk, Johnny. I've seen them every day, parked in unmarked cars. They don't fool your old man." He paused. "If they get you, they'll shoot you."

I put my arm on his shoulder. "I've come to say goodbye, Dad."

He was shaking. The reality of the situation was tragic. I had come to say goodbye to my father for possibly the last time and he was terrified that the cops would come bursting through the door and shoot me.

We hugged each other. There were tears in his eyes. "What are you going to do?"

"Don't worry, I'll be okay. I'll settle down in another state. When things quieten down, I'll come and see you."

"Listen to your old man for once. Go to Western Australia and get a job in the mines. They'll never find you."

He had to be kidding! I handed him $500. "Take this, Dad. It's the best I can do."

He looked at the money, then shook his head. "You'll need it more than me." He tried to hand it back.

I waved it aside. "I've got plenty."

"Your old man's never taken blood money in his life."

"It's not blood money. Harry took five hundred quid to cover the bail which he'll probably get back from the court."

He gave me a shocked look. "You gave Harry five hundred quid?"

"That's right. He's an honest guy, but he knows that it came from a bank. You're always telling me how the banks rip everyone off, how they ripped you off! Didn't you have to sell the house because of fucking banks? Well, this time we're ripping the bank off."

He pursed his lips, hesitated, then said: "I'll keep it in case you get into trouble. If you need it, it's there."

We shook hands. "I'd better go, Dad. Go easy on the booze, and give David my regards."

For a few moments we stood there staring at each other, neither of us knowing what to say. "Goodbye, Dad. I'll keep in touch." I turned and walked out the door.

"Keep your guard up, Johnny," was his parting advice.

I hurried to a nearby side door that opened into a small alcove where the garbage bins were stored. A startled cat that had been trying to pry the lid off a bin screeched its indignation as I leaped over the railing down onto the grass below.

As I jogged off into the darkness I couldn't get the words of the Seekers' song out of my mind:

"The Carnival is Over,

We may never meet again ..."

But it wasn't Dad I was thinking of, I was thinking of Cathy.

38

BOOKIES, BLONDES & BACCARAT
(February/April 1966)

I was now in a constant state of depression. At 24, no matter which way I looked at it, I had no future. And living on the run, I had no past.

I began to gamble heavily on the horses, mainly at the West Ryde TAB, but sometimes with an SP bookmaker at a nearby hotel. Although the introduction in 1964 of TABs in New South Wales hurt SP bookmakers, there were still a lot of them operating.

The stimulation I received from the gambling temporarily blunted my depressed state. But my losses exceeded my wins. I decided that, before decamping to Melbourne, I would have to make another hit. This time, instead of a bank, I intended to relieve the West Ryde bookie of his illegal takings. First, I would have to distance myself from the area.

When I gave Helen a week's notice she became upset.

"I thought things were serious between us," she said.

"You're married with a 10-year-old son."

"I'm separated, soon to be divorced. And Casper adores you. He thinks of you as a father."

I couldn't believe what I was hearing. Apart from having played a few games of chess with Casper, I'd had nothing to do with him. Some father I'd make, a bank robber on the run!

"I'm only fourteen years older than Casper," I said.

"And what about me? What do I mean to you?"

I shrugged. "You're a girlfriend. I really enjoyed being with you, but now I have to move on."

She stared at me, momentarily nonplussed. Then she nodded, more to herself than to me. "I knew you were too good to be true. You don't have a heart. I want you out of here today."

She walked away. I knew I had hurt her. But I had been truthful with her. I had never been emotionally involved with her. I was still in love with Cathy. My situation was horrific.

I rented a room in a guesthouse on the lower North Shore. Immediately, I felt out of place. It was expensive and all the guests were elderly.

The dining room contained three large tables. At meal times, regardless of where I chose to sit, I was always brought into the lively conversations. The three missing Beaumont children held a morbid fascination for most of the residents. They all had theories about what had happened to them. I had little doubt that some monster had murdered them, but I didn't voice my opinion. I had met such monsters.

Often I was asked the inevitable: "What is a young man like you doing in a place like this?"

It annoyed me. If only people would mind their own business.

An elderly English lady with blue rinse hair and precise manners, who claimed to have once met Princess Margaret, was more inquisitive than the others.

One day I stared at her and said: "I'm a bank robber on the run."

Her face registered shock and to me she looked exactly what she was: an old, pretentious blue-haired busybody.

An old guy who liked to tell jokes saved the situation. "Well, young Dillinger, your secret is safe with us."

The English lady managed a smile. That was the end of it. But I was angry with myself for my lack of discipline. It was time to hit the bookie and leave the state.

I chose Saturday night after the last greyhound race. Wearing a cap and dark glasses I followed at a discreet distance as the bookie, a small, balding middle-aged man, came out of the hotel with his minder, a big, gorilla-type ex-footballer. They walked towards the bookie's car in a nearby car park.

I waited until they arrived at the vehicle then I ran towards them and pointed the pistol at the minder. "Open the back door!" I said.

He hesitated then opened it. The bookie, standing near the driver's side was staring at me, his mouth open.

"Both of you get into the front," I said.

As they sidled into their seats, I glanced around. Although the area was well lit, there was no one in sight.

Getting into the seat behind the minder I pointed the pistol in his direction. "Give me the money, all of it."

"Look, mate," the bookie said, "I got cleaned out today. You picked a bad day. Why don't you try the TAB?"

"Listen, if you prefer the money to your head, tell me and I'll pull the trigger," I said.

The minder was glaring at me, his eyes narrowed. I read him like a book, he was close to jumping me.

"Don't even think about it," I said aggressively, meeting his gaze. "Believe me, you'll get shot."

The bookie handed me his wallet, it was crammed full of bank notes. "Take it!" he said. "But you won't get away with this, mate." He was glaring at me with undisguised rage.

"Give me your car keys," I said.

He flicked them at me. Catching them in my left hand, I grinned. "Even bookies lose sometimes. I'll toss the keys, you'll find 'em okay."

"What about my wallet?"

"Get a new one." I got out. "If either of you tries to follow me I'll shoot you."

"You're tough with a gun," the minder grumbled.

"That's true," I said. I hurled the keys as far as I could, then I ran off.

No one followed me. A few minutes later I hailed a taxi on Victoria Road. "Take me to the city," I said, getting into the back. If the robbery came over the radio I'd hear it. But we arrived in the city without incident. I caught a train home.

The wallet contained nearly $1,300. The favourites must have gone down like ninepins.

The robbery wasn't reported in the newspapers, which didn't surprise me. I figured the bookie had probably been paying off the cops and the publican to run his little business in direct opposition to the nearby TAB. If details of the robbery became known he would be out of business and the cops would lose one of their little golden geese.

A few days after the bookie robbery I caught a train to Melbourne. My state of mind was such that I knew I was on the borderline between sanity and insanity. I now had no interest in social conformity. I had stifled my emotions to the point where I had become a self-sufficient machine, detached from all groups. I resolved that, rather than be depressed, I would live each day as though it were my last and to derive as much pleasure from it as I could.

After renting a flatette in a rooming house near the lake at South Melbourne, I bought an old Holden for $300.

That night I dined at the Carousel Restaurant on the Albert Park Lake, less than a mile from where I lived. One of the drink waitresses was an attractive blonde who was in her early 20s. Each time I bought a drink I tipped her a dollar. After my fourth Bacardi I asked her for a date. She didn't hesitate to accept. When she finished work I drove her to my flat and poured her a drink. Five minutes later I had her in bed.

A few nights later I returned to the Carousal. Although the recently bedded blonde wasn't there, a Polish waitress named Marie, who had long blonde hair, blue eyes and a sexy accent, was friendly. When I asked her for a date she became a bit coy, but eventually accepted.

At my flat she reciprocated my kisses but when I began to undress her she resisted. As I pulled her panties down around her ankles she raked her fingernails down the side of my face.

Jumping from the bed I rushed over and looked in the mirror:

beginning just above my left eye, and extending about seven centimetres, were three deep scratches. "You've scarred me for life!"

I rushed over and pointed to my face. "Look!"

With her panties still around her ankles, she apologised.

I told her to take her panties off. She said she didn't know me well enough.

"You know me well enough to know that I won't force you," I said. "But after what you've done to me, scarred me for life, it's the least you can do for me."

She gave me a resigned sigh. "Let me clean your face first."

She bathed and dabbed my wounds until the bleeding ceased.

I began to undress. "Now take your clothes off."

Lowering her eyes she undressed and got under the sheets. While we made love my face began to bleed again; by the time we had finished we were both streaked with blood. I wondered what the housekeeper would think when she saw the sheets.

I liked Marie and took her out on a regular basis. But I wasn't in love with her and I had no intention of being faithful to her. On more than a few occasions I had one-night stands with women who took my fancy, usually blondes, the opposite of Cathy. Perhaps it was my couldn't give a damn attitude that attracted these women, or perhaps they sensed, and were perversely excited by, some portent of danger in me; but during that short period of time in my life, before my arrest, I usually got what I wanted from the women I pursued. The deep scratches on my face intrigued them. They all queried me about the obviously recent scars. I always delighted in telling them the truth, watching their reactions. It didn't discourage any of them.

Sometimes, after I had been with one of these women, I'd think of Cathy and self-loathing would pervade my being, until I reminded myself that Cathy and I were finished. But there was that illogical, optimistic idealistic part of me that wouldn't accept that fact, believing that somehow I would be reunited with her.

During these times, I became a tormented soul. Gambling was my only salvation. Ironically, for a while, I hit a winning streak. After winning more than $1,000 on the horses I began frequenting a baccarat game in the heart of the city. I applied my old system of wagering two dollars and doubling up until I won. With a bank of more than $2,000 I had to lose ten consecutive bets to go bust. I set myself to win $60 a night which more than covered living expenses.

With every win, my confidence soared and past losses became a distant memory. I discarded the reclusive type lifestyle to which I had strictly adhered to in Sydney. I grew a moustache and wore gold-rimmed glasses with plain glass. I was convinced that unless someone painted my name on my back the cops wouldn't know me. Sometimes I'd approach a cop in the street and ask for directions. My ego was taking control. I began to feel invincible.

39

THEY WERE JUST KIDDING
(March/April 1966)

After a while, I sold my Holden at a St Kilda car yard and, using another alias, bought a Ford for $400 at Caulfield. I also rented a flatette in Brighton. As an added precaution, I changed my gambling venues. I began to frequent Brewster's two-up game in Prahran, successfully using the same double up system on the two-up as I had used with the baccarat.

One of the regulars at Brewster's was Sparrow, whom I hadn't seen since 1960, the day I'd escaped from Bathurst Courthouse. During the ensuing six years he had earned a reputation as one of the best pickpockets in Australia. But, being a compulsive gambler, he rarely had much money. Despite my disguise he immediately recognised me. I told him that I was now John Clinton. He was too discreet to question me, probably half the patrons at Brewster's had something to hide. Brewster himself was an old gangster from the '30s and '40s era. When Sparrow realised that I was constantly winning he asked me for a loan of $20. This occurred three times a week and it was beginning to annoy me. The fourth time it happened, he approached me after I had just collected a winning bet. This time he had two mates with him: a tall, freckled redhead and a short, stocky guy who looked about as bright as a winter's night. Sparrow asked me for $50, he told me he needed it desperately and would repay it soon. While his two mates watched, I gave him the money and warned that it was the last loan he would get from me until he repaid me.

A few nights later, after winning $60, I left Brewster's and walked to my car. As I unlocked the car door Sparrow's two mates, Redhead and Shorty, approached me. The area was deserted, instinct warned me to be wary.

"How you going, mate?" Redhead said. Shorty stood just behind him, grinning.

"I'm fine." I stood facing them; aware of the two thousand plus dollars I had on me.

"We were wondering if you could loan us a couple of hundred, mate," Redhead said. "Sparrow'll vouch for us."

I smiled. Sparrow couldn't vouch for himself. I knew that if I refused them, there was a chance they would attack me. But during the past few months my ego had taken control to the point where I was confident that I could handle any situation. If they rushed me I'd immediately disable Redhead with a kick to the groin. "Sorry, boys. I can't help you."

Redhead, who was about six centimetres taller than me, stared at me, his eyes narrowed. Shorty's vacuous grin disappeared. A man walking with his dog approached us.

Redhead tried another tack. "Well, could you give us a lift to our mate's place?"

I didn't hesitate. "Sure, that's no problem."

The guy with the dog passed us without a sideways glance. The dog sniffed Shorty's leg, then hurried after its master.

By the time Redhead had got into the passenger's side next to me and Shorty was seated in the back, I had extracted my pistol from under the seat and placed it under my thigh. The adrenalin rushed through me as I imagined what might happen. These galahs were going to try to take me and the thought excited me. I was more than ready for them.

Redhead directed me to one of the outer suburbs. The two of them made inane attempts at conversation, which I discouraged by complaining of a headache. I wanted to concentrate on how I could handle a confrontation.

As we approached a large park, Redhead said: "Pull in here for a minute, mate – I'm busting for a piss."

I drove into the parking area and switched off the ignition. It was after midnight and the place was deserted.

Redhead turned to face me in the semi-darkness. "About that loan mate, would you like to reconsider?"

I feigned fear. "Yeah, okay fellas, I'll lend you a couple of hundred."

"Five hundred," Redhead said. Shorty gave an excited giggle.

I pointed the pistol at Redhead. "Do you think five hundred will pay for two funerals?"

Redhead instinctively put his hands to his face and leaned back against the door. "Take it easy, mate! We were only kidding."

I looked at Shorty. "Is that right? Were you only kidding?"

Shorty nodded four or five times before he said: "Yeah, we were just playing a joke."

"Oh," I said. "Well, in that case I'll just play a little joke on you. Now get out of the car, both of you. If you try to run, I'll shoot you."

The three of us got out. "All right, boys, strip off."

They stared at me. "What?" Redhead said.

"I know you're busting for a piss but get your gear off first!"

"Okay!" Shorty said quickly. "We'll do it." He started to undress. Reluctantly, Redhead followed suit.

When they were both standing naked, I smiled. "Now take a little run up the park and have a piss. Off you go."

They looked at each other. Shorty shrugged and began to jog up the park with Redhead following him. Picking up their clothes I put them in the car, then I got in and drove out of the park. After I'd driven a few miles I stopped and threw the clothing on to the side of the road.

As I drove I tried to imagine what Redhead and Shorty would do about their predicament. I had to laugh, life could be fun.

40

Four Drunks and a Bachelor Boy
(March/April 1966)

The incident with Redhead and Shorty compelled me to stay away from Brewster's and other illegal gaming houses. I knew that by frequenting them, I had been playing with fire. If the cops raided one of them while I was there it would almost certainly lead to my undoing. For an income I concentrated solely on gambling on horses. My winning streak continued when the great filly, *Storm Queen*, stormed home to win the Golden Slipper and my bank had increased to more than $4,000.

The women I dated were curious about what I did for a living. Although I was tempted to claim that I was a professional gambler, I knew that some people considered gamblers to be only one rung above bank robbers, so I posed as a 'singer from Sydney'. When questioned further, I purported to be forming a band. Most of the women were impressed by my claims. One of them, a shapely brunette named Louise, used her initiative to give me some free promotion. We were dining at the Cockpit Restaurant at Essendon Airport when she got up and approached the bandleader.

I thought she had merely requested a song and I was shocked when the bandleader announced: "Ladies and gentlemen, we have with us tonight, an up and coming young singer from the harbour city: Johnny Clinton! Come on up, Johnny, and give us a number."

Damn! Here we go again!

Louise came over; she was excited. "I used my womanly charms. Now go and knock 'em dead!"

Somehow, I managed to smile at her; it was either that or knock her out. Trying to gather my wits, I walked towards the stage and people began clapping.

"What are you going to sing, Johnny?" The bandleader asked.

My mind had been racing, trying to think of a song that didn't contain a high note. "Do you know *Bachelor Boy*?"

"We certainly do. Ladies and gentlemen, Johnny's going to give us his special rendition of the old Cliff Richards' number *Bachelor Boy*. Take it away, Johnny."

I had always fancied myself as a singer and after a nervous start I gave a reasonable performance. Four drunks at one of the front tables had been cheering and rallying me on. When I'd finished they shouted for more.

"Hey Johnny!" one of them yelled. "What about Frank's new one -- 'doo bee doo bee dah dah dah' ..."

A lot of people laughed. Sinatra had bounced back into the charts with *Strangers in the Night*. I smiled. "Sorry, I don't know it. I've got to get back to my girl."

I stepped from the stage and Doobeedoobeedah grabbed me by the arm. He was a big guy, with a strong grip. "Get your girl and come up and have a drink with us, Johnny." He sounded as though he was accustomed to giving orders.

I stared at him and my heart began to thump. Instinctively, I realised that he was a cop! The four of them were cops! Outwardly, I remained calm. "Yeah, okay. We'll come up and have a drink later."

He released his grip on my arm. "Make sure you do, you old bachelor boy. Ha ha."

One of the other guys at the table took a swig of his drink and yelled: "Good on ya, John!"

I returned to my table. "Come on Louise, time to leave."

She gave me a quizzical look. "Why?"

"Because I made a fool of myself."

"Rubbish. Everyone liked it. But you should have sung something a bit more modern."

I shrugged. "How about *These Boots Were Made for Walking*?"

She smiled. "Sit down. Dinner's on the way."

I looked across at the four drunks. Cops or not, they obviously had no idea who I was. Nevertheless, I wasn't prepared to push my luck. "I'm leaving, Louise. Are you coming or not?"

"No, I'm not."

I put $20 on the table. "In that case, adios." I walked out without looking back. I never saw her again.

My new resolve for women was don't get emotionally involved and this made her easy to forget.

41

WHY I CAN'T DO THE TANGO
(April 1966)

When I decided to avoid Brewster's I thought I had seen the last of Sparrow, but the day after the episode at the Cockpit Restaurant I encountered him at a TAB. He had lost his money and asked me for a loan. I gave him $20. We went for a drink and he told me that Redhead and Shorty were looking for me. I laughed and asked him why, but he said that neither of them would elaborate.

After his second beer, Sparrow said: "John, I need a favour."

I was cautious. "Depends what it is."

"I've been pinched for possession of housebreaking instruments." He paused; his shifty eyes looked at me pleadingly. "They want two spot to drop the charges, otherwise I'll cop six months."

Although I had no intention of giving him $200, I elected to stall him. He was no fool and probably suspected that I was on the run. If he believed that I would help him, he wouldn't be tempted to trade information to the cops. I told him I'd have the money for him within a week. Relieved, he gave me his address and we parted.

Common sense cautioned me that the recent series of incidents from which I had emerged unscathed, placed me in jeopardy. Although my good luck had been extraordinary, I had learned that luck was an ephemeral thing. I had departed Sydney at the right moment, it was now time to leave Melbourne. But I had signed up with the Fred Astaire Dance Studio for ten hours tuition in ballroom dancing. The course was expensive and I had paid in advance. I had only received four hours of lessons and I was reluctant to leave Melbourne until I had completed the contract. As usual, I decided to push my luck.

A few days later I lost about $4,000 at a TAB. That's the equivalent today of about $70,000. Imagine the effect on your mind if you wandered down to the TAB one afternoon and lost $70,000. All the money you had. You've also lost the love of your life. On top of that the Australian police, the Chicago cops and Interpol were looking for you. Your entire being wants to shut down. Hopelessness envelopes you, suffocates you, there's no one you can turn to. You are totally alone in the world. You feel like an alien totally disconnected from society. You know you are self-destructing but you don't know how to stop it.

For me, there was only one way to survive. I had to rob another bank. There were plenty of banks out there, money in abundance for a guy prepared to take a risk. No need to starve, no need to live on the street. Money was nothing but a commodity, easily replenished.

As always, I looked for an area that provided a good getaway route, eventually choosing a bank in Kensington. Later, I visited Sparrow, offering him a third share if he drove the getaway car.

At the mention of a bank robbery he paled, but was resolute. "I'm sick of being pinched for petty blues," he said. "As long as I've only got to drive the car, I'll be in it. Even a third split will be big money."

I didn't reveal to him which bank I had chosen. I arranged to meet him outside the Fred Astaire Dance Studio in town at 8.00 pm, the night before the planned robbery. From there I intended to take him to Kensington and show him the getaway route.

During my dancing lesson my thoughts were elsewhere and, to the frustration of my instructress, I floundered my way through an hour of the tango. At eight o'clock I eagerly departed the studio expecting to see Sparrow outside but he wasn't there. I waited for half an hour before cursing him and returning to my car. I drove to his place but no one was there. Accepting that he had no intention of being involved in a bank robbery, I drove to Marie's place and persuaded her to come for a drive. I intended to go ahead with the robbery and there was a chance that tomorrow I could be killed or captured. Tonight I needed Marie.

The following morning I stole an old Holden, gaining entry by smashing the side window with a brick. I drove the few miles to

Kensington and parked the car in a street diverging off the main road in which the bank was situated.

Carrying an overnight bag containing my pistol, I crossed the road and entered the bank, my only disguise was a pair of sunglasses. It was a small bank; there were two tellers and no customers inside.

I produced a pistol and pointed it at the tellers. "This is a hold-up! Get all the money from the drawers and put it in this bag!"

I put the bag on the counter. One of the tellers immediately began to fill it with money. The other teller stood near the phone, staring at me.

"You! Pull the phone out of the wall!"

He made a half-hearted attempt to rip the connection from the wall.

I pointed the pistol at his head. "Rip it right out!"

Slowly, grudgingly, he tore the connection from the wall.

The other teller pushed the bag towards me. "That's all there is, sir."

The Age, Saturday, April 9, 1966

The Commonwealth Bank branch at Kensington — scene of the armed hold-up.

I glanced in the bag. It appeared to contain a large amount of money. I ran out of the bank and across the street almost getting skittled by a car as the driver slammed on the brakes. Running towards my car I glanced over my shoulder, the two tellers were coming after me, both of them armed with pistols.

As I reached the car and opened the door one of them fired a shot at me. It hit the boot of the car.

I knelt behind the door and pointed my pistol at him. He and his mate scrambled behind a parked car. I jumped into the car and started it. I was quite calm; in some perverse way I was enjoying it. A truck pulled out from the kerb and stopped in the middle of the road, blocking my path. Cursing, I swerved onto the footpath and around it. As I sped down the street I checked my rear vision mirror, the truck was following me. And farther back the two tellers were running after both of us.

With the truck close behind me I drove down a few streets until I arrived at the end of a no through street. Jumping out of the car I looked around, the truck had stopped a few car lengths behind me. The driver sat there, staring at me.

I ran up to him. "What are you going to do now, hero?"

He sat there, fear in his eyes. I laughed and ran through the pedestrian exit and across a large field, which led to the railway station. I had timed my getaway to catch a train. I was halfway across the field when I saw the train coming into the station. Running as fast as I could with the bag of money I reached the station entrance only to find it closed by a barricade. I shouted at the railway attendant, who was standing on the other side of the barricade, to open it.

He shook his head. "Too late, fella. You should have got here earlier."

"I have to catch this train!"

Ignoring me, he blew his whistle. No passengers had alighted and the train began to pull away from the platform.

It had to be fate. All my life I had beaten the railway and its employees. Now, in the middle of a bank robbery, they had taken their revenge.

I looked back across the field. The truck driver was standing with the two tellers and another guy. The driver was pointing in my direction.

The attendant opened the barricade, gave me a superior smile and returned to his office, closing the door behind him.

On the other side of the railway track there was a three-metre high wire fence encompassing a large factory. Jumping down on to the track I rushed over to the fence and leapt on to it, gradually heaving myself to the top. Flinging the bag onto the other side, I climbed over and jumped to the ground. I was in the car park. I noticed two guys sitting in the front seat of one of the cars, eating sandwiches.

I opened the rear door and got in. They turned to stare at me. I showed them my pistol. "Take it easy, boys. I'm in a bit of trouble and I want you to drive me out of here".

They looked at each other. They guy in the driver's seat who wore glasses and looked to be about forty, said: "I'll do that for you. Where would you like to go?"

"Take me into town."

Nodding, he started the car and drove towards the exit. An old security guard sitting in the cubicle gave him a wave and lifted the barrier. As we drove past the guard we could hear police sirens in the distance.

The guy in the passenger seat who was younger and more solidly built than the driver, said: "I wonder who they're looking for?"

I smiled. "Could be anybody."

As we drove along we chatted about Melbourne football. They were both Collingwood supporters and confident of winning the premiership this year. Twice, we saw police cars, with sirens blaring, rush past us.

When we reached the outskirts of the city I told the driver to stop. I handed him $40. "Here, take this for petrol."

He gave me a surprised look. "It wouldn't come to that."

I shrugged. "Next time I might want to go further." I handed $40 to his mate. "I'm a Geelong supporter myself," I said. "But you might as well put this on the Magpies to win the flag. If they win, remember me."

He took the money. "Thanks, mate. I'll whack this on the Maggies for sure."

I got out of the car. "I hope they win for you." Collingwood went on to reach the Grand Final, only to lose by a point to St Kilda. Geelong finished fourth.

They drove off. Instinct told me that they wouldn't go to the police.

As soon as I arrived home I counted the money, $3,400. Despite having been shot at, I considered it to be a nice day's work.

The robbery was given headline coverage on the TV news. They interviewed the truck driver, proclaiming him to be a hero who had valiantly risked his life trying to capture the bandit. When a police spokesman claimed that the bandit had escaped via train, I knew that my intuition regarding the two factory workers had proven to be correct. Since then I've always had a soft spot for Collingwood supporters.

My main concern about the robbery was Sparrow. He would read about it and almost certainly conclude that I had been the perpetrator. I recalled the night we had robbed the Western Stores at Bathurst and Sparrow had hidden some diamond rings in his socks. I felt that if he couldn't raise the $200 to have his charges dropped, there was a distinct possibility he would try to trade my freedom for his. I considered gong to his place and giving him the money, but the irresponsible manner that he had displayed towards me in all my dealings with him had antagonised me towards him to such an extent that I resolved he would never get another cent from me. At least he didn't know where I lived.

I sold my Ford and caught a taxi to a large second hand car yard on the Princes Highway where I bought another Holden. Although I felt I now had covered my tracks, I determined to soon move to Perth and make a fresh start.

At my next visit to the TAB I had another disastrous day losing more than $2,000. Some of the horses I had backed were beaten by centimetres. I contemplated robbing another bank, but decided to battle on with the $1,200 that I had. There were some good horses entered for the big races over the next few weeks and I was confident that if I kept my cool I would recoup the $6,000 in losses I'd incurred during the past eight days.

On the Monday I had a good win on *Prince Grant* in the Sydney Cup but overall I only managed to finish even on the day. Two days later I backed up and won $800 on *Prince Grant* after he won a titanic struggle with the old champion *Craftsman* in the Queen Elizabeth Stakes. That night I set out for the dance studio in high spirits. I had managed to restore my bank to $2,000. And there were lots of good things coming up in the next few weeks.

As I stopped at the traffic lights outside Flinders Street Station a car stopped alongside me. Glancing across, I instinctively knew that although the four occupants wore plain clothes, they were cops.

The lights changed to green and they sped off. I drove slowly, still shaken by the incident. Twice, in a few weeks, I had come into close contact with a bunch of detectives. My luck couldn't hold out much longer. I was wanted for multiple bank robberies in Sydney, and less than a week ago I had robbed a bank in Melbourne. Every cop in Sydney and Melbourne would be looking for me. Sooner or later I'd run into a cop who would recognise me or at least be suspicious enough to question me. Suddenly I had a strong urge to turn around and start driving to Perth. The instinct I had developed for danger was on red alert. I made a snap decision. This would be my last dancing lesson. After the appointment I would go home, pack and start driving towards Perth.

I drove around the city block twice, unable to find a parking spot. I was already seven minutes late for the appointment. Cursing, I decided to go home.

At that moment a lady in a blue Volkswagen pulled out from the kerb. After manoeuvring my car into the parking space, I got out and began running toward the studio.

I ran down the steps of the studio and, out of breath, grinned at the receptionist. "Sorry I'm late." Even as I spoke, I realised, too late, by the look of fear and apprehension in her eyes that I had walked into a trap.

Police, male and female, posing as dancers were pointing guns at me. "Don't move!" one of them shouted.

For a split second my mind was paralysed with shock. Someone from behind grabbed me in a half nelson. "I've got him!" he yelled.

Other cops grabbed hold of me and dragged me into the back room.

"What the hell's going on?" I shouted.

Someone punched me hard on the side of the head, stunning me. My arms were pinned from behind me and my wrists quickly handcuffed behind my back, the handcuffs cutting into my wrists.

"Are you sure you guys have got the right guy?" I said. "I'm just here to learn to tango."

"Shut up!" someone yelled.

They half dragged and half shoved me to the stairs. A thin guy with a sallow complexion said: "Don't try anything stupid."

I couldn't help myself. As they dragged me up the stairs, I twisted my head to look at him. "You picked it," I yelled. "I was going to make a run for it."

One of the policewomen giggled.

At Russell Street they took me to one of the upstairs offices, undid the handcuffs and handcuffed my right wrist to a chair. They had been on so tight that they had pierced my skin.

A short, chubby guy with a round pink face entered the room and walked up to me. "You're a bloody hard man to catch, John."

I studied my injured wrist and shrugged. "You guys just look in the wrong places."

A couple of cops sniggered. "We looked in the right place tonight," one of them said.

"Only because a little bird told you where to look," I said.

"We've been hot on your trail for a while, John," Chubby said. "We know it was you who hit the bank at Kensington."

Instead of denying it, I remained silent. I knew that the bank tellers and the truck driver would identify me.

Chubby stared at me. "You've caused us a lot of trouble, John. We grabbed the wrong bloke tonight."

"I've been trying to tell these guys that all night," I said.

He smiled. "No, we've got the right bloke this time. But the other bloke who fitted your description walked in about the time you were due. Some of our blokes jumped on him, threw him to the ground and put a pistol to his head. He wasn't too happy, I can tell you. He reckons he's going to sue us."

"Not as much as I'll be suing you for," I said. But we all knew I was bluffing. They had me well and truly wrapped up on the Kensington bank.

"The Sydney boys will want to come down and have a chat to you, too, John," Chubby said.

"Tell them I'm not interested."

Chubby pretended to examine a document he held in his hand. "How about the Commonwealth Bank at Canley Heights," he said, watching for my reaction.

I frowned. "I used to live at Canley Heights. Never banked there, though."

"Well, that's for the Sydney blokes to find out. We've got a few jobs down here we went to talk to you about."

They questioned me until after midnight about various armed robberies that had been committed in Melbourne during the past six months. When they showed me the pistol they had found in my car, I admitted to having robbed the Kensington bank, but denied knowledge of any others. I had expected them to bash me, but apart from a few threats they didn't apply any real pressure on me. I suppose they were pleased to clear up the Kensington robbery.

They took all my money and winning TAB tickets and asked me to sign a receipt for it. I was told the money and the tickets would go to the bank as part of my restitution. Later on, they took my car as well.

Before I was taken across the street to the cells I said to Chubby: "It was Sparrow who put me in, wasn't it?"

For a few moments he met my gaze before he slowly shook his head. "You're on the wrong track, John. We received our information from a female."

I was stunned. "But none of them knew about me."

He gave me a knowing smile. "One of them did. You had too many girlfriends, mate."

I was put in an unoccupied cell. I stretched out on the bench and wondered if Chubby had been covering for Sparrow or if I had slipped up somewhere and one of the women I had been dating suspected that I was a bank robber. But who? Apart from Sparrow, only Marie and Louise had been aware that I took dancing lessons.

Before I drifted off into an exhausted sleep I had concluded that if Sparrow hadn't informed on me, it must have been Louise. I shouldn't have walked out on her at the Cockpit Restaurant.

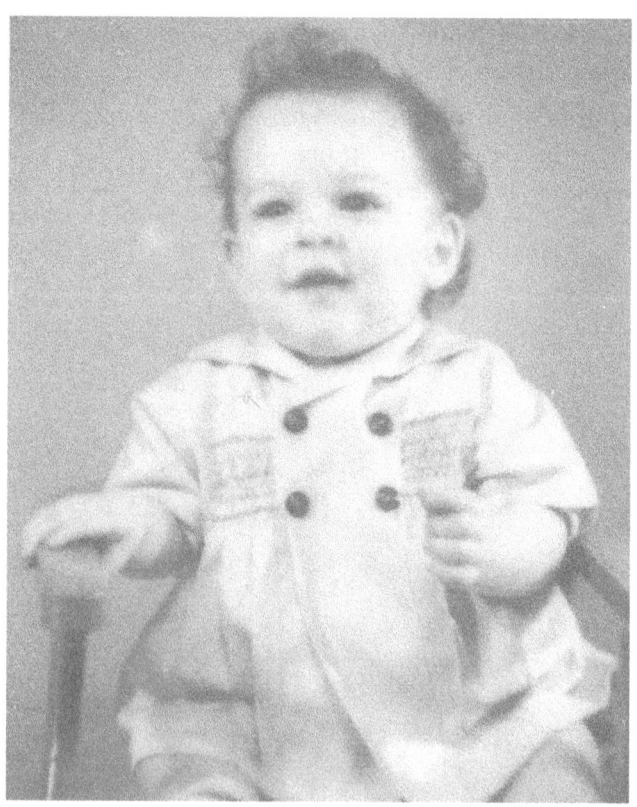

John holding Whisky, 1955

John, December 1942

David at ferry jetty at Taronga Park Zoo, c. 1957

John's father mowing the lawn, North Ryde, 1952

John as a baby in basket with his mother, Coogee, 1942

John's brother David and father at Luna Park on TV, 1957

John with father, mother and relatives at Bankstown, 1944

The Killick house in Macquarie Street, Fairfield, where John's mother died in 1959. This house was older and more run down than the one in Lombard Street

Cathy with her dog in Oaklawn, Chicago, 1965

John and friend at the Royal Easter Show, April 1958

Cathy in Chicago, 1970

John after release and hair dye, 1973

John's mother and father on verandah at Lombard Street, Fairfield, 1955

John's mother with Whisky, 1956

John in tree and mother seated in the backyard at Lombard Street, Fairfield, 1957

John's mother seated at table wearing a cross at Macquarie Street, Fairfield, two weeks before she died in June 1959

42

HOW THE COPS SOLVED THE RAILWAY ROBBERY
(April 1966)

I had been asleep for about an hour when the cell door opened and a young, dark-haired guy was shoved into the cell. As they slammed and locked the door, I noticed he was crying.

I sat up. "Looks like they've given you a rough time, eh?" I asked.

He sat down on the bench opposite me. "They've charged me with strangling an old lady," he said. "They said they found one of my hairs on her pillow."

Stunned, I was unable to think of something appropriate to say. The lights in the cell were on 24 hours a day and I scrutinised him while he continued to cry. He was an exceptionally good-looking youth who, I later discovered, was only 18. It was hard to fit him to the image of a strangler of old ladies.

I wondered why the cops had put him in the cell with me. Could he be a spy, posing as a murderer in the hope that I would tell him about some of my crimes? I dismissed the idea. His tears were real; he was in a distressed state. They had probably put him in my cell to ensure that he didn't try to hang himself.

"I'm John. What's your name?"

"David." He paused and wiped his eyes. "My wife will probably leave me."

I thought that would be a safe bet, but I didn't comment.

"I don't know if I did it or not," he said. "I was drunk."

I nodded. I thought of the hair on the pillow. It was irrefutable evidence. It made me aware of how easy it would be to convict someone with forensic evidence. It also occurred to me that it wouldn't be too difficult for the cops to take a hair from a person's hairbrush and plant it on a pillow.

He continued to cry. There wasn't much I could do. I had my own problems. If he had murdered an old lady, he must be insane.

After a while he went to sleep. Unable to sleep, I began to devise possible scenarios where I would have a chance to escape. I was confident that, sooner or later, I would get the opportunity. When it came, there would be no time to weigh up the chances, and I had to be psyched up and ready to act instinctively.

After an early breakfast of stale bread and two cold sausages I paced the small cell while David stared at the wall. At ten o'clock I was handcuffed and escorted by four cops into court. The magistrate remanded me for a week. With nothing to lose, I asked him for bail. He had a sense of humour and smiled as he refused my request. Later that day David was put on a van to Pentridge. When I asked one of the uniformed cops why I wasn't going with David I was told that "the detectives haven't finished with you yet."

I spent the remainder of the day and night alone in the cell. I had recovered from the initial shock of arrest and, after pacing up and down all day, I had convinced myself that this would be only a temporary setback. I was extremely confident that I would escape. Believing this, I was able to think rationally without being overcome by depression.

The following day I was handcuffed and taken to the detectives' office. This time a softly spoken guy named Ainesley, who had been there when I was arrested, was in charge. He was about forty, tall and thin with kindly features. He could have been mistaken for a minister of religion. Pointing to two overweight cops, he introduced them, and told me they had flown from Sydney to interview me.

"Well at least they got a nice trip for nothing," I said.

Ainesley gave a sad smile. "The pistol we found in your possession has been identified as the one taken from the Commonwealth Bank at Canley Heights."

Although that type of evidence was just as conclusive as David's hair on the pillow, it didn't overly concern me; I had been expecting it. If things went according to plan, they would never get the opportunity to take me to Sydney.

I smiled at the two overweight cops. "Well, if I'm ever up Sydney way I'll drop in and discuss it with you."

"You'll be extradited to Sydney after you serve your sentence down here, whenever that may be," one of them said.

Ainesley cut in: "John likes to be funny, it keeps him going."

The cop who looked to be the fatter of the two, said: "Yeah? Well, I'll tell him something he might find hilarious." He paused and looked at his mate who nodded. He continued: "The lady you gave ten shillings to after you made the phone call, remember her?"

I gave him a blank look.

"Well, she remembers you. She picked you out from dozens of photos."

"She framed the ten bob and hung it on the wall," the other cop said.

I believed him. In her own little way it would make her a celebrity. "How much money was stolen?" I asked.

"A bit over a thousand quid, as you very well know."

As I had suspected, the £8,000 quoted by the newspaper had been a fabrication, probably a police ploy to try to cause dissension between the two robbers. I knew that if I couldn't escape and was eventually extradited to Sydney, they would have no difficulties convicting me on the Canley Heights robbery. I told them I would make their jobs easy and give them a statement if they gave me a pen and some writing paper and later posted some letters for me. Ainesley said he would supply the writing materials and ensure that the letters were posted. The Sydney cops weren't satisfied. They told me that the butcher who had been robbed while he was in the bank at Cabramatta on C-Day had positively identified me as the bandit. They also suspected me of at least four other robberies, but they had no evidence. Nevertheless, they tried to persuade me to confess to all six robberies, promising me that they would put in a good word for me at court. I commented that if I pleaded guilty to six armed robberies a good word from the Pope would be to no avail.

After I had given them a handwritten statement admitting to the Canley Heights robbery, Ainesley brought me a hot meal, an apple pie and a cup of coffee. When I returned to the cell he arranged for me to have writing materials in the cell. Of all the cops I've met, he was the most obliging and understanding. I could sense that he sympathised with my situation.

I wrote a short letter to Cathy telling her that I had foxtrotted into a dance studio and had been waltzed out by police. I wrote that I would be at Pentridge for a while and I would leave it up to her whether she wanted to write or not. I wasn't too hopeful of her replying. In my letter to Dad I told him that things weren't as bad as they seemed and I'd probably be out of gaol a lot sooner than he expected. Until then, I promised to write regularly. I then wrote to Harry and thanked him and his family for their kindness. I commented on his luck, from half a dozen applicants for the room he had chosen me! My fourth letter was to Marie. I explained that I hadn't been too serious in our relationship because I had been wanted for bank robbery. I asked her to come and visit me at Pentridge to enable me sign over some of my belongings to her, including my record player and approximately 50 records.

Later that night I flushed the letter to Marie down the toilet. If I escaped I would need her and it was imperative that the police weren't aware of her existence. I had decided to take a gamble and set the stage for an escape bid. Thus far, the security on me had been rigid. Each time I had been taken from the cell I had been handcuffed and escorted by at least three cops. I knew that once I was behind the walls of Pentridge it would be extremely difficult to escape. It had been less than five months since a prison officer had been killed during the successful escape of Ryan and Walker. According to all reports, security in all areas at Pentridge had been extensively tightened.

The next morning when Ainesley came to collect the letter I told him that I wanted to clear up another robbery. He was momentarily nonplussed.

"I want to get it off my chest and make a fresh start," I said.

He nodded. "What robbery are we talking about?"

"A railway station. I was drunk at the time and I can't remember where it was."

"What if we take you around a few railways that have been held up? Would that jog your memory?"

"If I saw the right one it would."

"All right, John. I'll arrange for you to have a day out." Taking the letters, he hurried off.

I knew that all I had to do was to tell him I had forced the railway attendant to take off his pants and they immediately would be able to locate the robbery. But my escape plan was contingent on my being able to go to various railway stations where, hopefully, I would get a chance to make a run for it. I had practised running up and down in my cell with my wrists held together as though they were handcuffed. I was confident that, even with handcuffs on, I would be able to out run most cops. If I managed to get away I would have to hide somewhere until dark. Then I could phone Marie and ask her to meet me. Hopefully, when she came I'd be able to persuade her to help me.

A few hours later Ainesley and three plain clothes cops escorted me, handcuffed, to the detectives' office.

"John," Ainesley said, handing me a cup of coffee, "we've checked out the railway robberies of the past 12 months and there's only one that hasn't been cleared up."

"Well, let's go and have a look at it," I said. "I'll soon tell you if it's the one I did."

"If you stuck up a railway station, it had to be the one," Ainesley said. He indicated one of the cops who had escorted me from the cells. "Terry here is a photographer. He'll be coming with us and can take some photos of you pointing to various parts of the station."

They hadn't requested similar photos in regards to the Kensington bank. "Why do you want photos?"

"Because the bandit was masked. We've got no identification. If you give us a statement and later change your mind and claim the confession was forced, we'll have no evidence."

I shrugged. It suited me. While they were taking photos I might be able to jump down onto the railway line and run along the track.

"We'll get you to give us a statement first," Ainesley said.

I gave him a handwritten statement admitting to the robbery. I did it with trepidation. I knew that if things didn't go to plan and I was unable to escape, I was virtually signing my life away.

The five of us had a hot meal and dessert before leaving for the scene of the crime.

When we arrived at the railway station, I vaguely recognised it, although I wasn't certain if it was the one I had robbed.

Ainesley then played his ace and I realised I had underrated the man. He unlocked my handcuffs and cuffed my left wrist to his right wrist. When I protested he gave me his sad smile. "Just an extra precaution, John. We know how fast you are."

"You have to be kidding. You don't think I'd be stupid enough to try and get away while I'm handcuffed, do you?"

The cop who had been driving, a big, slow-talking guy with a prominent broken nose, cut in: "If I had my way you'd be wearing a ball and chain."

"If I had a chain I'd flush it and that'd be the end of you," I said.

The other cops laughed. The driver glared at me, but unable to think of a suitable retort, remained silent.

"I'm not going anywhere," I said. "Take me back to my cell."

"Be reasonable, John," Ainesley said. "What difference does it make whether you're handcuffed to me or on your own?"

"I've still got my dignity. I'm not walking around a railway station handcuffed to a cop as though I'm a dog on a leash."

"You lost your dignity a long time ago," the driver said.

"And when you lose your virginity we'll be even," I said.

Ainesley grinned. "Cut it out you two. Look, John, if you're concerned about people seeing you handcuffed to a policeman, we'll pretend I'm the crim. You're dressed in a suit, you can lead the way."

I still had one chance, the toilet. "On one condition," I said. "I wear your hat."

"It's a deal," Ainesley said, relieved.

The driver shook his head in disgust.

I put on Ainesley's hat and led the way to the station. As the five of us walked through the entrance a girl, aged about ten, who was standing with a fat lady, stared at us. I winked at her.

"Come on, fella," I said, jerking Ainesley forward. "Let's have a look at this railway station that you stuck up."

Ainesley flushed. Even the driver was grinning. When I saw the office I realised that it was the station I had held up. We spent about three minutes on the platform while the photographer took some photos of me pointing towards the door of the office where I had committed the robbery.

"Before we go back I have to go to the toilet," I said.

Ainesley gave me a suspicious look. "Can't it wait?"

"I'm afraid not. I think it was the dessert."

As we walked to the toilet I was aware that six or seven people on the platform were watching us. No doubt we had provided them with a topic of conversation for the day. If I suddenly came bursting out of the toilet with four cops in hot pursuit they would have something to talk about for weeks. Most of them thought Ainesley was the prisoner.

Inside the toilet I insisted Ainesley uncuffed my wrist while I went to the toilet. I could see he was apprehensive about it, but his gentlemanly nature prevailed. While the other cops stood guard inside the entrance he undid the handcuff on his wrist. I went into the cubicle and closed the door. As I sat on the toilet my heart was thumping. Was it worth the risk? Even if I came rushing out of the cubicle throwing punches my chances of getting past them were almost nil. They were on the alert, half-expecting me to try something. If he got the chance the driver might shoot me. Reluctantly, I decided against making a desperate bid that would be almost certain to fail. I had to wait for the right moment and that moment wasn't now.

After flushing the toilet, I walked out grinning. "You guys are a bit on edge, what's the matter?"

Ainesley smiled as he handcuffed his wrist to mine. "If we lost you, John, it could cost all of us our jobs."

"I'm glad I didn't try anything, I wouldn't be able to cope knowing you guys were unemployed because of me."

"You're full of bullshit, Killick," the driver said.

We were all smiling as we walked out of the toilet.

On the way back to Russell Street I extracted a promise from Ainesley, much to the driver's vexation, to supply me with a hot meal and a large block of chocolate before I returned to my cell.

43

PENTRIDGE
(1966)

The following day I appeared before a magistrate in Court No 1. It is one of the original three that stand on the site of the old Supreme Court where Ned Kelly was sentenced to death. I was remanded in custody and returned to the City Watch House that was next door to the Old Melbourne Gaol where Ned Kelly and 134 other unfortunates were hung. It's estimated that up to 19,000 prisoners a year passed through the City Watch House until it was closed in 1994. Although it had been described as a monument to human misery, these types of places are much the same everywhere. I found it much the same as Central cells in Sydney.

After lunch I was handcuffed to another prisoner and placed in the back of a prison van. We were the only prisoners in it.

I looked at the guy. He had red hair and looked to be about my age. "We must be special," I said, grinning.

He didn't reply, just stared straight ahead.

I shrugged and remained silent for the remainder of the trip.

When we arrived at Pentridge we were taken into a large reception area where two screws took charge of us. After our handcuffs had been taken off, one of the screws said: "Which one of you is Keith Ryrie?"

I shrugged. "I'm John Killick."

"Come with me, Killick," he said, walking away with the other guard.

As I followed them, three prisoners who had been standing nearby moved towards Ryrie. Hearing a scream I turned and saw the prisoners bashing him. "What's going on?" I said to the screws.

One of them gave me a hard stare. "I didn't see anything." He turned to his mate. "Did you see anything?"

"Not a thing."

Ryrie who was now on the ground had stopped screaming. One of the prisoners was kicking him. Ryrie wasn't moving.

I didn't pursue it. I followed the screws to the shower room where I luxuriated under a hot shower. When I returned to the reception area, Ryrie and his three attackers were gone. I later learnt that he had been taken to the notorious punishment section, H Division, for his own protection. He had been charged with raping and murdering both a six-year-old and a 15-year-old girl. The treatment meted out to him had been a typical Pentridge reception given to men charged with heinous crimes against children.

Pentridge was larger in area than Long Bay. In 1966 it was capable of holding 1,374 prisoners. Unlike Long Bay, apart from a few dormitories, all the cells were one out.

While on remand I was housed in D Division, the larger of the two remand Divisions. The other one, F Division, contained a dormitory. D Division has since been redeveloped into a tourist site. Apart from general tours of the gaol, you can arrange to be locked in a cell for a night. Some of the cells have been leased as storerooms. In an ironic twist, in 2007, Graeme Alford, who spent nearly eight years in gaol during the '70s for embezzlement and armed robbery, bought cell number 43. It was a cell he had spent nine months in as a prisoner.

There were six small exercise yards outside D Division where the prisoners had to spend the day until we were locked in our cells at about 4.00 pm. Although conditions were archaic, it had a few advantages in comparison to the remand section at Long Bay. The meals were served in a mess hall and were of superior quality to those I had received at the Bay. The cells were equipped with flush toilets, compared to tin buckets at the Bay, and each cell had a set of headphones that tuned into two radio stations. Each yard had an open shower and although it was demeaning to have to shower in the open yard, often in freezing conditions, it was preferable to the two showers a week system at the Bay. I noticed that some of the prisoners never took a shower. My cell was on the second tier, not far from the crosswalk that also served as the gallows. There was a trap in the catwalk and, above it, a large beam from which the hangman could suspend his noose. Even then, the feeling throughout the prison was that Ronald Ryan would be the next man for whom the hangman would suspend his noose.

I was allowed to make a reception phone call. I left a message with Marie's mother, requesting Marie to visit me and pick up some property.

She came on the first Sunday. Although the visits were non-contact, I enjoyed seeing and talking to her. She commented that although she had regarded me as a mystery man, she had been shocked to learn that I was in gaol for robbing banks. I had arranged for her to pick up my record player and records, and when she offered to put $20 in my property, I accepted it; the cops had taken all my money. Before she left she blew me a kiss and promised to visit me every Sunday. She was an attractive girl and as she walked off I noticed a few guys staring at her.

Before I went to court again I was told I had a security alert on me. A chief prison officer told me that the fact I was on armed robbery charges and the police intended to extradite me to Sydney after I served my sentence in Victoria, made me an escape risk.

I didn't argue. In fact I wholeheartedly agreed with him, but I didn't tell him that.

Each time before I was taken to court I was handcuffed and placed alone in a small compartment of the van known as the dog-box. I dreaded these trips. The confined space and lack of air conditioning always made me nauseous.

At court I represented myself. In those days if you had a criminal record it was difficult to get Legal Aid. I didn't even try. With extradition hanging like a storm cloud over my head I wasn't concerned with whatever sentence I might get in Victoria. My mind was like a rat trapped in a cage, racing around in circles, trying to find a way out when there appeared to be no escape. I tried to rationalise. If I was a rat trapped in a cage, then

Pentridge and the dog-box and the cells were cages. With the security that had been placed on me it would be nearly impossible to escape from any of them. I would have to make a bid for freedom when I was out of the cages at court. It would be the only chance I would get. In deference to court etiquette, the screws always took the handcuffs off me while I was in court. As there were always plenty of cops around it didn't offer much chance of escape but it would be the best chance I would get. I simply had to choose the right time. I had the element of surprise in my favour and if, somehow, I managed to get out of the courtroom I would have a good chance of getting away. I was desperate. They weren't.

After four or five visits, Marie dropped off. She didn't say anything, she simply didn't come again. I didn't pursue it by writing to her. There had never been anything special between us and I guessed that she wanted to get on with her life without feeling obligated to a guy in gaol.

Cathy didn't reply to my letter.

David, the young guy charged with strangling the old lady, often walked up and down the yard with me. I found him to be an intelligent but highly emotional youth. One day after a visit from his wife he returned to the yard visibly upset. He told me that she wanted to terminate their relationship and he had threatened that if she left him he would hang himself.

"What did she say to that?" I asked.

He rubbed his eyes. "She said she'll still visit me but she can't promise there won't be other men in her life."

I didn't tell him that when a woman said that, there was already another man in her life. "Well, at least you'll have a good friend."

"I don't want a good friend," he said. "I want a wife. I love her."

He was eventually convicted of murder and sentenced to 30 years. His wife left him and be became a passive homosexual. I suppose he felt he didn't have much choice.

44

IT'S NOW OR NEVER
(1966)

About two months after my arrest I was scheduled for sentencing at Hawthorn Court. To that stage the security on me had been so tight that an escape attempt would have been futile perhaps even suicidal. Nevertheless, I had decided that Hawthorn Court would be my last chance and I would have to take it. After I was sentenced, I would be confined to many years behind the grim grey walls of Pentridge and after that I would be extradited to Sydney to face more of the same at the Bay. It was enough incentive for me to try to escape against overwhelming odds even though I knew that failure would result in my going to H Division. The day I went to Hawthorn Court for sentencing the odds swung back in my favour. The van was running late and the court was waiting for me. The judge was handling a trial and I was listed to be sentenced before the trial began. Although Ainesley assured me he would be there to put in a good word for me to the judge, he wasn't there. Nor were any of his cronies. I was taken handcuffed from the dog-box to the foyer of the courtroom by two screws. Both of them were about my size and build. Outside the door to the courtroom, one of them held on to me while the other took off my handcuffs. We then entered the courtroom. I stood in the dock while the two screws stood either side of me. The adrenalin rushed through my body, not because I was about to be sentenced for two armed robberies, but because my instinct told me this was it. I would never get a better chance to escape. If Ainesley and his cronies didn't arrive, I would only have two screws to beat and I was not handcuffed.

As the court assistant read out the charges, I prayed Ainesley wouldn't suddenly appear. Even though his favourable testimony would undoubtedly impress the judge and influence him towards imposing a lighter sentence, I was prepared to gamble on a possible heavier sentence, knowing that my chances of escaping would be greatly enhanced if Ainesley and his cronies weren't there.

The judge, whose name was Winowski, asked me if I had anything to say before he passed sentence.

I met his gaze. He had that inscrutable countenance that all judges seemed to possess before they handed down a sentence. I had to make it short. "Your Honour, I don't want to make excuses. I had a girl in America who I loved very much but they wouldn't let me into America because of my record. Something happened in my mind. I find it hard to believe the trouble I'm in. It all seems a bit unreal. I realise that the charges are serious and that you will have to send me to gaol for quite a while. All I can say in my favour is that I co-operated with police in every way and I ask that you take it into consideration."

He stared at me. "Is that all?"

"Well I didn't hurt anyone. Even though the bank teller fired a shot at me, I didn't fire back."

He nodded. "Yes, I noticed that in the police record. It's the one redeeming factor for you. Nevertheless ..." He went on for nearly five minutes about how decent, law-abiding citizens had to be protected from gun-wielding hoodlums from interstate. He emphasised the interstate and I realised it was true: Melbournians really do hate Sydneysiders. He finally sentenced me to five years for the bank robbery and two years for the railway, the sentences to run cumulatively. All things considered it was a fair sentence. He ordered a non-parole period of five years.

As we walked from the court both guards held on to me. When we entered the foyer one of them released his grip and held out the handcuffs. "Seven years isn't bad for two armed robs," he said. "You should have thanked the judge."

He was about 40 and had a slight paunch. I punched him in the solar plexus, sending him reeling back across the room clutching his stomach. The other screw, younger and more athletic looking grabbed me in a bear hug and began yelling for help. With the strength of desperation I broke free and flung him aside and ran towards the exit only metres away. I had to stop to open the door and the young screw came rushing towards me screaming for me to stop. I leapt down the steps, only to be brought to the ground by a diving rugby tackle from the screw. We rolled on to the grass. I kicked and punched him, trying to break his grip as he held on to me like a limpet, yelling for help. Just as I managed to break free and jump to my feet the cavalry arrived. Cops came from all directions and with a barrage of punches knocked me down again.

A few of them started kicking me. I vaguely recall being dragged to a cell where I copped a bit of a flogging. Nothing more than I expected. After they had gone my entire body ached but I was able to stand up. After a while, although I was in considerable pain, I was satisfied that no bones were broken.

I was sitting on the bench feeling sorry for myself when the small trap in the door opened and Ainesley called out to me.

Painfully, I walked across to the door. "Thanks for putting in a good word for me to the judge," I said.

He peered at me through the trap. "I'm sorry John, we broke down on the way. I only just arrived." He gave me a sad smile. "You gave 'em a hell of a fright, mate."

"Yeah. And they gave me a hell of a kicking."

"I've had a word with them, they won't charge you with the escape."

"I couldn't give a stuff whether they charge me or not. I'll counter charge them with assault."

"You know you'll be going to H Division for a while."

I shrugged. "Doesn't bother me."

He nodded. We both knew I was lying. H Division was the Victorian equivalent of Grafton. "You had lunch?"

"I'm too sick to eat anything."

"Even a chocolate?"

I grinned. "Even a chocolate."

"I sincerely wish you luck, John."

"Luck has deserted me. Have a look at today. I get sentenced to seven years, might have got less if you'd been there. I try to escape, actually made the break and I get rugby tackled by a screw in a State where they don't even know how to play rugby. He must be the only screw in Victoria who knows how to tackle. Now I'm off to H Division."

"You've got a way of putting things, John. But, remember, you are still young, mate. Do something useful with your time." He paused. "If I can ever do anything for you, you know where to contact me." He closed the trap.

I sat down and wondered what the dreaded H Division held in store for me.

45

H Division
(1966)

At about noon I was handcuffed and taken by van to Pentridge. Despite being inside the gaol, the handcuffs remained on while two screws escorted me to H Division. When we arrived at the entrance to H Division I noticed a round mirror positioned inside and above the grille gate, enabling anyone inside the office to see who was coming down the path. Three screws came to the gate. One, who was the senior, was small and thin. The other two were both tall and solidly built. The senior unlocked the gate and told me to step forward. After one of the two screws that had escorted me had taken off my handcuffs, they both left H Division. Curiously, I felt no fear. The beating I had received at the police station had blunted my senses, and I was so depressed by my failure to escape that I had resigned myself to accepting whatever happened.

The senior locked the gate. I turned to watch him and one of the other screws belted me across the back of the head with a baton. I felt excruciating pain and fell to the floor.

"Get to your feet!" the senior shouted.

Clutching the back of my head, I staggered to my feet.

"Stand to attention, hands by your sides!" the senior screamed. His eyes were bulging and the veins in his neck protruded against his shirt collar. His small, pinched face had an unhealthy pallor. I concluded that he was insane and dangerous.

I stood at attention and he stepped forward and, only centimetres away, looked up into my face. "You are here because no one else wants you," he said, blowing bits of spittle on to my face. "Whether you survive while you're here depends on me and the other officers in this

Division. And from what I see, I'm not impressed. You're nothing! Do you understand! Nothing!"

Hitler had nothing on this guy. One of the big screws whacked my left arm with his baton. "Answer the officer!"

Although it hurt, I was becoming accustomed to pain. Using all my willpower I held my arms by my side without flinching. "Yes, sir," I said, deciding that if I didn't go along with these maniacs I'd be seriously maimed.

"Strip off," the senior said.

My left arm had gone numb. I struggled to undress.

"Hurry up!" the other big screw said, pushing his baton into my side.

After stripping naked, I stood to attention.

"Open your mouth," the senior said.

I opened my mouth and he looked inside for contraband. Finding nothing but blood he told me to lift my feet one at a time and show my heels.

After he had found nothing adhered to the soles of my feet he said: "Now bend over and pull your cheeks apart."

For a split second I was tempted to hit him with a right uppercut and break his jaw. I knew that if I did it, there was a good chance they would kill me with their batons. But there are times where pride shuts out all logical thoughts to the point where one becomes irrationally prepared to suffer all forms of hardship for the sake of self esteem and dignity.

I stared at the senior whom I had silently nicknamed 'Hitler'. "I'm not pulling my cheeks apart for anyone."

I knew the two gorillas would lash out with their batons and I tried to protect my head as they swung at me. I was slow raising my injured left arm and a baton thudded against the side of my head. It must have knocked me unconscious; the next thing I knew I was on the floor trying to cover up as the three of them began kicking me. Although they administered some powerful kicks I had reached the stage where I didn't feel a lot of pain. To stop myself from crying out, I bit my lip, eventually biting right through it.

After what seemed minutes but was probably only 30 seconds, they stopped when I began coughing and spitting blood.

"Get up!" Hitler said.

Still spitting blood, I rose unsteadily to my feet. Everything was hazy. For some reason I thought of Cathy, I wondered what she would think if she could see me now.

Hitler stared at me. He looked a trifle worried.

"He's not a very tough bank robber, is he?" one of the other screws said.

"They're all the fuckin' same," Hitler said. "Put them under a bit of pressure and they fold like a bag of shit."

He pointed to a pile of clothing, a hat and a pair of heavy boots on the floor. "That's yours. Pick it up."

I gathered up the boots and clothing.

"Now right turn, quick march!" Hitler said. One of the screws pushed me and I limped forward. Someone belted me twice across the buttocks with a baton and I grimaced from the humiliation more than pain. Despite everything, I told myself that I had beaten them: I hadn't pulled my cheeks apart and, with the exception of a few grunts, I hadn't uttered a sound during the beating.

I was taken to a cell that was about three metres long and two metres wide. The door had a trap in it. Inside were a bed, mattress, sheets, blankets and a pillow. There was a small wooden stand with a drawer and shelves. In the far corner was a tap but no basin. A shiny aluminium bowl rested above the toilet. There was a strip of matting on the floor with a black cross painted in the middle.

The sheets and blankets were folded with exactness to a rectangular display with a blanket folded around the outside. One of the screws picked them up and threw them on the floor. He then unravelled the blankets and sheets. "Make sure they're folded in the correct manner before you come out in the morning," he said, smirking.

Hitler said: "There's a rule book there. Read it."

They went out and locked the door.

Although I was stiff and sore for about a week, the beating I had received that day did no permanent damage to my body. The effect on my mind was more complex. Despite having been aware of what happened in places like Grafton and H Division, my experiencing it personally distorted my perception of human nature and the value of life. Put enough pressure on a person and sooner or later the civilized being breaks down. I was at the mercy of evil men in the name of the law and it caused me to expand my code of ethics to the point where I found I could justify killing someone. I knew, with certainty, that if I had the chance I would be capable of killing one of the screws and enjoying the act, particularly Hitler. As time went on, I even concocted various ways to kill him, all of them slow and painful. Just as he hated me, I hated and despised the man and everything he represented. I sensed that without his uniform and henchmen to protect him, he would be a coward. I vowed to myself that when I was finally released I would, one day, put him to the test.

During my first week in H Division I learnt a lot about the psychology behind the administration of the place. It operated mainly on fear. The prisoners knew that if they didn't obey all orders they would be beaten. Sometimes, even if they did obey all the rules they would be beaten. H Division had a total of 39 cells on two tiers. It was established in 1958 ostensibly to contain men who had made escape attempts, who had assaulted screws or stabbed another prisoner. But after a while prisoners were sent there for minor breaches of regulations. It was the authorities' way of establishing that they held the whip hand.

When a prisoner first entered H Division, whether it be for assaulting a screw or having excess tobacco, he was usually given a beating. That was the softening-up process to demonstrate who was boss. The prisoner had to work in one of the labour yards of which there were 12. Each yard was about seven metres long by four metres wide. Each morning the prisoner had to break large rocks with a big hammer to fragments the size of a fist. In the afternoon, he had to pulverise with a small hammer the fist-sized rocks to the size of a thumb nail. If the fragments were too large or too small the prisoner could be charged with disobeying orders or maybe he would simply be beaten. Each morning when a prisoner's cell was opened, he had to stand to attention on the cross on the mat in his cell while a screw wearing white gloves came in and ran his fingers along the walls and even the floor looking for dust. If he found any, the prisoner would be charged or beaten. The bedding had to be made with an exactness that could only be acquired after much practise. The dish inside and out had to resemble a mirror. Shirts and jackets had to be buttoned to the neck and the canvas hat had to sit precisely on the prisoner's head.

Prisoners were not permitted to walk, they had to march everywhere. When asked his name he had to state his name, say Sir and salute in a correct and precise manner. When he marched from his cell to go to the labour yards he had to salute the chief screw who usually stood near the entrance to the passageway that led to the labour yards. Sometimes the chief wasn't there, but the prisoners still had to salute. On my second morning in the Division I found myself saluting the chief's cat.

It was impossible to comply with all the rules and regulations in a correct manner. There was always something they could get you for. Not bringing your arm up in the correct way when saluting, not marching correctly, not holding your salute for three paces when saluting the chief's cat, having dust in your cell, dish not shiny enough, a button on your shirt or jacket undone, hat not on straight, bedding not exact, rocks not broken to the correct size etc.

For me, the most harrowing part of each day was the waiting in the cell while they inspected other cells. They always let out one prisoner at a time; sometimes it took ten minutes before they let out the next one. During that time the rest of us could hear what was happening. A dish being thrown on the floor or belted over a prisoner's head, Hitler screaming out in his degrading manner that the prisoner was a nothing, or sometimes the unmistakable sounds of a prisoner being beaten could be heard, or a prisoner screaming out. The effect of listening to these happenings every morning, knowing that your turn was coming, played havoc with your nerves, regardless of how tough you might consider yourself to be.

H Division was a fertile breeding ground for blind hate and revenge. No matter how minor the offence the prisoner had committed before coming to H Division, the administration and screws provided all the necessary ingredients for the prisoner to become a snivelling wreck of a man or a hard, ruthless and violent criminal. I knew that, with me, the pent-up resentfulness, hatred and desire for revenge would one day manifest itself in violence and probable self-destruction. I was hopeful that when it did happen, I would be out of gaol so that I would have a chance to unleash my fury on a few of my oppressors. I had read that time healed, hate waned and the mind played tricks and tried to convince itself that things weren't as bad as you had imagined. I vowed to myself that I wouldn't allow time to heal. I would work at picking the scabs.

I spent six weeks in the labour yards. It was virtually solitary confinement. During that period, the only time I saw other prisoners was when I went for a shower. Prisoners in the labour yards were, with the exception of public holidays, permitted to shower on Mondays, Wednesdays and Fridays. They showered in pairs in one of the two exercise yards, each of which held two showers. But conversation between the two prisoners was forbidden. We had to shower under surveillance from both a screw standing by the door and a screw standing in a gallery above the yards. The gallery, which extended all the way above the yards to the end of the Division, was enclosed by windows that enabled the screw in it to see down into the yards. He also controlled the door of each yard with a locking mechanism contained in the gallery. Each yard was overlaid with strong wire mesh and any attempt by a prisoner to get into the gallery would have been suicidal.

Most of the prisoners I saw during shower time were too frightened to even look at me, although one little guy I saw on a few occasions would always wink at me and say: "Ain't no lions and tigers down here." I always returned the wink and replied: "Only pussycats." It was our way of telling each other that some of us weren't broken by the system. With the omnipresent risk of being bashed if caught, our conversation never extended beyond this point.

The ironic part about the showers was that after we had finished showering, we had to return to the labour yards and break more rocks. If there was a holiday on the Monday, it resulted in the labour yard prisoners going without a shower for five days. Sometimes I would be so repulsed by my body odour that I would wash at night using water from the toilet. I had discovered that if I used the dish it was nearly impossible to polish it back to its normal mirror sheen. I later learnt that nearly all the prisoners used the same procedure to wash in their cells.

After six weeks of breaking rocks in the labour yards, I was given a job as a billet. When the food was brought to the scullery it was my job, with the help of two other billets, to distribute it into the metal dixies for the chief to hand to the men as they came up from the yards. Apart from dishing out the meals and washing up, the three of us were responsible for sweeping and cleaning the Division. It was a welcome change from the labour yards and we were the only prisoners in the Division who didn't have to march everywhere. We spent an hour each day in one of the exercise yards where we could walk up and down and talk, play cards and shower when we wanted to.

I was moved to another cell that was equipped with a pair of earphones that were linked to a radio in the Division controlled by the screws. The attitude of the screws towards us was almost civil, possibly due to the fact that a former billet had been caught urinating into the screws' tea. I suppose they figured that if they treated us as human beings we wouldn't resort to such low deeds. I had no intention of doing anything of such petty nature. Although my hatred for these men remained, I had resolved to nurture it until I was out of gaol.

One morning while I was locked in my cell I heard a young man named Poole being hassled by the screws. Although, in the preceding weeks, I had listened to dozens of prisoners being given a hard time, on this occasion the chief was involved. I heard him say to Poole: "Who do you think you are!"

Poole's reply was inaudible to me.

"That's right," the chief said. "Bloody no one. Have a look at you, you're good for nothing, you little turd! Would you agree with that?"

"Yes, sir."

"Then how dare you tell your mother you don't want anything to do with her. You let her make that decision, not you! Do you understand!"

Poole began to cry. "I'm ashamed of myself, sir. She's better off without me."

"Of course she's better off without you! What mother would want a son like you! But you let her tell you. You don't tell her! I've destroyed the letter. You can write her another one."

That night Stephen Poole hanged himself.

46

RYAN AND WALKER
(1965-1967)

During my first confinement in H Division, Ronald Ryan was in an observation cell opposite the scullery. The front of the cell consisted of steel bars and a steel bar door. A guard sat outside his cell watching everything he did. His light was always on and the guards worked on a roster to ensure he was observed 24 hours a day. The only time he left his cell was for a shower and one hour's exercise in one of the labour yards each day. Before he was taken from the cell they fastened a leather security belt around his waist with handcuffs attached to the front of the belt. From 30th March 1966, the day he had been found guilty of murder and sentenced to death, his life belonged to the state and they made certain that he knew it.

The escape of Ryan and Walker generated the largest manhunt in Australian history, even surpassing that of Simmonds and Newcombe in 1959.

On 19 December 1965, Ronald Ryan, 40, serving 13 years for shopbreaking, possession of explosives and broken parole, and Peter Walker, 24, serving 12 years for bank robbery, used a long wooden plank to scale a five metre high wall and climb onto a tower outside B Division. It was cunningly planned. A lot of the guards were attending a Christmas party. Brandishing an iron bar, Ryan confronted the startled guard on the tower and took his carbine. He then forced him to operate the locking mechanism, lifting the levers on two doors that led to the prison car park. As they rushed towards the street they were confronted by a Salvation Army brigadier, James Hewitt. Ryan demanded Hewitt's car keys. When the brigadier said he hadn't brought his car that day, Ryan knocked him to the ground.

Meanwhile the guard on the tower had sounded the alarm and sirens were blaring from all parts of the prison. Guards were running towards the troubled area.

Ryan ran to nearby Sydney Road where he commandeered a car at gunpoint. Forcing the couple inside to get out, he got into the driver's seat. A guard ran up and tried to open one of the doors. Meanwhile, another guard, George Hodson, had cut Walker off and began hitting him over the head with a piece of pipe. Walker managed to fend him off and started running again with Hodson, still brandishing the pipe, in hot pursuit.

Getting out of the car Ryan pointed the carbine at Hodson. Simultaneously, a guard from a tower aimed his rifle at Walker.

Hodson fell to the ground dead, hit in the heart with a single bullet. A ballistics expert later testified that the angle of the bullet wound showed that the bullet had entered at a downward angle.

Ryan and Walker commandeered another vehicle and drove off at high speed. Although police set up numerous roadblocks around the city, their quarry eluded them.

Despite an intensive manhunt, police had no definite sightings of the pair until four days later when they held up the ANZ bank in Ormond and escaped with more than £4,000 ($8,000) and two bank pistols.

The following day the Victorian government announced a £5,000 reward for information leading to their capture. The same day, Christmas Eve, Ryan and Walker held a party in a flat in Elwood where they had been hiding out. One of the guests, a truck driver named Arthur Henderson, who was the boyfriend of the tenant, recognized Ryan. His fatal mistake was that he didn't recognise Walker. When Henderson declared he would go and buy some more beer, Walker decided to accompany him. Less than an hour later, Walker returned alone. Shortly afterwards, they left in a hurry.

On Christmas Day, Henderson's body was found on the floor of a toilet block in Middle Park. He had been shot in the back of the head.

The hunt for Ryan and Walker intensified to the point where Victorian police were raiding an estimated forty houses a day. But the pair had driven to Sydney where they rented a flat in Coogee.

On 5 January, a woman rang the Sydney CIB and said that Walker had phoned her and asked her to arrange a double date. She had known Walker a few years earlier when he had used an assumed name. Apparently, due to the alias, Walker thought she wouldn't know that he was one of the most wanted men in Australia. She had arranged to meet Walker and his friend at 9.00 pm outside the Concord Repatriation Hospital where she worked.

When Ryan and Walker arrived, more than 50 specially selected police were waiting at various vantage points. The pair was arrested without a struggle.

Extradited to Melbourne both Ryan and Walker were charged with the murder of Hodson. Walker was also charged with the murder of Henderson. The Crown alleged he had killed Henderson to prevent him from informing. Walker claimed that Henderson had attacked him and the shooting had been accidental. The jury convicted him of manslaughter for which he was sentenced to 12 years. He was also convicted of the manslaughter of Hodson and received 12 years cumulative, leaving him with a total sentence of 36 years. He served almost 19 years before he was released in December 1984.

Despite persuasive arguments put forward by Ryan's counsel, Philip Opas QC, that Hodson could have been killed accidentally by another guard trying to prevent the escape, the jury found Ryan guilty. Although the bullet that killed Hodson was never found and the gun used by Ryan never tested to see whether it had been fired, the judge had no option other than to sentence him to the mandatory death sentence.

I once saw Ryan's mother when she came to visit him; she was a saddened little old lady who had suddenly found herself thrust into a nightmarish limelight. The strain of her visiting the son whom she loved in a condemned cell must have been enormous on her.

In late November 1966 I was transferred from H Division to B Division. I was allocated a cell on the bottom section named Six Tier, where the men considered to be high security risks were housed. I was given a job in the mat yard where I was taught to operate an ancient pedal-operated weaving machine that produced coir matting. It was token work. Most of us only worked for an hour or two and then spent the remainder of the day playing cards or walking up and down. Although the old overseer often complained that most of us wouldn't work in an iron lung, he rarely charged anyone.

As the scheduled date of Ryan's execution drew near, there were Australia-wide protests by all classes of people in an effort to save his life. Petitions to stop the hanging, containing thousands of signatures, were ignored by the Victorian Premier, Sir Henry Bolte, who made it clear that he was determined to ensure the execution would be carried out. He publicly stated that while he was Premier, any person who killed a police officer or prison officer would be hanged. This statement provoked widespread criticism and anger, particularly when the child killer Keith Ryrie, who was also sentenced to death, had his sentence commuted. Even Dad was outraged about it. In a letter to me, he wrote: "Your old man is keeping up with what is going on down there. It's okay for some mongrel to rape and murder little girls, but kill a screw or a copper and they neck you."

After an appeal to both the Victorian Supreme Court and the High Court of Australia failed, the Victorian Executive Council granted a stay of execution pending the outcome of an appeal to the Privy Council in England. On 24 January 1967, the Privy Council rescheduled the execution for 31 January. On 27 January the Queen rejected an appeal to commute the sentence. On 30 January, while thousands of protesters and members of anti-hanging groups gathered outside Pentridge, an ex-prisoner signed an affidavit claiming he had overheard a prison guard admit he had fired the shot that had killed Hodson.

Nine hours before Ryan was due to be hanged, an enormous roar erupted inside and outside Pentridge. It had been announced on the radio that Justice Stark, acting on the affidavit from the ex-prisoner, had ordered a stay of execution. Men were banging on cell walls and yelling out: "Ronny's got a reprieve!"

When I heard the news I wondered how Ryan felt. Undoubtedly, he would have prepared himself for death. Now, nine hours before the scheduled execution, he had again been given hope. I wondered about what it would do to a person inside. If I were in Ryan's shoes, how would I react?

The evidence given by the ex-prisoner in the affidavit could not be substantiated and another date was set for the execution, 3 February. The ex-prisoner had gained Ryan a mere 72 hours of life. It seemed that the authorities were becoming impatient to get it over with.

On 2 February the crowd of anti-hanging groups outside Pentridge was larger than at any other time. The atmosphere inside the gaol was one that I have never experienced before or since. Everyone seemed to possess the prescience that, this time, the hanging would be carried out. Pentridge, particularly B Division, was literally a powder keg. It would have taken only one minor incident to set it off. The guards, who normally walked around the Divisions on their own, were particularly vigilant and walked in threes.

On 3 February they opened our cells at 7.00 am. There had been no mention of a last minute reprieve on the news. Although, as we picked up our breakfast, no mention was made of it, all of us were aware that Ronald Ryan had less than an hour to live. I was reminded of Oscar Wilde's *The Ballad of Reading Gaol*:

"*For the Lord of Death with icy breath*

Had entered in to kill…"

At about 7.30 am word was passed around that everyone should refuse to go to work. If the guards wanted trouble and tried to force us to go, there would be a full-scale riot. But discretion prevailed. No one was asked to go to work.

A few minutes after 8.00 am the news came on the radio that Ronald Ryan was dead. Although it was the last legal execution in Australia, it wasn't until 1985 that capital punishment was abolished in Australia.

47

BORG, BAZLEY AND BOOKMAKING
(1967)

After a while I settled into the dull routine of prison life in Pentridge. The Ryan and Walker affair had forced the authorities to take a rigid approach towards security. The cells on Six Tier were checked twice a day. But some things remained unchanged. Although officially gambling was not permitted, in reality it flourished. Usually the guards turned a blind eye to the numerous card games that took place every day. There was also a bookmaker in B Division who took bets of tobacco, chocolates and, occasionally, money on the races. The unofficial attitude of the Governor was that while the prisoners were playing card games and listening to the races, they weren't causing problems elsewhere.

One Friday afternoon in April a prisoner in the mat yard gave me a race guide. As a precautionary measure I put it inside my shoe. All the prisoners were given a cursory search before returning from the workshop to the Divisions. The screws that conducted the search were security screws. Due to the fact that they had the power to search anyone anywhere at any time, they considered themselves to be an elite group. But the crims and some of the other screws called them the Keystone Kops because they rarely found anything.

Unfortunately for me, someone had informed the Keystone Kops that I had hidden contraband in my shoes. They escorted me to a small room and ordered me to strip off. When they found the race guide some of them couldn't contain their excitement.

One of them said: "What's this?"

I frowned. "It looks like a race guide."

Another screw said: "It is race guide. What's it doing in your shoe?"

"It's not in my shoe." Fuck 'em.

"It was in your shoe! What was it doing there?"

"I'm trying to give up gambling and I felt that if I put it in my shoe I wouldn't read it."

"Smart cunt. Well, you can forget about the races this week, you're going to H Division."

I shrugged. "There aren't any lions or tigers down there."

They handcuffed me and escorted me to H Division. On the way, I decided that rather than be bashed senseless again, I would, if asked, pull my cheeks apart. My day would come.

When we arrived at the entrance to H Division I was relieved to see that the senior screw was not Hitler. I had arrived at an auspicious time, most of the screws were waiting to go home and were impatient to get me processed and locked away. I was told to strip off, put on the H Division clothing and quick march to the cells area where I was locked in a cell. They didn't even bother to throw the blankets in the air.

My having worked in H Division as a billet for three months must have moderated the screws' hostility towards me, particularly after they learnt that I was there for possession of a race guide. Although, during my seven days there, I was occasionally abused and shouted at, particularly by Hitler, I didn't have a hand, or a baton, laid on me. Nevertheless, it remained unnerving to listen to other prisoners being abused and bashed. When my week was finished and I returned to B Division I was relieved.

A few weeks after returning from H Division I received a letter from my brother David. He and his friend John had gone to New Zealand where John had been arrested for larceny and sentenced to three years' imprisonment. David had met a girl named Colleen and they were engaged.

The days at Pentridge passed slowly. With escape never far from my mind, I did hundreds of push-ups and sit-ups and running on the spot in my cell each night. If the chance to escape came, fitness would be the deciding factor on whether I failed or succeeded.

A few months after my second stay in H Division the gaol bookie, James Bazley, asked me if I wanted to operate business for him. Although he was in gaol for bank robbery, the distinguished-looking Bazley, whose curly, dark brown hair was beginning to grey, looked more like a bank manager. He told me that he was tired of being a bookmaker, but I knew he had been experiencing difficulties in collecting some of the debts and had, in fact, recently came off second best in a fight with a young crim who had reneged on a debt. Jim was about forty and wanted to avoid confrontation with the young hotheads and gaol heavies and the possibilities of going to H Division. His proposition was that I run the business and he would finance it and we would equally share the profits. I didn't hesitate to accept his offer. Within a month I had become established as the gaol bookmaker.

Then I struck trouble. A fool with a star tattooed on his forehead who owed me two ounces of tobacco approached me in the mat yard and shouted: "You're brassed, Killick!"

This was his way of telling me that he wouldn't pay. Although I knew that he was tough, I couldn't afford to show any sign of weakness. If I allowed him to get away with it, others would be encouraged to do the same. I had to make an example of him.

"All right, goose," I said. "Get in the shed and we'll settle it."

I knew I had a battle on my hands. I had once seen him fight. His opponent had smashed a full jar of polish on his head and he had merely shook his head, growled like a grizzly bear and rushed at his hapless foe and threw him to the ground and grabbed him around the throat, nearly killing him before some guys dragged him away.

When we entered the large shed, most of the crims stopped work and came in to watch. I suspected that because I was the bookie, most of them would be hoping to see me get a battering.

I stood in the middle of the room and shaped up, the Star put his head down and rushed at me like a bull. I stepped to the side and hit him with a hard right to the side of the head, knocking him sideways. Before he could regain his balance I moved in and hit him with a barrage of punches to the head. Blood spurted from both his mouth and his nose. Shaking his head he growled and tried to grab hold of me. I jumped back. He rushed forward, wildly throwing punches. I danced around him and hit him with three or four left jabs and a hard right cross. His knees buckled, but the fool kept coming. The crims were screaming out encouragement, some for me, most for him. I continued to dance around him, hitting him with quick left jabs. His lack of condition combined with the battering he had taken had effectively slowed him down to the point where he could hardly hold up his hands. I knew I had him, I intended to systematically cut him to pieces to set an example to anyone else who might consider brassing me.

A short while later I asked him if he had had enough, he was gasping for breath and his face was a battered mess. I was now hitting him at will, but I was only jabbing him. I was feeling sorry for him, admiring his courage. Some of the guys were yelling at him to throw in the towel. But a fool never knows when he is beaten. He shook his head and gasped: "I never surrender!"

Then someone stuck out his foot and tripped me. I fell to my knees. Before I could scramble to my feet the Star leapt on me and we crashed to the floor. We began to roll around on the floor, wrestling. I tried to break free but, despite the battering he had taken, he had the strength of a madman. He managed to pin me down and sit astride me. I tried to jab him in the eyes but he twisted his head away and grabbed me around the throat, shouting: "I'm going to kill you!"

The logical part of me told me that this wasn't worth two ounces of tobacco. He was choking me! In desperation, I was trying to pry his hands off my throat when the screws alerted by the crims yelling out ran in and dragged him off me. It is the only time in my life that I was glad to be caught breaking the law, if that's what I was doing by being choked to death by a raving lunatic.

Both of us were taken before the Governor who took one look at the Star and sentenced me to two weeks confinement in H Division. He gave the Star a caution. Five days later the Star had his fine paid and was released.

As I was being escorted to H Division I could hear music from the loudspeaker of one of the yards. Scott McKenzie was singing:

"*If you're goin' to San Francisco*

Be sure to wear some flowers in your hair..."

I wondered what Hitler would do if I came through the gate wearing flowers in my hair. Would he take it as a sign of peace?

As we entered the lane that led to the entrance of H Division I heard the words:

"*If you're goin' to San Francisco*

You're goin' to meet some gentle people there..."

I smiled grimly at the irony of the situation. I felt it would be more appropriate if they had a sign over the entrance like the one Dante saw in *The Inferno* preceding his descent into Hell, *Abandon all hope ye who enter here.*

On arrival in H Division I received a moderate reception biff. Nothing too serious, but severe enough to augment my resolve to kill some of my oppressors after I was released.

For the next two weeks I was abused and shouted at every day, occasionally, I was given a backhand or a belt across the buttocks with a baton. Hitler screamed at me that I was a three time loser and that anyone who came to H Division three times was either insane or doomed, or both.

When my fourteen days had passed and I was due to return to B Division, Hitler pushed his twisted face centimetres from mine and said: "If you come back here again, I personally promise you that when you leave you'll be carried out."

I met his gaze. "Yes, sir." One day I'll bury you, you bastard.

After I had returned to B Division, Jim told me that although he had operated the book while I had been away, he was pleased to again hand over the reins to me.

Although the fight with the Star had demonstrated my willingness to fight punters who didn't pay, I knew there were a few who would see it as a challenge. It would be only a matter of time before I either finished in hospital or in H Division again. I decided to pre-empt either situation by employing two minders. One of them, Bill, was a solidly-built guy of 25, who had a reputation for being violent. The other one, a big, strong, slow-thinking guy named Jack, was Bill's best mate. Both of them were tough and ruthless. The first job I gave them served a dual purpose. It settled a debt and set an example to others as to what they could expect if they crossed me. It was something both Bill and Jack excelled at: bashing someone. I asked them to belt the guy who had tripped me during my fight with the Star. I believed that not only had he been the cause of my almost being strangled, but also due to his action, I had been discovered fighting by the screws and sent to H Division. I told Bill and Jack to be careful not to break any bones, to simply make him sore for a week. They did a good job.

One of my clients was Ray Borg who, before his arrest, had owned racehorses and had been a mammoth punter. Borg, who was reputed to have a near genius IQ, was serving nine years for embezzlement and was housed in E Division. He worked for the director of prison industries and had his own office. Apparently he had saved the administration nearly $50,000 per annum by devising more efficient ways to run the industries and cookhouse, thus depriving many crims and screws of the little rorts they had been operating for years. Although Borg was the most hated man in the system, by both crims and screws, it was acknowledged throughout the gaol that he had virtual immunity from gaol discipline and the only way the screws would get him into H Division would be to catch him with a machine gun and then it would have to be loaded. Borg, who was about forty, had Arabic features and a large, balding head. He was one of the few punters who wagered in cash rather than tobacco and chocolate. He told me he had thousands stashed away and wanted me to raise the limit of $20 that Jim had imposed on me. When I discussed it with Jim he was emphatic that the limit remain. Jim's attitude upset me. I was convinced that if we raised the limit we could eventually get Borg for all he had. I suspected that Jim's trust of me was limited. Perhaps he thought that if we raised the limit, I would collude with Borg and bankrupt him. Borg was accustomed to getting his own way; when I told him the limit would remain he petulantly declared that he wouldn't bet with small fry.

Nevertheless business flourished. Most of the punters lost. It soon became necessary to trade the excess tobacco and chocolate at a cut rate for cash. The guys who operated the card games usually arranged this transaction for me.

After four months I had $500 hidden away in the mat yard.

A few days before the Melbourne Cup, Borg came to see me. He wanted to place some $50 wagers on horses during the Cup carnival and asked me if I would accept them. I reminded him that I had an agreement with Jim that the limit was $20.

"Look, Ray," I said, "why don't you pull a few strings and get me transferred to E Division. I could run the book on my own without any limit."

He hesitated. I knew that the computer-like brain would be figuring out all the angles.

"You'll virtually have your own private bookmaker," I urged.

He rubbed his hand up and down his bald head. I wondered if that's why it was so shiny. "How can I get you to E Division?"

"You've got a lot of influence with the Governor. If anyone can do it, you can."

He gave me an earnest look. "You'll break away from Bazley?"

I nodded. "Definitely."

He raised his eyebrows. He was the most calculating person I had known. "How much money have you got?"

"As much as you."

"You're not kidding me?"

I gave him a wink. "Bookies' honour."

"Leave it with me." He handed me a slip of paper. "Here's four hundred dollars' worth of bets for today's meeting. Will you take them in good faith?"

I glanced at the list. There were a few $50 wagers, but nothing I couldn't cover. "Sure, I'll take them in good faith. But if I'm not in E Division in a few weeks we revert to the $20 limit."

That day, he lost about $100.

Before the races began, I had a talk to Jim. I explained to him that it was imperative for me to get to E Division and that's why I had accepted the wagers. Although he didn't ask me why I wanted to go to E Division, I sensed that he had a good idea. He possessed a sharp criminal mind.

"I understand, John. Just a word of advice. Watch Borg, he's a treacherous, clever son-of-a-bitch with a lot of pull. If you have a fall out with him you'll finish up back in H Division and for a long time."

Bazley was an enigmatic personality. He was in Pentridge for robbing three banks with a machine gun and earning the nickname Machine Gun Bazley. But there were others, myself included, who referred to him as Gentleman Jim. In April 1986, he was sentenced to life imprisonment for murdering drug couriers Douglas and Isabel Wilson and conspiracy to murder Donald Mackay in 1977. He was released in 2001, aged 75.

It took Borg a few weeks before he could wield enough influence to have me transferred to E Division. He explained that he had encountered strong opposition; even the Governor had remarked: "Killick has hit more hurdles than a one-legged steeplechaser."

"I gave him my personal guarantee that all you needed was a chance," Borg said. "So don't let me down."

I felt no loyalty or obligation towards Borg. He had arranged for my transfer solely for his own benefit.

E Division consisted of seven dormitories, four on top and three on the bottom. Two of the dormitories on the top level each contained forty prisoners. I was housed in one of these. Each day we were locked away at 4.30 pm. On each side of the room were ten double bunks. At the front of the room there was a TV on a rack attached to the wall. Two toilets were situated near the TV. There were no doors on the cubicles; anyone using the toilet was on open display to everyone in the dormitory. It was summer and sometimes the stench of forty bodies, some of them unwashed, caused me to yearn for the luxury of my old cell in B Division.

In contrast to my living quarters, Borg lived in a small, luxurious dormitory that housed three prisoners. It had a bathroom, TV, radio, toaster, heater, electric jug and fan. Borg even had a remote control for the TV. Although there were two other prisoners in the dormitory, Borg was the unchallenged boss. The crims in other dormitories referred to it as Toorak Towers.

Most of the men in E Division welcomed the news that they now had a resident bookie. To safeguard myself against possible confrontation over bad debts, I refused to accept credit wagers. Although I knew this would severely decrease my turnover, I couldn't afford the risk of trouble and probable expulsion from E Division. I was confident that if I made the right preparations, I would be able to escape from E Division. But it would be necessary to work my way into one of the smaller dormitories downstairs. The screw on night duty always sat upstairs, only occasionally going downstairs for routine checks.

Being in the dormitory made it difficult to train, although I was able to do push-ups and sit-ups, I couldn't run on the spot. To compensate, I ran up and down the mat yard for 15 minutes every working day.

Eight days before Christmas, Prime Minister Harold Holt went missing in the surf at Portsea, believed drowned. When the tragic news was announced on the TV in the dormitory, some of the crims cracked jokes about it, no one expressed sympathy. It confirmed my belief that prisoners, myself included, were a unique breed of people. The basic niceties and hypocrisies that existed in a normal society to enable people to live and work in harmony were virtually non-existent among prisoners. The harsh reality was that not one of us cared that Holt was dead and we didn't conceal the fact.

48

THE PUGNACIOUS PUNTER
(1967-1968)

During the Christmas period a sports carnival was conducted at the sports oval, a large sporting area surrounded by walls and towers. One of the scheduled events was my old speciality, the 440. After entering for the race, I let it be known that I would accept wagers on the event. Most of the crims wanted to back a guy named Davis who was a top all-round sportsman. Although I offered the short odds of even money for Davis, it didn't deter a lot of guys from wagering their weekly tobacco ration on him. No one backed me. After I easily won my heat a few of the punters complained that the bookie shouldn't be allowed to run in the race. I told them that if they could show me a rulebook where it stated that a bookie couldn't compete in a race, I would, if I won, refund their money.

The final was held on Sunday afternoon. I had watched the other heats and I knew that my only danger was Davis. There were 20 runners in the final. Not wanting to risk being caught up behind stragglers, I immediately raced to the lead and set a fairly solid pace. Approaching the turn Davis moved up alongside me but I could see he was under pressure. I imagined that I had just escaped and Davis was a cop trying to catch me. If I reached the finish line first, I would escape.

I raced away to win by about five metres from Davis.

Some of the crims wanted to lynch me. It just wasn't fair. The bookie taking bets on a race and then winning it himself.

Borg was upset that I hadn't told him I would win. He could have backed me with Bazley.

One night the Keystone Kops came to our dormitory and strip-searched all of us. After finding a small amount of marijuana in a crim's underpants they bustled the guy off to H Division. No doubts someone had informed on him. In those days it was rare for anyone to be caught with drugs. Although there was the occasional heroin addict, pot smoker, barbiturate or amphetamine user in gaol, the vast majority of crims shunned drugs and regarded drug users with suspicion and contempt. Today, approximately eighty per cent of people in gaol are there for drug-related offences and the gaols are filled with junkies.

My brother David wrote that he had married the New Zealand girl, Colleen. Included with his letter was a wedding photo. Although I was pleased for him, the irony of it depressed me. Two years ago I had promised to send him some wedding photos of Cathy and me. Despite the hopelessness of my situation, I often thought about Cathy. I was still in love with her. I realised with a shock that I hadn't seen her for four and a half years. Where was my life going? I *had* to get out.

In late January, I made an application to be transferred to one of the smaller dormitories, but the request was denied. I asked Borg to wield some influence but he told me to be patient.

January and February is often a good period for punters. The tracks are usually good and the top horses are competing. During that period, Borg managed to hold his own with me. Sometimes he would win a bit, sometimes he'd lose a bit, but there was never much in it. I was confident that it would be only a matter of time before he had a bad run.

In March, Borg demonstrated just how much influence he had. He procured for me a job in an office next to him in the industries administration block. The job was simple: to sort out invoices, record them in a book and file them. My first reaction was to conclude that Borg wasn't such a bad guy and that his action had been of an altruistic nature. Within a week I realised that he had manoeuvred my transfer to enable him to have me on hand so that he could bet every day, race after race.

The boss, Mr Maher, a clean cut, well-spoken man in his thirties, told me that he had gone against all advice by employing me. He had done it as a personal favour to Ray and if I made one mistake I would be back in the mat yard and B Division. I gave him an assurance that I would do the right thing. At least until I escaped.

A few weeks after I started the job a guy named Bob Johannsen asked me if I would accept a $40 all up bet. The horses were both at short odds. I estimated that if they both won I would only lose about $100 or $120. Bob, a big blonde Swede who was reputedly the best fighter in Pentridge was one of a group of six guys who had formed a betting syndicate. They had chosen what appeared to be the two best bets on the programme. I had robbed banks because good things had a habit of being beaten. I accepted the wager. Then it rained. In fact it poured. Both horses had to carry heavy weights and they drifted in the betting. The first horse went from odds-on to 2 to 1, the second horse drifted from 6 to 4 to 7 to 1.

Naturally, they both won. I owed the syndicate $960. My entire bank was less than $600. I had no doubts that if I gave them $500 and told them that was all I had, they would be more than satisfied. But my escape plan was contingent on my having enough money to hide out for a while without having to commit a robbery. Regardless of the consequences, I decided that I wouldn't pay.

With the exception of a guy named Russell, Bob and his syndicate were housed in another dormitory. After work, I walked into their dormitory, psyched up and prepared for a beating. Bob and two others from the syndicate were seated at a table.

Bob stood up. His huge, powerful arms hung by his side.

I stopped about a metre from him. "Hi, Bob."

He gave a twisted smile. "You payin' us, John?"

I met his gaze. "I can't. I haven't got it."

One of the other syndicate members, a slow-thinking Greek, jumped up from the table. "I fuckin' knew it!"

Bob gestured at him with a wave of the hand to sit down. "Shut up, Nick." He again focused his attention on me. "How much can you pay?"

I watched his hands. He had a reputation of being able to knock out a man with one punch, with either hand. "You know the rules, Bob. A gaol bookie either pays all, or else he declares and pays nothing."

For a few moments he stood staring at me, his face inscrutable. I was tense, prepared for him to attack.

Suddenly, he threw his head back and laughed. "Why would you? I wouldn't be fuckin' paying, either. Just give us our money back."

Trying to conceal my relief, I nodded. "I'll give it to you in the morning. I'll let everyone know that I've declared and they'll have to find a new bookmaker."

"What? Don't be stupid. You're the best bookie we've had. You'll bet on anything. Just forget this ever happened. Next time you take a big bet, make sure you can cover it."

I gave him a look that implied there was camaraderie between us. "When I accepted the bet I could've covered it. But the fuckin' things blew out to ridiculous odds."

"Yeah, I know." He paused, a wistful look in his eyes at the thought of what might have been. "Well, I've gotta have a shower. I'll get that forty off you tomorrow."

Later that night the guy Russell, who was in my dormitory, approached me. He was a good-looking, dark haired 20-year-old who had a quick temper. From the moment I had told him of the agreement between Bob and I that the winning wager was null and void he had moped around, brooding.

I was doing some sit-ups on the floor between my bunk and the adjoining one. Looking down at me, he said: "I've been thinking about that money you owe us. It ain't right."

I stood up. "I'm not the first bookie who couldn't cover a bet in gaol. Our resources are limited. I can't very well go and rob a bank, can I?"

He gave me a sombre look. He was about ten centimetres shorter than me, but he was solidly built. He edged closer to me. "How about you just pay me. Five quid of the bet was mine. That's a hundred and twenty quid you owe me, give me a hundred and we'll call it quits."

"You know I can't do that. If I pay you, I have to pay everyone."

He smiled conspiratorially. "No one'll know. We'll just keep it between ourselves."

"That wouldn't be very fair to Bob and your mates, would it?" I began to push past him.

He half turned away, then pivoted around and punched me in the mouth. I staggered back. He rushed forward throwing punches at me, knocking me to the ground. It was a confined space, as I tried to get up he kicked me in the face, snapping my head back against the small cupboard behind me. Only half-conscious, I jumped to my feet throwing ineffectual punches. He didn't back off, we stood there trading punches for about 30 seconds until one of my friends, Rex, grabbed him and pulled him away. I was virtually out on my feet. Dazed, I sat on the edge of the bottom bunk; blood was flowing freely from the wounds in my face.

Rex, a tall, dark-haired guy of 25, grabbed a towel and dabbed at my wounds. "Mate, you'll have to get some stitches over your eye."

I grabbed a mirror and looked at my face. It was a mess. There was a deep gash over my left eye; my nose was swollen and bleeding and my top lip was badly gashed. My face was swollen and I had a lump on the back of my head where I had hit the cupboard.

"He did a good job, didn't he?" I said.

"I'll bang up for a doctor," Rex said. He walked to the entrance and began kicking the metal gate and rattling the lock. When the night-duty screw came to the grille I walked over and told him I needed some stitches over my eye.

"What happened?"

"I fell off the top bunk."

"Yeah, it looks like it. All right, I'll get the medical officer."

Fifteen minutes later a male nurse who walked like a fairy came and stitched the gash above my eye.

"It must have been a bad fall," he commented sceptically.

"I was having a nightmare at the time," I said. "Dreamt I was being chased by a poofter."

The screw laughed. Before they left, the screw asked me if I wanted to change dormitories. I told him I wouldn't be having any more nightmares.

After they had gone Russell came and apologised. "I was upset," he explained.

It peeved me to see that he only had a few superficial marks on his face. I nodded sympathetically. "I know how it is. I hate bookies myself."

He held out his hand. "Do you want to call it quits?"

I shook his hand. "All's fair in love and war." Which you have yet to learn, you poor, simple bastard.

As soon as the dormitories were unlocked the next morning, Borg rushed in to see me. Apparently, the night screw had told him I had been badly bashed. By now, both my eyes had blackened. Although I sensed that Borg wanted to admonish me, he could see that I was in no mood for a lecture. He lent me a pair of sunglasses.

About 20 minutes after we arrived for work, Mr Maher walked to the door of my office and stood staring at me. Pretending I didn't see him I concentrated on entering some invoices. After a few moments he shook his head and walked away muttering.

A week passed before I decided it was time for round two. Although, for a few days, Russell had been wary, he had now dropped his guard.

It was about 15 minutes before the morning work muster. Russell was standing by one of the bunks talking to one of his mates, a flat slob named Danny who had cheered him on while he had pummelled me. I causally walked up to him and, as hard as I could, punched Russell on the side of the jaw. I heard his jaw snap. Without a sound, he fell to the ground. Stepping forward I gave him one swift, hard kick in the ribs. He screamed out.

"Fair go!" Danny yelled.

Grabbing him by the hair I pulled him forward and punched him in the mouth. He collapsed on the floor and covered his head with his hands and shouted: "I haven't done nothin'!"

"You didn't yell out for a fair go when this cunt king hit me, did you!" I yelled.

I had psyched myself up to the point where the violence in me had taken control. I rushed out to Johannsen's dormitory. Bob was standing by the large mirror, shaving.

I walked over to him. "I just broke Russell's jaw and probably his ribs. I also clouted his mate, Danny."

Bob turned to face me. He was smiling. "I thought you'd get around to it, it's between you and him, isn't it?"

We stared at each other. I felt the adrenalin drain from my body. I smiled. "Yeah." I began to walk away.

"He'll back up," Bob warned.

Nodding, I kept on walking. I had no doubt that there would be round three. But at least I had ascertained that Bob, and therefore the syndicate, would remain neutral. I was thankful that Bob had remained cool. Even psyched up as I had been, I doubted that I would have been a match for him.

Russell was taken to hospital with a broken jaw. If he'd told the authorities that I had assaulted him, I would have been taken to H Division. But Russell, as I knew he would, abided by the criminal code and told the screws he had fallen down the stairs. As it saved the administration a lot of paperwork, they usually accepted these types of explanations.

A few weeks later Borg, after I had offered him a $50 bonus, managed to have me transferred to a smaller dormitory downstairs that housed twelve prisoners. This was the chance I had been waiting for, the fact that it was on the ground floor would facilitate my escape plan as the night duty screw only occasionally came downstairs for routine checks. If I tried to escape from the top dormitory he would probably see me the moment I came out the door and shoot me. The only way to escape from the top dormitory would be to saw the bars of one of the outside windows; but the screws regularly patrolled the area flashing torches at the bars. The chances of sawing through the bars without detection were minuscule.

There was an old guy in B Division who had taken an impression of a set of keys that a careless screw had left on a table in the storeroom. Although the panic-stricken screw had retrieved the keys ten minutes later, the old guy claimed to have taken a perfect impression of each key. After discussing it with him, I offered him $200 if he could use the impression to make a set of keys that worked. He said it would take him about a month, but he was confident he could do it. Fortune was finally favouring me. If I could obtain a set of keys I would be able to escape while the screw upstairs read his *Footy Week*.

The day Martin Luther King was assassinated, one of the crims in my dormitory, a big, ginger-haired guy nicknamed Bluey, commented: "That's the best thing that ever could have happened to America. That bloke was ruining the country."

His attitude infuriated me. "You don't know what you're talking about," I said. "He was a great man. He helped give the Negroes their freedom."

He stared at me. "Have you ever been to America?"

He had hit a sore point. "No, but it's not from the want of trying."

"Well, I have. The Negroes are a real problem. They think they own the country."

I recalled that Cathy's father, Roland, had held similar views. "I suppose you feel that the Australian Aboriginals shouldn't be allowed to vote?" It had been less than a year since the Aboriginals had become eligible to vote. A referendum had shown that 95 percent of Australians believed that Aboriginals should have that right. I sometimes wondered about the other five percent.

"That's right," Bluey said. "If we left it to the Abos we'd all be living in huts and eating witchetty grubs."

A little guy who rarely spoke, jumped down from his bunk, picked up a chair and hit Bluey over the head with it. "My mother's an Abo!" he shouted.

Bluey run up to the other end of the room. The little guy, still gripping the chair, went after him. I rushed up and grabbed him. "Take it easy, fella," I said. "You'll only get yourself a trip to H Division."

Although he was much bigger than the other guy, Bluey was terrified. "I'm sorry," he said. "I didn't know you were an Abo."

The little guy hurled the chair at him. It missed. I put my arm around his shoulder. "Come on, forget it, Bluey's got a big mouth, haven't you Blue?"

"Yeah," Bluey said.

The little guy calmed down. He was one of those people you rarely noticed and it was only after closely scrutinising him that I discerned unmistakable physiognomical aspects of the Aboriginal race. He later boasted that he was a cousin of Lionel Rose who had recently become the first Aboriginal to win a world boxing title. I didn't believe him because since Rose had won the title, he had gained a lot of lost cousins. But I think Bluey believed him and it was the last time he made a disparaging remark about blacks.

The guy who had taken the impression of keys told me he was having difficulties duplicating a set. Late in May, frustrated, I raised my offer to $300.

Then Russell, who had been convalescing for two months in G Division with a wired jaw, returned to E Division. I was sitting down eating lunch when Rex approached me and said: "John, Russell's back. He's upstairs telling everyone how he's going to break every bone in your body."

The adrenalin rushed through me, my heart began to race. I had dreaded this moment as it could destroy everything I had worked towards. Rex was staring at me. Was I scared? Sighing, I got up. Unless I went on protection, there was no way I could avoid a confrontation.

As I entered the dormitory where Russell was waiting, he shaped up in a classical boxing stance and yelled: "We'll see who goes to hospital this time, cunt!"

"I hope you've booked your bed," I said.

A lot of the guys had congregated to watch the expected bloodbath. Smiling grimly at the absurdity and futility of the situation, I took a defensive stance and waited for him to come to me.

For about five minutes the fight was evenly balanced as both of us had taken a bit of a battering. Then his lack of condition began to tell; his footwork slackened and his punches became ineffectual. I knew I had him. I backed him into a corner and began to pummel him. He went into a crouch and covered up.

I stepped back. I had no animosity or anger towards this young guy. "You had enough?" I said.

He nodded. "Yeah. A good fight."

We shook hands. "I'm glad all my punters aren't like you," I said. A couple of guys laughed.

Both of us were covered in blood. I surveyed myself in the mirror. My left cheek was cut and the old wound above my left eye had reopened and was bleeding profusely. I also had no doubts that my swollen left eye would soon be black. This time I had no intention of asking for stitches. I had pushed my luck to the limit.

Before returning to work I borrowed Borg's sunglasses. Later in the afternoon Mr Maher called me into his office.

"John, I'm not going to beat around the bush. I like you, you're a good worker, but I think you've got problems."

Of course I've got fucking problems. I'm doing seven years and then they're going to extradite me to Sydney for half a dozen bank robberies! I gave him an innocent look.

"Problems, sir? What makes you think that?"

"Because every time I see you wearing sunglasses, I wonder who they've taken to hospital. I went out on a limb to give you this job."

"Oh, you mean the cut eye. It's nothing serious, Mr Maher. You can rest assured that no one is going to hospital and you've got my word from now on I'll avoid all trouble, no matter what."

He gave me an exasperated look. "All right, John. You're skating on thin ice, but I'm going to give you one more chance. If you let me down I doubt that you'll ever be given another chance in Pentridge. You'll rot in B Division and the mat yard."

I walked away resolving to put my escape plan into action as soon as possible. It was hard to stay out of trouble in gaol.

49

DESPERATION STAKES
(April/June 1968)

I still had the hint of a black eye from my final fight with Russell when Robert Kennedy, the man tipped by many astute judges to become the next President of the United States, was assassinated. Incredibly, in less than two months, two of the most powerful men in America had been cut down in their prime by a pair of social misfits. The TV coverage sickened me. Kennedy lying on the floor mortally wounded while people grappled with the assassin, an unstable Arab named Sirhan Sirhan.

As much as I hated Hitler and most of the other screws that worked in H Division, I began to question my ability to kill someone in cold blood. Although Hitler and his cronies had unlawfully and maliciously assaulted me and hundreds of others, making life hell for us. But the other part of me, the side that couldn't stand to be beaten, argued that until I had avenged myself I would be less than a man. It was this dominant side to me that Hitler and others would one day have to contend with.

About mid May, Borg encountered what every gambler will inevitably experience, a bad losing streak. This particular day Borg didn't back one winner. The next day I told him he owed me $500. He gave me an engaging smile. "You don't expect me to pay it do you, Johnny?"

"Yes, I do, Ray."

He looked hurt. "But we're buddies."

I nodded. "Betting buddies."

He was exasperated. "Oh, come on, Johnny. You don't really expect me to pay you five hundred, do you? When you lost a lot of money you didn't pay."

"I know. But I got into a couple of vicious fights because of it. When you don't pay, you have to fight."

He paled. "I see. Very well, you'll have your money in the morning." He walked away.

I knew that I now had an enemy more dangerous than any I had thus far encountered in Pentridge.

The following morning at work he paid me the money then, for the remainder of the day, ignored me. My bank now totalled almost $1100 that I entrusted with Bill and Jack who had a good hiding spot in the mat yard. Although it was a risk leaving it there, I had no alternatives.

The guy who had been trying to make me a set of keys finally admitted defeat. He claimed that without the proper tools it was an impossible task. I wondered why it had taken him two months before he had come to this conclusion. Probably the promised monetary reward had proved tantalising enough for him to persevere. His failure to produce the keys was an enormous setback to my escape plans. I would have to do it the hard way.

I arranged for a guy to smuggle a hacksaw blade from his workshop to E Division where I hid it behind the large metal mirror that was attached to the wall in my dormitory. Unless someone tore the mirror from its fixture, the blade would remain undetected.

Geoff Ponton, who worked in the office next to mine, confided to me that he had overheard Borg tell Mr Maher that it was time Killick went to H Division.

I was running out of time. I decided that on Sunday, three days away, I would make my escape bid.

On Friday, I arranged for Bill and Jack to bring the money from the mat yard. When Bill brought me the money he warned me to be careful. A few crims had seen him digging in the garden where he had hidden the money. I gave Bill and Jack $100 and hid the remainder in my mattress. Although this was risky, there was nowhere else I could hide it. I felt that with only two days remaining before I escaped, the risk was worthwhile.

Aware that Borg would seize any opportunity to get me into trouble, I announced on the Saturday that I had finished with bookmaking. Although a lot of the crims were disappointed, another guy declared that he would be the new bookie thus appeasing most of the punters who had been horrified at the thought of a Saturday going by without them being able to have a bet.

Borg was immediately suspicious and questioned me as to my motives for renouncing such a lucrative business. I told him I had become tired of it. I could see that he didn't believe me.

"What are you going to do with all your money?" he asked.

"I sent most of it out to my family."

"You're a bad liar, Killick." He paused, eyeing me suspiciously. "What are you up to?"

"Even if I was up to something, I wouldn't tell you about it, Borg." I walked away.

On Sunday morning I approached Geoff Ponton, who was about my age, and asked him if he was interested in escaping. I had watched him closely and I knew he was doing his time hard. He was also one of the few people whom I trusted. Although he wore glasses, parted his black hair down the middle and spoke like an English scholar, I sensed that behind the college boy exterior was a ruthless criminal. He confirmed my intuition by nodding in agreement when I confided that a successful escape would necessitate the overpowering of a screw.

I then approached a guy named Mac. Although he wasn't overly endowed with intelligence, my escape plan was contingent on my having two accomplices and Mac was the only other guy in my dormitory whom I felt might be persuaded to undertake such a dangerous venture.

Mac, who was in his early twenties, was excited at the prospect of escaping. Although he didn't have a long time left to serve, as Geoff and I did, he looked upon an escape as a great adventure. When I warned him that we would have to overpower a screw, he gave me a toothless grin and said he was all for it.

That afternoon I confided to Rex that I intended to escape that night. Rex, who was in gaol for having kidnapped his estranged girlfriend, immediately declared that he wanted to come with us. I told him it would be impossible as he was in one of the top dormitories.

"But if you are going to take the screw and get his keys," Rex said, "you can come up and get me."

I thought about it. "I suppose I could get you out." I paused. Why not unlock all the dormitories? The thought of 140 crims making a run for the wall at midnight gave me an adrenalin rush. The screws and the cops would have nightmares! It was an outrageous idea but it was also brilliant. Even if only 20 of them decided to escape, the cops would have to look for 24 of us instead of four. My chances of eluding capture would be considerably enhanced. I told Rex that not only would I come and get him but I would also give everyone in the dormitory the option of escaping.

"Whatever you do," I told Rex, "don't mention this to anyone. If the screws get an inkling of what we're up to they'll kill us."

Before lock up I smuggled an iron bar from the weights area into my dormitory; it was about half a metre long and 10 centimetres in circumference.

After we had been locked away I went to the mattress to retrieve the money, it wasn't there! For a moment I was stunned, unable to accept that it was gone. While some of the others watched with fascination, I began rummaging through the mattress like a man possessed. Finally, in a state of shock, I accepted that the money was gone.

Geoff came over. He looked worried. "What have you lost?"

"A lot of money. Some dog's pinched it." I looked around the dormitory. A few of the guys were staring at me.

Mac got off his bunk and walked over. "What's wrong, mate?"

"Nothing serious." I looked at Geoff. "Be ready for trouble, it's time to make a move."

Grabbing the iron bar I walked over to the TV and turned down the sound. Before anyone could protest I jumped on to one of the tables and said: "I've got a few things to tell you guys." Pausing, I looked around; I had gained everyone's attention.

"First, someone has stolen some money I had hidden in my mattress.

If they return it now, we'll leave it at that. No repercussions. But, if it isn't returned, I'm going to search the dormitory and if I find it I'm going to iron bar whoever's responsible." I paused. "Now who's got it?" There was silence; some of them looked at each other, some stared at me while others just stared at the floor. I knew a search would prove futile. I was almost certain that Borg had taken the money. He had spies all over the gaol. He had probably been told that Bill and Jack had given me the money and he would have realised that there weren't many hiding spots available to me. By simple process of elimination, he would have eventually figured on the mattress. The dormitory was often unoccupied. There would have been ample opportunities for Borg to come in and search the mattress.

"All right," I said. "Now listen carefully, everyone. Geoff, Mac and me are busting out of here tonight." There were a few shocked murmurs. I smiled. "As long as no one tries to interfere, no one will get hurt. But if anyone tries to stop us or alert a screw, I'll belt his brains out with this." I held up the iron bar. There was stunned silence. "Anyone who wants to come with us," I said, "is welcome. But it's not just a case of walking out, we're going to have to overpower the screw and take his keys." Mac giggled excitedly. Some of the others stared at me as though they couldn't believe what they had just heard.

An old guy of about 55 with greying hair and glasses was outraged. "You can't do this to us," he said. "It isn't fair. If you blokes hurt an officer and then piss off, we'll all cop the blame. They'll throw us all in H Division and bash the lot of us."

I stared at him. I could understand his concern. "All you have to do is tell the truth," I said. "You tell the screws that I threatened to cave your head in with an iron bar if you do anything to alert them."

"I still say you're doing the wrong thing," the old guy mumbled. "You've got no right to do it."

"Well, come with us if you don't want to get it from the screws after we've gone."

"I wouldn't come with you, you're crazy, the lot of you. They'll catch you soon enough and I'd hate to be in your shoes when they do."

I looked around. "Is there anyone who wants to come with us?"

There were no takers. "All right. Then just get on with what you were doing. If a screw comes around to check on us, act normal. Anyone who tries to give us away, I promise I'll get you before they get us."

"You don't scare me," the old guy said.

I jumped down from the table and walked over to him. "Have you ever been to H Division?"

He gave me a defiant look. "No."

"That's what I thought. So don't preach to me about my rights. When you've been bashed and humiliated and forced to break rocks just because you had a race guide, then you'll consider it not only your right, but your duty to escape."

"I'd never escape."

"That's your choice. But if you try to stop me getting out of here I won't hesitate to use this on you instead of the screw." I waved the bar at him.

He was an old man and he couldn't disguise the fear in his eyes. His blustering manner gone, he got into bed without another word. I looked around at the others, silently daring them to protest, but all of them had been intimidated by the threat of violence and my manner. In the psyched up mood that I was in, I was dangerous and the others had picked up the vibes. Part of me recoiled at the idea of hitting anyone with an iron bar yet I had resolved to do just that to the night duty screw. It had to be the other side of me, Paleface, who took control when the going got tough. That part of me that disregarded consequences and could justify any action, even hitting someone with an iron bar. All I had to do was focus on the treatment I had received in H Division. The vicious blow from the screw's baton felling me, the soul destroying humiliation and degradation that I had been forced to endure. The blue uniform would be the catalyst motivating and justifying whatever action I had to take to ensure a successful escape.

Geoff and Mac were watching me, waiting for instructions. "Come on, guys," I said. "Give me a hand to get the mirror off the wall."

The three of us managed to wrench the mirror from its fixture; the hacksaw blade fell to the ground. One of the guys in the dormitory did a bit of woodwork as a hobby. I asked him for a loan of a piece of tabletop he had been working on and a sheet of emery paper.

"Mac," I said, "you sit opposite the door with the woodwork and sand paper. Watch closely; if you see the screw's shadow under the door, start sanding the piece of wood. I'll immediately stop sawing the bars and he'll think the noise he heard was you sand-papering."

The wooden door had a peephole from which the night duty screw occasionally peered through to check on us. Although the door was bolted from the outside, I knew it wasn't locked. But before I could get to the door I would have to saw through two of the bars in the steel grille. The wooden door had some thin panelling across the centre, it wouldn't be difficult to force a hole through it enabling me to reach through and slide the bolt off. Once we were out of the dormitory we could overpower the screw, take his keys, open the other dormitories giving everyone an opportunity to escape and then unlock the entrance to the Division. From there it was only a short distance to the wall.

"Geoff, use some sheets to knot up a rope about 30 feet long."

Geoff nodded. "What do we use for a grappling hook?"

"A broom."

He gave me a puzzled look. I grinned. An old crim had once told me that a broom attached to a rope was the best way to get over a wall. Once you threw the broom over the wall and tugged on the rope, the end of the broom dug in against the outside wall. "Don't worry, Geoff, it works."

While Geoff worked at knotting some sheets together and Mac sat with the emery paper and tabletop watching the door, I got under the bed near the grille and began sawing the bottom bar. It was a slow process and it took about forty minutes to cut through it. My arms were aching and I swapped places with Mac. Most of the guys pretended to watch TV, some feigned sleep. When Mac had nearly finished cutting through the top part of the bar I again changed places with him. I left the bar intact and began sawing on the next one. I had been at it for about ten minutes when Mac began to rapidly sand paper the piece of wood. I immediately stopped sawing and withdrew from under the bed. The door opened. The screw, a tall, gangling guy with a long neck and a large Adam's apple stood staring for a few moments at Mac, and then looked around the dormitory. I held my breath; if he looked down at the bars I had cut, we were history.

"You lot are pretty quiet tonight, aren't youse?"

I gripped the iron bar. Would someone give us away? No one answered him. Frowning, he took a step forward. Geoff, who had managed to conceal the knotted sheets, walked over.

"You picked a bad time to come for a chat, officer. We're watching the news. But I'll have a chat with you."

It was good psychology. Geoff was no fool. The screw gave him a scathing look and said: "I don't want to have a chat with you." He turned around and walked out, bolting the door behind him.

I scrambled out from under the bed. "Nice work, Geoff. But we'll have to be careful. I think he's a bit suspicious. We'll take a break for an hour." I walked over and turned the sound down on the TV. "Listen you guys we're not fucking idiots, some of you thought that by ignoring the screw he would become suspicious and that's exactly what happened. If he comes around again, act normal. We're close to busting out of here and if some of you bring us undone, I swear I won't be responsible for my actions."

Although a few of them nodded, I could sense the hostility. I had no doubt that if they could alert the screw to what was happening without me or the other two being aware of it, they would do it.

After an hour had elapsed without a sign of the screw, Mac and I took turns at sawing through the second bar. By 9.30 pm both bars were held together by little more than a thread. Geoff had knotted the sheets together and tied a broom to one end. Everything was now in readiness for the escape. I had decided to wait until the screws changed shifts at

11.30 pm as the tall, gangling screw was already suspicious and might be alert enough to cause us some trouble.

At 10.30 pm the screw came and peered through the peephole, then walked away. By now I was tense with anticipation and anxiety. The venture I was about to embark on was far more risky and dangerous than anything I had ever done. Failure and its consequences were too horrific for me to even contemplate. The gambler in me was prepared to take the chance and refused to acknowledge that the gamble could fail.

Geoff's calm demeanour was belied by the paleness of his face and the fear in his eyes. Mac was excited and had a craziness in his eyes.

At about 11.20 pm I sat by the bars of one of the windows waiting to see who the relieving screw would be. The lights and the TV had been switched off. As I sat there in the darkness gripping an iron bar, it all began to seem unreal. A dream…or a nightmare. The waiting was the worst part and the tension was becoming unbearable.

When I saw the relieving screw walking towards the Division my heart sank. John De Boer. He was a big, good-natured screw. As far as I knew, he hadn't committed a bad act against anyone. How the hell could I belt him over the head with an iron bar? What alternative did I have? Even if the bars hadn't been cut, most of the crims in the dormitory would be straight into the chief's office in the morning to tell on us. I had a choice. I could be a nice guy and not assault De Boer and wait with Geoff and Mac to be carted off to H Division; or, regardless of what screw got hurt, I could go ahead with my original plan. Thinking about it, I knew there was no decision to make. For a long time now it had been me against THEM. Only De Boer and a brick wall stood between freedom and me. I resolved to try not to hit him too hard.

About 20 minutes after the screws had changed shifts I decided it was time to make our move. It took a few minutes to wrench the sawn bars free and climb through the gap. Using a screwdriver I began to grind a hole in the thinly partitioned section of the door. All my senses were on red alert, the slight sounds of the screwdriver forcing its way through the wood caused me to wince with anxiety. If the screw heard the sounds and came to investigate we were shot ducks.

Eventually I made a hole large enough to get my arm through. Reaching through I carefully slid back the bolt. My heart was thumping so hard I had to momentarily close my eyes to regain control. What would happen when I opened the door? Would the screw be standing outside ready to shoot me? Only one way to find out. I opened the door. I was greeted by a cold draft. I turned to Geoff and Mac who were staring wide-eyed at me through the bars.

I handed Mac the screwdriver. "Mac, you keep an eye on this lot of sleeping beauties. If one of them wakes up and tries to raise the alarm put this screwdriver through his guts."

"Come on, Geoff," I said. "Let's get the screw."

Geoff climbed through the gap on the bars and joined me at the door.

"Give us 30 seconds and then bang up," I said to Mac.

Geoff and I crept down the passageway to the entrance that led to the stairs. As Mac banged on the gate and yelled for a doctor, Geoff stood on the other side of the entrance facing me. His job was to help me if I encountered difficulties with the screw. We could hear De Boer descending the stairs. Gripping the iron bar in my right hand I stared across the entranceway at Geoff. He was pale and trembling uncontrollably; although it was winter, I knew he wasn't trembling due to the cold. Instinctively, I realised he wouldn't be capable of helping me if things went wrong. This realisation had an instantaneous calming effect on me. I would do what had to be done.

When De Boer turned towards me in the passageway a look of shocked disbelief showed on his face. Instinctively, his hand went towards the pistol in the holster on his hip. I lunged at him and restraining the force of the blow hit him over the head with the iron bar. He wasn't wearing his cap and blood spurted from his head. He screamed out and reeled backwards. Horrified, Geoff jumped out of his way. Leaping forward, I hit him again with the bar, once more restraining the force of impact. He screamed out again and staggered towards the alarm bell on the side of the wall. Blood was streaming from his head. I couldn't hit him again with the bar. Cursing, I dropped the bar and grabbed him, dragging him away from the alarm.

"Don't hit me again," he pleaded.

For a split second I stared into his eyes; I saw abject terror. His head and face were covered in blood. Did I do this? Surely this couldn't be happening. It was a nightmare. I punched him on the jaw and he collapsed to the floor.

Mac had come into the passageway to see what was happening. Geoff stood staring at De Boer. Kneeling down, I took De Boer's pistol from its holster. De Boer, softly moaning, didn't resist.

"Geoff, pull yourself together and get the rope. And hurry. We made a lot of noise and we mightn't have much time. And bring a towel to wrap around the screw's head to try and stop the bleeding."

I searched De Boer's pockets for his keys. They weren't there. "De Boer, where are your keys?"

"I haven't got any keys." His voice was barely audible. "Don't hit me anymore."

I tried to contain the panic rising within me. "I'm not going to hit you. Where did you leave the keys?"

"We're not allowed to have keys while we're locked in the Division after Ryan and Walker escaped. The night senior's got them."

Ugh! What a fuck up!

Mac was moving around and rubbing his hands together as though he were performing some crazy dance. "Mac, tie his hands behind his back with his belt so he can't get to the alarm. We're going to have to shoot the lock off the gate and make a run for the wall before they can get organised and man the towers."

As Mac fumbled with the hapless screw's belt, I thought of Rex. There's no way now I could get him and the others out.

I heard someone running towards the entrance of the Division. "John! Are you all right?"

John De Boer groaned. I ran through the passageway towards

the front entrance where a screw was standing at the gate peering through.

I pointed the pistol at him. "Don't move or you're dead!"

He dived to the left out of sight. I heard him running away shouting for help. Sirens began to blare all around the gaol. To make a dash now for the wall would be suicide. I smiled grimly. When it came to escaping, I didn't have a lot of luck. I was quite calm. The gamble, like many others in my life, had failed. This time it would probably cost me my life. I had no illusions about that. In some perverse way I welcomed the thought of death. I felt empty inside; the future held nothing for people like me. The tragic Bobby Walker case flashed through my mind. Walker, who had been sentenced to life imprisonment in 1953, had a gun smuggled in and commandeered part of B Division. After being surrounded by armed screws he ran back to his cell and shot himself through the brain.

I walked inside to where Geoff and Mac were waiting. "We're off tap, boys. It's up to you what you want to do. I'm going upstairs to barricade the top of the stairs. They'll have trouble getting to us from there."

"I'll come with you!" Mac said.

Geoff, who was holding the knotted sheets and broom, looked as though he was in a trance. "What's my mother going to think?"

I knew how he felt. I had already experienced similar thoughts about Dad and Cathy. "She'll understand," I lied. "If we were prisoners of war we'd be heroes for trying this."

I looked down at De Boer. The towel wrapped around his head was already soaked in blood. I had no doubts that if I'd hit him full force with the iron bar I would have killed him. Mac had done a clumsy job of securing his hands behind his back. Not that it mattered.

Apart from the gaol sirens I could hear police sirens in the background. I could also hear screws running and shouting outside the Division. This was going to be one hell of a night!

I grabbed Geoff by the arm and shook him. "What you are doing, Geoff? Are you coming upstairs with us, or are you going to stay down here and surrender and hope they don't shoot your head off?"

He shook his head. "I'm going with you."

The three of us rushed upstairs to the large rectangular area that was encompassed by four dormitories. The steel bars on the dormitory windows would keep the cops and screws out. The only way they would be able to get to us would be by coming up the stairs. There was a fairly large organ standing in a corner that was used for the E Division church services. The three of us managed to drag it across the room to block the stairs entrance.

The sirens were becoming deafening. I had to almost shout to make myself heard. "Geoff, stay by the organ and watch the stairs. If you see anyone, sing out and I'll come over."

He gave me an uncertain look. I patted his shoulder. "Don't worry, they won't come rushing up the stairs and risk getting shot. They'll try to negotiate first."

"Are we going to negotiate?"

"That's a decision each of us will have to make independently." I turned to Mac. "Mac, you open the dormitory doors and switch on the lights. I'll be around to talk to everyone."

I hurried over to Rex's dormitory, switched on the lights and opened the door. Rex and nine or ten others were gathered around the grille. I walked inside the steel gate and grinned at Rex. "We didn't quite pull it off, mate."

Rex stared at me. "Where's the screw?"

"He's downstairs with a headache."

"What are you going to do?"

"I don't know. I think they'll kill me."

"Oh, mate!"

"We'll see what happens." Pausing, I looked at the crims who were gaping at me with inordinate curiosity. "Look, you guys, I was going to let the lot of you out tonight, but things went wrong. Now I want you all to do me a favour and tell me if the cops try to cut through the bars or come in via the roof."

There was a roar of assent. "We'll do better than that," one of them said. "If they try to come in we'll piss on them while they're cutting the bars." There was raucous laughter. The men were caught up in the excitement.

I shook hands with Rex through the bars.

"I'll get back to you later, Rex."

Leaving Borg's dormitory until last, I went to the other dormitories and explained the situation to the men. Most of them pledged their support and assured me they would warn me if anyone tried to break in.

Pausing outside Borg's dormitory I looked at Geoff. "See anyone, Geoff?"

He seemed calm. "Not yet."

Nodding, I switched on the light and swung Borg's dormitory door open. Borg was sitting up in bed, ashen-faced, staring at me.

I smiled. "Hello, Borg."

He tried to return the smile; his features were so taut his face reminded me of a death mask. "Hello, Johnny."

I almost burst out laughing. Yesterday I had been Killick. Now, as I stood in his doorway in the early hours of the morning pointing a pistol at him with sirens blaring all over the gaol, he greeted me with "Hello, Johnny" as though everything was perfectly normal.

The two other guys in the dormitory were also sitting up in their beds watching me.

"Where's my money, Borg?"

"What money, Johnny?"

"I haven't got time to argue with you, Raymond. I want the money you stole from under my mattress."

"I swear I don't know what you're talking about, Johnny."

I shrugged. "There's a good chance I'll be dead shortly. And before I go, I'll be taking you with me."

His eyes were almost staring out of their sockets. "But I've always helped you, Johnny."

"Sure. You were going to help me to H Division. You know what the H Stands for? It stands for Hell, and that's where you and I are going tonight." I slammed the door shut.

Suddenly, a voice came booming through the loudspeaker. It was loud enough for everyone in the gaol to hear. "Attention! Attention! This is the Governor, Mr Grindlay, speaking. You men up there might as well come down now before it's too late. The Division is surrounded by police marksmen. You can't get away."

Mac rushed over to the organ. "Get fucked, Grindlay!" A chorus of cheering and whistling erupted from the dormitories.

I pushed Mac aside. "Let me handle this." I looked downstairs, but couldn't see anyone. "Mr Grindlay!" I shouted.

"Yes?"

"We're not coming down. If anyone tries to rush the stairs they'll need more than bulletproof vests because I'll shoot their eyes out. You can check my record – I'm an expert shot," I lied.

"Who am I talking to?"

"John Killick."

"Who else is up there with you?"

"Geoff Ponton and Daryl Cormick."

"Where's the officer?"

"He's downstairs."

I heard a rush of feet as cops ran inside to the passageway where we had left De Boer.

"He's alive!" someone shouted.

For a few minutes there was a lot of commotion downstairs, then Grindlay spoke in the loudspeaker: "Killick, the officer is all right. He's on his feet and walking. Now why don't you men come down?"

"Why should we?"

"Well, you'll have to come down sooner or later. Why not get it over with?"

"Because we're up here and you can't get us." There was laughter and cheering from the dormitories.

"Don't you believe it. There are 50 highly trained policemen here. I'm trying to get you down here before they rush the place and someone gets killed."

"The first one to get killed will be Borg. We've got him tied to the bars. If you try to rush the place I'll put a bullet in his head." Borg was Grindlay's favourite prisoner.

"Why would you want to hurt Borg?"

"I don't like him."

"You know what will happen if you shoot someone. Remember Ronny Ryan. At the moment things aren't too serious."

"Oh, sorry! Gee, for a while there, I thought it was serious. How's De Boer's head?"

"Officer De Boer is fine. At the moment he's drinking a cup of coffee. Now how about coming down? The police are becoming impatient."

"Well, seeing things aren't too serious, why don't you send the 50 policemen home and handle this with your men?"

"You know I can't do that."

De Boer had left a jar of coffee and an electric jug on the table. Mac had made some coffee and handed me a cup. The banter between Grindlay and I continued for a while, then he said: "I'll give you ten minutes to talk it over between yourselves. If you don't come down then it will be out of my hands. The police will come in and get you."

"The first one up will be a dead man!" I yelled.

I looked at Geoff and Mac. "I'm staying up here but if you guys want to go down, I'll understand."

"I'm staying," Mac said.

Geoff hesitated. "Do you think they'll rush us?"

I met his gaze. "Eventually they will. They'll negotiate for a while. But if we don't come down they'll have to do something. They'll probably throw tear gas up here."

Geoff said, "We'll have to go down then. They might even shoot us on the way down."

I shrugged. "Getting shot might be better than going to H Division. We caved a screw's head in. If they get us down in H Division the screws will kill us."

Mac giggled, he was close to hysteria. Ignoring him, I said to Geoff: "I'll see what sort of deal I can get for us. You can make your own decision then." I paused. "Keep an eye on the stairs for a minute."

Hurrying across to Borg's dormitory I swung the door open. Borg wasn't in sight. "Where's Borg?" I asked the thin, shifty-eyed crim in the bed opposite Borg's.

"He's in the bathroom with a mattress wrapped around him."

I laughed. "Hey, Raymond! You can't hide. I can blow the lock off this gate with one shot. And unless you can find another mattress to wrap around your big head you've backed your last winner. I'm going to get you, Borg! Oh, Mr Grindlay sends his regards. Can't understand why I'd want to shoot a nice guy like you." I slammed the door shut. Although I had no intention of shooting Borg, hopefully, if I put him under enough pressure he might finish with ulcers.

Mac had calmed down, but I knew he was on the verge of a complete breakdown. "What are you going to do, John?" he said.

"We'll try to get some sort of deal," I said. I walked over to the organ. "Mr Grindlay!"

"I'm here. Are you coming down?"

"We want a deal."

"What type of deal?"

"We want a plane to Cuba."

He gave a condescending laugh. "Get serious, Killick. What type of deal do you have in mind?"

"I am serious. We want a safe escort from here to the airport and a waiting plane."

A new voice boomed through the loud speaker. "Listen, Killick! I represent the Police Commissioner. You can forget about aeroplanes and escorts out of here. If you don't come down we'll throw tear gas up there."

"Go ahead. We'll hold out up here until we're nearly dead. By the time we come down and you get up here and release a hundred innocent tear gassed prisoners your career will be finished. The press will have a field day with you. They'll call you a Nazi war criminal."

"Now you listen to me, Killick! There are 20 car loads of police here. I've got marksmen all over the gaol. If they have to come up there and get you they may be forced to shoot you."

"Then you'll have a real bloodbath on your hands. First sign of one of your gorillas coming up here I'll shoot Borg and a few other dog crims up here and then I'll shoot myself. And I'm not bluffing! Try explaining that to the Police Commissioner!"

Grindlay returned to the loudspeaker. "There's no need for those drastic measures, Killick. You mentioned a deal. We're prepared to listen to anything reasonable."

I thought of Cathy. Maybe I could get a phone call with her. It would be my last chance to speak to her. What could I say? "Hi sweetheart. Sorry to call unexpectedly like this, but I'm in the middle of a siege at the prison and I just wanted to take this opportunity to personally apologise for things not working out." No, I couldn't call her. She wouldn't understand.

It was time to negotiate. "Mr. Grindlay, I won't be coming down but Geoff and Mac may, depending on the circumstances."

"Let me talk to them."

"No. I'll be doing the negotiation. They want to know why they should come down. They're looking at getting another 15 years gaol and a flogging every day in H Division. Would you come down under those circumstances?"

"I can't speak for what sentence the court might impose, but I can assure you that Officer De Boer is all right. You won't receive anything like 15 years. As for being flogged in H Division, you have my word that you won't have a hand laid on you."

"I believe you're a man of your word, Mr Grindlay, but you're rarely in H Division. The officers there are a law unto themselves."

"They will do what I tell them to do. I'll say it again, and no doubt every man in Pentridge is listening to this. If you men come down now without hurting anyone else, you will not have a finger laid on you while you are in H Division."

"What do you think, John?" Geoff said.

"We've got to get a better deal in court," I said. "Otherwise we'll be old men when we get out."

"Are any of you men coming down?" Grindlay said. "I've given my word that you won't be harmed."

"You said De Boer's all right," I yelled. "How about charging us with assault and keeping it in low court?"

"It's not within my power to do that."

"Well, get fucked!" Mac yelled.

"Who was that?" Grindlay asked, peeved.

"I don't know," I said. "But there's no way I'll be coming down unless I've got an assurance that it'll be kept in low court."

"Well, let the other two speak for themselves."

I looked at Mac and Geoff. "If you guys want to do another 15 years, go on down."

"Mr Grindlay!" Mac shouted.

"Yes?"

"This is Daryl Cormick and I ain't coming down! Ha ha ha ha ha!"

Loud cheering and whistling erupted from the dormitories.

"Quiet, you men!" Grindlay yelled. "Give these men a chance. What about you, Ponton? I'm surprised at you being involved in this."

Geoff had the look of a man who couldn't really believe what was happening. "I'll only come down if it's kept in low court," Geoff said, resolutely.

Suddenly, the sound of rifle shots and breaking glass sent the three of us diving to the floor. The cops had shot out all the lights! Darkness enveloped the entire building. For the first time that night, I experienced fear, a dread of the unknown. Until now, I had been in control of the situation. But what now? Were they playing on our nerves, or did they intend to rush us in the dark? If they did rush us what would I do? Try to shoot a few of them, or shoot myself? What if they only wounded me and I recovered and had to spend another 15 or 20 years in gaol? Surely death was the preferable alternative. All I had to do was put the gun to my head and pull the trigger. I thought of Cathy. If I died here now, with a bullet through my brain like a crazed dog, she would eventually find out. It would be the final cruel blow to the girl who, despite everything, had believed in me. We would never meet again. Never. At that moment, there in the darkness, frightened and devoid of all hope, I saw her face, so real and beautiful that for a few wonderful moments I believed she was there. "Don't do it, John. I still love you." Then she was gone. Immediately, I felt the strength flowing back into my body. I was John Killick and I could take anything these bastards could hand out. No matter what happened, I would live and I would come through all this and I would see Cathy again.

Grindlay broke the silence: "This is your last chance. If you don't come down now, the police will be coming in to get you. Now, what is it to be?"

"I'm going down, John," Geoff said.

I touched him on the shoulder. I knew he'd reached his breaking point. "All right, Geoff. Do us a favour, though. When they question you, tell them we've got Borg tied to the bars. If you do that you could save our lives."

"What are you going to do?"

"I'm going to try and get us a better deal in court. Cross your fingers, I can pull it off otherwise we're all fucked."

"I'm waiting for an answer!" Grindlay said.

"This is Ponton! I'm coming down if you promise I won't be bashed."

"I gave my word. Now, put your hands on your head and come down the stairs very slowly."

"I can't see."

Suddenly powerful torches lit up the stairway. With his hands on his head Geoff began a slow descent of the stairs. After reaching the bottom, he disappeared from my sight. I heard some shouting. At least they hadn't shot him.

"What about you, Cormick?" Grindlay said. "Are you ready to come down now?"

Mac, who had been unusually quiet, came to life. "I'll never surrender! Come and get me, coppers! Ha ha ha!"

Damn it! He might provoke them too far. "We're not coming down unless we can do a deal on what sentence we receive," I yelled.

"I told you, Killick, I have no control over these matters."

"Well you'd better get someone who has. Do you want to know why I won't come down?"

"I'm listening."

"I've got three years to go here. Then I have to face numerous armed robbery charges in Sydney. If I get a big sentence on this as well, I'll never get out of gaol. I might as well finish here, tonight."

"You might not get as long as you think."

"No. I might get longer. I'll only come down if the matter is kept in low court."

"That's impossible."

"Well, I'm not coming down."

For the next hour the police did most of the negotiating. Although, on more than one occasion, they threatened to storm up the stairs with high-powered weapons blazing, both Mac and I refused to budge. The strain of knowing that at any moment I could be dead, made each minute seem like ten; sometimes, the police would say nothing for ten or 15 minutes. During these periods of eerie silence in the darkness, my nerves were stretched to breaking point. At one stage I had to control the impulse to scream out that I was coming down. While I had accepted death as a probability, I had experienced no fear and now that I wanted to survive, fear, stress and extreme anxiety were opposing my resolve to hold out for a deal that seemed impossible to obtain.

At one stage, they almost persuaded Mac to go down, but at the last moment he changed his mind.

Eventually, Grindlay returned to the loud speaker. He told us that he didn't want any more bloodshed and consequently he had managed to get an assurance from the authorities that if Mac and I came down without harming anyone the three of us would be dealt with by a magistrate. But each of us would have to spend the remainder of his sentence in H Division.

At the time, two years was the maximum sentence that a magistrate could impose; I wouldn't have to worry about a judge considering me to be a menace to society and adding 12 or 15 years to my sentence. But if I received another two years from a magistrate I would have to spend the next five years in H Division! Could I survive five years of hell at the hands of Hitler and his cronies? And if I did survive would I be able to retain my sanity? If, by some miracle, I came through it all, I still had to face extradition to Sydney. How many years up there? By the time I got out, Cathy would be a middle-aged housewife.

Grindlay cut into my thoughts: "What are you men waiting for? You've got what you asked for. You have my word that this whole episode will be dealt with by a magistrate and you won't have a hand laid on you in H Division. I'm going to be the subject of a lot of criticism for agreeing to these terms. But I've explained that I want to prevent further bloodshed. Now be sensible and come down while the offer still stands. It's nearly sunrise and I have to have the gaol back to normal before then. Now who's coming down first?"

Damn it! Whatever happened, time would pass. One day all this would be behind me. "Mr Grindlay! I'm coming down!"

Torches again lit up the stairway. "All right, Killick. First, throw the pistol down the stairs. Then come out with your hands on your head."

Mac grabbed me by the arm. "You can't go down, mate. They'll kill you."

"They'll kill us if we stay up here," I said grimly. "You'd better come down with me, Mac. We've pushed our luck as far as it'll go."

Mac couldn't contain the panic in his voice. "I'm not going down."

I handed him the pistol. "Well, you'd better take this." I shook his hand. "Good luck, Mac."

I stood up. "I'm coming down! I haven't got the gun, Cormick's got it."

This time one of the cops said: "All right. Put your hands on your head and slowly proceed down the stairs."

As I began the slow descent down the stairs there was a tightness in my chest and I found it difficult to breathe. Nearing the bottom I looked to the side. At least six cops were pointing rifles at me. It would take only one of them to press on the trigger and I would be blown to oblivion. When I came to the bottom of the stairs I was ordered to walk up the passageway. After I'd gone a few metres I was grabbed by three cops who quickly handcuffed my hands behind my back.

Grindlay, a distinguished looking grey-haired man in his early fifties, approached me. We looked at each other. He was pale and drawn. I dreaded to think of how I must have looked. The experience had taken its toll on both of us. Grindlay later wrote a book entitled *Pentridge Papers* in which he described the entire episode.

"You are a foolish fellow, Killick."

"I won't argue about that."

"Is Borg all right?"

"I'd say he needs clean underwear."

Grindlay gave a faint smile. "Take him to H Division."

As three screws escorted me along the familiar path to H Division, I looked up at the sky. It was still dark and I took in the beauty of the stars contrasted against the vast blackness of the sky.

It would be a long time before I saw it again.

3 foiled escapees to be tried by gaol court

Charges against three Pentridge convicts over an abortive escape attempt yesterday will be heard in the gaol by a visiting magistrate and a justice of the peace — probably next month.

The Age, 18 June 1968

50

Confession to Murder

When I arrived there were seven regular H Division screws waiting. Although I had steeled myself for a savage beating, it didn't come. After being strip-searched and changing clothes I was placed in an observation cell, the only furniture being a mattress on the floor. The screws stood outside the cell staring at me through the grille. Eventually one of them gripped the bars and spat at me. "You fucking bastard!" he said.

I spat back at him. "Get fucked, dog!" I had psyched myself to the point where I was ready for anything. If Grindlay kept his word, these bastards wouldn't be able to touch me. If he didn't, my abusing one of them would be of little consequence to what they would do to me.

About 15 minutes after I had arrived I heard them bring Mac in. I was relieved. I'd had my doubts about him surrendering and I had been half-expecting them to shoot him.

During the next five days Grindlay came down to H Division every morning and asked each of us if we were all right. He would stare at me and say: "Has anyone laid a hand on you?"

I would hold his gaze and reply. "No sir."

He would nod with satisfaction and, I suspect, a little pride. He again had proven himself to be a man of his word.

Once, after Grindlay had gone, Hitler came to the grille and said: "Your mate Cormick cracked up and was taken to J Ward." J Ward was an asylum at Ararat for the criminally insane.

The news didn't surprise me. "At least he won't have to break rocks," I said.

He glared at me, the hate in his eyes evident. "Don't think you're going to get away with this, Killick. We've all got long memories down here."

I glared back. "So have I."

His ugly, twisted features suffused with rage. "Do you know what you've done? You've assaulted an officer with an iron bar! Do you think you're going to get away with that because the Governor comes down to see how you are?"

"I'm not going to get away with anything. I have to be sentenced yet and I have to spend the remainder of my sentence down here."

"Sentenced by a magistrate. Do you call that justice for what you did?"

"I don't know what justice is any more."

"Don't you. Well I'll tell you what it is. In your case, it would be when they carry you out of here in a box or a strait jacket like your mate. You're here for a long, long time, Killick. You belong to us."

On the Friday evening after everyone had been locked away for the night, a group of screws came to my cell and unlocked it. "Step out, Killick," one of them said.

"Here it comes," I thought, trying to psyche myself for what I was certain would be the worst beating of my life. Instead, I was taken to the observation cell where Ronald Ryan had been held.

Hitler wasn't among the screws. The senior in charge, a thickset guy in his forties who had the complexion of a chronic drunk, said: "You're going into the death cell. Officer De Boer suffered a stroke and died at two o'clock this afternoon. You'll be charged with murder on Monday."

Momentarily shocked, I stared at him. I couldn't think of anything to say.

"You know they'll hang you, don't you," the senior said. "How do you feel about that?"

By now I had regained my composure. I looked at this man who represented everything I hated. There was no sign of sorrow or sadness in his eyes. He was gloating. "I always did envy Ryan, all the publicity he got," I said casually.

"Put the cunt in the cell before I kill him here and now," the senior said.

For the next 48 hours the screws took turns sitting outside the grille watching everything I did. The light remained on all night. When I managed to fall asleep one of the screws would make a noise, waking me with a start. Although I concentrated on appearing nonchalant, I was stressed to the breaking point. I tried to rationalise: If De Boer had died, surely the police immediately would have been down to interview me and charge me. I thought it probable that because Grindlay didn't work on weekends, the screws had waited until now to stage their scenario in the hope that the additional pressure and fear would break me. Despite my scepticism about De Boer's supposed death, nagging doubts remained. What if it was true? I had no doubts they would hang me. My crime would be considered worse than Ryan's. He had fired a shot in the heat of the moment during a frantic chase. I had premeditatedly waited for De Boer and, when the first blow hadn't felled him, struck him again. The strain of it all would probably kill Dad. And what about Cathy? "Dear Cathy, I have to see you one more time. Could you come and see me before they hang me?"

To think that I had once been ashamed to tell her that I had been in gaol for selling raffle tickets!

On Sunday evening I was taken from the death cell and placed in a normal routine cell.

"You're lucky, Killick," one of the screws said. "Officer De Boer was resuscitated."

That night I slept peacefully. The following morning I was marched to the labour yards. After having spent a weekend locked in an observation cell, I was relieved to be able to get some fresh air, even if it meant I had to break rocks all day.

When Grindlay came down and asked me if I was all right I didn't mention the death cell incident. If the screws gave me a severe beating I would have the marks to prove it but I was certain they would deny having placed me in the death cell and would claim I was going insane and suffering delusions. This would put Grindlay in the predicament of either having to believe them or me. I felt it would be in my interest to avoid such a situation. Apart from that, I wanted to demonstrate I had the mental strength to remain unaffected by any mind games they wanted to play.

After my first day in the labour yards, Grindlay ceased his visits to me. From that point I was subjected to increased verbal abuse and threats, but apart from an occasional whack across the buttocks with a baton while I was marching, no one physically assaulted me. I had learned to cope with stress, but the vitriolic abuse of myself and others, or the sounds of someone being mercilessly beaten, frayed at my nerves, causing me to become jumpy and agitated. The only diversion I had from the omnipresent fear and depression that pervaded H Division was my access to books. Each evening as I came up from the labour yards I was permitted 20 seconds to choose a book from a small bookcase situated at the bottom of the stairs. Although most of the books were old, I discovered some gems: a book of hilarious short stories by the legendary Damon Runyon; an anthology of stories by that other great American humourist, Ring Lardner; and two voluminous novels, each containing more than 1,000 pages that influenced my way of thinking and helped me to survive. One, *Atlas Shrugged* by Ayn Rand, was about a small group of brilliant individuals who, disillusioned with the corruption of power and society, took on the world and brought it to its knees; the other, *The Count of Monte Cristo* by Alexandre Dumas, had such an effect on me that I read it twice. The story of a man thrown into solitary confinement in a dungeon for 15 years for a crime he didn't commit fascinated me. Although it was fiction, I was inspired by the manner in which, after 20 years absence, he returned to destroy his enemies. He didn't resort to violence; he became rich and powerful and, with obsessive purposefulness and diabolical planning, put into motion events that resulted in each of his enemies destroying himself. I dreamed of one day emulating the fabulous *Count of Monte Cristo*.

Dad wrote to me, commenting: "It was on the TV that there was a bit of trouble down there the other night. Keep your chin up. Love, Dad."

It was his way of telling me that he knew of the trouble that I was in and that I still had his support. This gave me a lift.

A few weeks after the bungled escape attempt, a magistrate came to H Division specifically to sentence Geoff, Mac and I. By then, Mac had returned from J Ward. Although I pleaded guilty to attempted escape and assault, Geoff and Mac pleaded not guilty to assault. I had written a statement explaining that the entire venture had been my idea and that I was the only one who had assaulted De Boer. Nevertheless, the magistrate found the three of us guilty. When he sentenced each of us to 18 months, the screws were outraged. The following day they held a stop work meeting to discuss whether or not to go on strike and demand Grindlay's resignation. But it all came to nothing and, to my relief, Grindlay continued on as Governor. I had no doubts that if he were replaced as Governor, Hitler and his cronies would be given free rein to do as they pleased with Geoff, Mac and me.

A few days after receiving the extra sentence I wrote to Cathy. I explained that I had struck a bit of trouble and was a bit depressed at the moment. Would she write as a friend? It was a letter written out of desperation. It had been more than two years since I had written to her and I doubted she would reply. Although I couldn't bear to think about it, I knew it was possible she had married.

About ten days later I received a reply:

> Dear John,
>
> I wish I could say it was a pleasure to hear from you, but on the contrary. One of Mum's friends in Fairfield wrote and told her about your latest escapade. John, if only you would try as hard in life as you do at robbing banks and trying to escape, you could be anything you want to be. I must admit I thought about writing (as a friend) when I heard that you were in more trouble, but I can't do it without hurting others, and I'm no longer prepared to put you before everyone else. But, no, I'm not married.

John, this letter may seem cruel, but I can't take any more. You have the capacity to bring joy to others, but you are also capable of ruthlessly hurting all those who love you. Take care, John. Cathy.

Tearing it up, I flushed it down the toilet. There was a tightness in my chest and tears in my eyes. She was still hurting from what I had done. For the first time in my life, I felt utterly worthless. I was powerless to change the situation. The only girl I had ever loved despised me. No matter what misery I had to endure, I had to survive and one day restore her faith in me.

Unable to physically harm me, the screws concentrated on breaking my spirit by maximising the stress. Sometimes, usually on a Friday, I would miss out on a shower, thus forcing me to go from Wednesday to Monday without a shower. Covered in sweat and grime after breaking rocks, being deprived of a precious shower always increased my depression and feeling of degradation. Often I would be the last one brought out for a thrice-weekly shave. Two electric razors had to suffice for 39 men. In most instances, when it was my turn to shave, the razor was hot, close to being ineffective, and emanated a foul odour. The screws would wait until I was half finished, and then order me to return to my cell. I was always shocked by my image in the mirror; much of my jet back hair had turned white and my features were taut and drawn; in a few months I seemed to have aged ten years. No matter what I did the screws would find fault with it. My cell was always dirty; the rocks I smashed were never the correct size; letters I wrote were destroyed because of their offensive content; my hat was never on straight; I always saluted incorrectly; I didn't march in a correct manner; why had I only half shaved? Why didn't I shower properly? I stank! My toilet was dirty; my dish didn't resemble a mirror. These things, and more, gave the screws the opportunity to scream abuse and ridicule me. Sometimes they would bang on my door in the early hours of the morning and demand that I stop snoring.

Every morning I psyched myself to get through the day, to ignore the abuse and insults and accept the treatment for what it was: frustration on their behalf. Despite all the regulations I was accused of violating, I was never charged and taken before the Governor. Grindlay soon would have realised I was being subjected to a persecution campaign and he would have been honour bound to do something about it.

With abundant time to scheme, I eventually came up with what I believed to be an ingenious plan. One morning when Hitler asked me if I had any requests, I told him I wanted to see Detective Ainseley.

He gave me a suspicious look. "What do you want to see him for?"

"It's about a murder I committed."

For the first time since I had known him, Hitler momentarily was at a loss for words. Recovering his composure, he said: "What murder?"

"I'm only prepared to tell Detective Ainesley about that."

His eyes narrowed to a slit. "All right Killick, I'll contact him for you."

I knew what he was thinking: This stupid bastard is about to get himself a life sentence, or even hanged. But the way I figured it, I had everything to gain and nothing to lose. I intended to tell Ainesley that I had killed Arthur, the guy I had bashed in the park. If I could convince Ainesley that it was true, the authorities would promptly arrange to have me paroled from Victoria and extradited to Sydney to enable me to show them where the body was buried. Once in Sydney I would renounce the story. No doubt, the armed hold up cops would then charge me with the Sydney bank robberies. Not only would I be finished with H Division, but I also wouldn't have to worry about extradition when I finished my sentence. I would have a release date and could start counting down and planning for the future.

The day after I had spoken to Hitler, Ainesley came to interview me. He had brought me a large Cadbury's chocolate, but the screw standing guard by the door of the small interview room wouldn't allow me to have it.

"Make sure you put it in my property," I told the screw. "I'll eat it when I get out."

Ainesley grinned. "You haven't changed, John."

"You're kidding, aren't you? What about my white hair?"

"It makes you look distinguished." He paused and gave me a concerned look. "What's this about a murder, John?"

I gave him an accurate, detailed account of how I had bashed Arthur and then taken him by taxi to Dad's place where Dad had bathed and dressed his wounds. I then ventured into fantasy.

"After we left Dad's place I walked with him to Fairfield Park on the way to Carramar railway station," I said. "But he started complaining about his head aching and insisted on going to Fairfield Hospital. I knew that if he went to hospital they would call the police and I'd be arrested." I paused and stared at Ainesley. I could see he was hanging on every word. I shrugged. "We argued about it and I hit him. He fell down and hit his head on a rock. When I examined him he was dead."

Ainesley nodded sympathetically. "It was an accident. You could get off on manslaughter."

My mind began to race. A manslaughter charge mightn't be enough to get me paroled to Sydney. I hesitated, then said: "At least I thought he was dead. But he started to moan. I panicked and picked up the rock and smashed his head in."

Ainesley paled. "John, are you telling me the truth?"

I nodded. "I do these things without thinking. Look at that screw De Boer. I nearly killed him with an iron bar."

Ainesley grimaced. "I always thought of you as a gentleman bank robber. I'm afraid you've surprised me a bit, John."

I rubbed my forehead and looked at the floor. "I surprise myself sometimes. Anyway, after I killed him I stole an early model Holden, put him in the boot and drove him to the Blue Mountains where I buried him."

"Do you remember exactly where you buried him?"

"Yes. I wouldn't be able to point it out on a map, but if I was driven there I could show you exactly where it was."

Ainesley spent the next hour going over the story with me and asking me questions and trying to trap me. Eventually he was satisfied. "All right, John. I believe you did kill this person. I want you to write a detailed account of how it happened."

"What will happen then?"

"I'll be contacting the Sydney Homicide Squad. They'll interview your father. If the story checks out, I'd say you will be on a plane to Sydney within a month."

The adrenalin rushed through me. The entire legal system in two States was about to fall prey to the chicanery of the rock-breaking raconteur extraordinaire of H Division. I had to suppress a strong urge to smile with satisfaction.

It was probable that my plan would have succeeded but for Dad's determination to discredit my story. When the Sydney Homicide cops interviewed him he assured them that after I'd left the house with Arthur I had returned in less than half an hour – hardly enough time to have killed Arthur, stolen a car, driven to the Blue Mountains, buried him and driven back. Although he would never admit to it, Dad was a frustrated detective and delighted in telling the cops that Arthur had been a first class deviate.

"You're bound to have him on your files," Dad told them. "If you take me down to headquarters and show me the poofters' mug book I'll point him out for you."

And that's what happened. Dad, glorifying in the VIP treatment he was receiving, identified Arthur from a photo in one of the police albums containing known homosexuals. Within 24 hours the police had tracked him down. He was working as a chef in a North Shore nursing home.

Ainesley didn't bother to come and admonish me. He would have understood that, in my position, if I could rort the system I would. It was his job to see that I didn't.

I learned of the failure of my scheme via a letter from Dad: "I don't know what happened to make you confess to a crime that didn't happen, but your old man set the record straight."

Hitler must have told the screws. For weeks I was taunted with remarks such as: "Can't handle the pressure, eh, Killick? Cracking up, are we?"

"I committed a murder, sir! You couldn't kill a cockroach, Killick. You had your chance up in E Division and you shit yourself."

These childish taunts had little effect on me. I comforted myself with the thought that if I ever did kill someone, he would wear a screw's uniform.

51

THE IRON MAN OF PENTRIDGE

A few weeks before Christmas, I was taken from the labour yards and placed in No. 2 Security Workshop. This was where prisoners who had escaped or committed a serious offence while in gaol were confined after serving penance in the labour yards. It held a maximum of 12 prisoners. It was a large concrete room with two long tables situated in the centre. As with the labour yards, the sectioned off catwalk was situated above, enabling a screw, whenever he chose, to stand and watch us. Each table had three steel vices attached on both sides; they were used as clamps for wooden broom heads that the prisoners had to thread with coarse fibre and horsehair. Each prisoner was expected to complete at least eight brooms a day. Some prisoners, who had been there a long time, managed twelve.

Ponton and Cormick both were allocated to work in No. 1 Security Workshop that reputedly held the less dangerous prisoners. The concept behind the shops was that the prisoners, by working hard, could eventually work their way out of H Division. The average term spent in the shops was from two to three months.

One man, the much-publicised William John O'Mealley, had been in H Division for ten years. At the time, he was something of a legend in the Victorian penal system. He was known as The Iron Man of Pentridge. Although he was seated at the same table as me, we weren't permitted to talk during working hours. It wasn't until lunch break when we were transferred to the exercise yard that he spoke to me. He was a short, solidly-built man of 48 and, although his wavy grey hair was still prominent at the sides, he had a large, bald spot on top which he tried to cover by combing the side hair across. When he smiled, it was a grimace: during the past 16 years William O'Mealley hadn't had much to smile about. A petty thief, whose specialty was stealing from cars, he had been convicted in May 1952 of shooting dead a young police constable who had interrupted him breaking into a car. Although originally sentenced to death, the Victorian Labor Party came to power in December 1952 and commuted his sentence to life. O'Mealley always insisted he was innocent. At his trial he produced a diary showing that, at the time the cop had been killed, he had been miles away. In the diary he described that day as cool; unfortunately for him the diary was proven to be a fake. The day in question had reached a temperature of 100 degrees (40 degrees C).

In August 1955, O'Mealley escaped but, a few hours later, was found not far from the gaol hiding in the grass. With John Henry Taylor, O'Mealley again escaped in March 1957, this time shooting a guard in the process. Both men were sentenced to an additional six years and twelve strokes of a water-soaked cat-o'-nine tails administered by a masked man. It was the last time in Victoria that corporal punishment was administered, although the screws had tried to have it reinstated and applied to Ponton, Cormick and me.

When O'Mealley approached me in the exercise yard he gave me his grimace of a smile. "You're Killick, aren't you?"

I nodded. "You're Bill O'Mealley." I held out my hand. "Pleased to meet you. I've heard a lot about you."

He squeezed my hand in a vice-like grip; I had to make an effort not to react to the pain. "You know you've done the wrong thing," he said softly. "I was due to get out of here, but what you did will set me back two years. You should have waited."

I couldn't believe my ears. Was he serious? Or was he testing me? "I had no idea that you were due to get out of here, Bill," I said. "But it wouldn't have made any difference. I was desperate to get out. Nothing else mattered. Surely you, of all people, can understand that."

His face suffused with anger. "When I escaped there was no Bill O'Mealley in H Division. I've been here for *ten* years. Ten years of living Hell."

I met his gaze. "I'm sorry about that, but it's not my problem. I've got enough problems of my own."

"You should have waited," he mumbled and walked away.

A tall, good-looking guy came over and held out his hand. "How are you? I'm Peter Walker."

I shook his hand. "I thought I recognised you from the newspaper photos."

Unlike O'Mealley, his smile came easy; he rubbed his hand through his wavy, brown hair that was rapidly receding at the forehead. "I've lost a bit of hair since then."

I grinned. "Mine's turned white. It must be the life we lead."

"Let's go for a walk," he said.

When we reached the other side of the yard he said: "Did O'Mealley blame you for keeping him down here?"

"Just about. He reckons I should have waited."

"Don't take any notice of him. He said the same thing to me two years ago."

"What did you say?"

"I told him to get stuffed. We don't get on too well. He's even dirty on his mate, Taylor, getting out of here."

"He got out of here three or four years ago, didn't he?"

"Yeah. O'Mealley was the ringleader. He's the one they wanted. It'll be the same with you. After a while they'll let the other blokes out of here, but you'll stay here with me for a long, long time."

Peter Walker and I were in a remarkably similar situation. Both of us were 26; we were both in gaol for bank robbery and both of us had been involved in desperate escape bids where, in each instance, a screw had been assaulted and had his firearm taken by a prisoner armed with an iron bar. Although, from that point, Walker and I had taken different paths, events culminated with our being incarcerated in H Division for many years. Our circumstances created a degree of camaraderie between us that existed for the entire time I was in H Division.

My new cell was security cell number six, next door to Walker. It had a radio receiver; with the aid of the radio and some *Time* magazines that Walker gave me, I was able to catch up on what had happened on the world scene during the latter part of 1968. It had been a year of dissention and protests.

Richard Nixon had won a close Presidential election against an uninspiring Hubert Humphrey after President Johnson, due to the increasing anti-war movement, had decided not to run.

The communists seemed to be getting the best of the Vietnam War. The Americans and Australians were beginning to realise that the result of the war was far from a foregone conclusion. In Mexico City, days before the opening of the Olympic Games, police had killed dozens of anti-war demonstrators. At the Democratic National Convention in Chicago, police and protesters had waged violent battles in the streets. Czech leader Alexander Dubcek had tried to bring political liberalisation to his country, but as in Hungary 22 years previously, the Soviets moved in with their tanks and killed more than 150 Czechs. At least a million Biafrans had starved to death after a disastrous civil war against the Nigerian government. Add the assassinations of Martin Luther King and Robert Kennedy and 1968 had been a particularly barbarous year.

On a lighter note, Jacqueline Kennedy had shocked a lot of snobs by marrying Greek shipping tycoon Aristotle Onassis. The Beatles confirmed my suspicion that they were oddballs by becoming devotees of the Maharishi Malesh Yogi. In Australia a horse named *Rain Lover* had won the Melbourne Cup by an incredible eight lengths.

As 1968 drew to a close, life in H Division became a little easier after the unexpected departure of Hitler. Apparently he received a promotion and was transferred to another gaol. The replacement senior, Lindgren, was harsh in his attitude but he didn't menace the prisoners in the same manner as the maniacal Hitler had done.

52

THE SHORT STORY WRITER

Although I didn't receive visits, I derived some support from letters. Apart from corresponding with Dad, I received an occasional letter from either David or his wife, Colleen. They now had a son, David John. In one of her letters Colleen included a photo of the child, a fine-looking, blue-eyed, blonde boy. I had to give David credit; he had managed to overcome adversity to make a decent life for himself.

In April 1969, overall conditions in H Division improved with the appointment of Robert James Carrolan as permanent chief. The previous chief, Mr H Clark, who had ruled with an iron hand since the inception of H Division in 1958, graduated in rank and became head of Pentridge security and the Keystone Kops. Immediately Carrolan became chief he abolished the rule prohibiting prisoners to talk while working in the workshop. The bashings in H Division became less frequent and the amount of time spent in the labour yards was reduced.

Confined as I was in H Division, I had an intense desire to do something constructive with my time. After the repressive Clark had gone, I requested permission from Carrolan to do a course on short story writing. He denied the request on the ground that prisoners in H Division weren't permitted to do educational courses. I waited for a month and then requested to see Grindlay. I pointed out to him that most prisoners in H Division only stayed for a maximum of three months. My case was an exceptional one, as I had to spend the remainder of my sentence there. Grindlay agreed with my logic and granted permission for me to apply to the education officer for a course on short story writing. A few days later the education officer, a nervous little guy in his thirties, came to see me. He told me that I had set a precedent by becoming the first man in H Division to do an educational course; he hoped I was prepared to persevere because a lot of people were putting themselves out to enable me to do it. Twice he looked around to see what the screw at the door was doing. Maybe the screws had intimidated him. I gained the impression that he would have been pleased if I'd have changed my mind about doing the course and he could have avoided H Division. When he remarked that my having failed the Intermediate Certificate was hardly a recommendation for a writing course, I pointed out that I had later gained a pass in Leaving Certificate English.

Eventually I was enrolled as a student with the South Australian Technical Correspondence School. My tutor was Ian Mudie who, I later learned, was a poet of some renown. He soon made it evident that I had a lot to learn about writing. For my first assignment, a brief story about an old trotter, I received a C. Mudie used one and a half pages pointing out where I had gone wrong. Determined to improve, I bombarded him with queries about various aspects of writing. When he realised I was serious and that I had talent, he was painstaking in his effort to teach me everything he knew about the craft. No matter how hard I tried to write a flawless story, it would always return with marks in red biro pointing out where I could improve on it. But always, he would conclude with words of encouragement.

Despite my progressing from the labour yards to the workshop, the campaign against me by the screws continued. Sometimes David would send me books and I'd discover that the last few pages had been torn out. Often I'd return to my cell to find course materials scattered on the floor with boot prints on some of the pages. One of my assignments would be missing and, even though I'd arranged with Dad, David and Colleen to acknowledge each letter I sent, some of my letters were never mentioned. Under normal circumstance these incidents merely would have irritated me but due to the desolate conditions I was forced to live under, the accumulation of petty vendettas against me succeeded in stressing and angering me.

One day, discouraged and depressed, I decided to give up my literary pursuits. I convinced myself that, because of the rage and resentment I harboured, the sword would be mightier than the pen. Others could write about it. I would do it.

That afternoon when I returned to my cell, a story I had sent a month ago to Mudie was on my table. Opening the envelope, I looked at the mark. An A+! I couldn't believe it. I read his comments:

"John, congratulations. This is a great story. It held me riveted from start to finish. Couldn't fault it."

The A+ and Mudie's remarks revived the motivation and stimulation I needed to carry on with my writing. From that day on I achieved either an A or an A+ for every story I wrote, some of which were published after my release.

Relations between O'Mealley and I gradually deteriorated to the stage where we pointedly ignored each other. Although I knew it would be only a matter of time before we clashed, when it happened I was unprepared. I was sitting down in the exercise yard playing cards with Walker and two others when O'Mealley rushed over and punched me in the face.

"You're not the king of the yard!" he shouted.

Dazed, I jumped up and grabbed hold of him. Although he was nearly 50, he was still fit and strong. Breaking free from my grip, he began throwing punches. I retaliated. Both of us took some heavy punches to the head and body before I knocked him down. Stepping back, I allowed him to get to his feet before we carried on. Although he was tough, I was younger and fitter. Eventually, with blood streaming from both of us, I backed him into a corner and began to hit him with a flurry of punches. Suddenly, I was hit with such force that I was flung halfway across the yard into the urinal. A screw, leaning out of the gallery window, had turned the fire hose on me. After about 30 seconds, he switched it off; the door opened and three screws rushed in and grabbed me, dragging me out of the yard. As I was pushed and pulled to my cell I was given a few resounding whacks on the buttocks with a baton and someone punched me on the back of the head.

After being locked in my cell, I washed myself as best I could in the toilet bowl before scrutinising myself in the mirror sheen dish. Apart from a busted lip, a bleeding nose and a spilt eyebrow, I hadn't fared too badly.

The next day I was taken before Grindlay and charged with fighting.

For a few moments he surveyed me in silence, then he said: "Is it beyond you to stay out of trouble, Killick?"

Although, according to the criminal code, I should have accepted equal blame for the incident, I now lived by my own code of ethics that didn't include covering for a man who, unprovoked, had savagely attacked me while I had been sitting down.

"O'Mealley started it, sir. I merely defended myself."

"You weren't defending yourself when you had him in a corner pummelling the crap out of him."

"O'Mealley is the type of man you have to subdue. If I had eased up on him, he would have flogged me."

"Well, I can't be accused of favouring you, Killick." I've given you too many chances. You can spend a month breaking rocks." He paused. "If it's any consolation, O'Mealley will spend two months down there."

A few weeks later, while I was breaking rocks, Neil Armstrong walked on the Moon. Although most of the world watched it on TV, I was unaware of the historic feat until I returned to the workshop in August.

When O'Mealley returned to the workshop a month after me, he came over and held out his hand. "Let's forget it happened," he said.

I shook his hand. "Might as well." I harboured no grudges against O'Mealley. Anyone who had spent 10 years in H Division could be excused for being full of hate and violence.

Another example of what pent-up hate and bitterness can do to a person, is the case of Stanley Brian Taylor. A balding, solidly built guy of medium height, Stan, originally had been sentenced to nine years for a TAB robbery. But after he and another prisoner, Martin Nagle, escaped from Ararat Gaol, they held up three service stations before being recaptured. Both of them were sentenced to an additional twelve-and-a-half years. Taylor became embittered with the fact that he was doing twenty-one-and-a-half years for four robberies that had netted him a few thousand dollars. He particularly hated police who, he claimed, had often bashed and verballed him. "By the time I get out I'll be nearly 50," he often said. At the time he was 32. "I'll be a stuffed unit. But the dogs will pay. One day I'll walk into Russell Street headquarters with sticks of gelly taped all around me and I'll take all the fuckin' dogs with me."

Although it didn't happen that way, Stanley Brian Taylor tried to take his revenge on the police on 27 March 1986 when, with the aid of three accomplices, he placed a Holden Commodore loaded with 50 sticks of gelignite outside the Russell Street Police Complex. At about 1.00 pm that day the car exploded. Shrapnel from the car and rubble from the police building coated buildings and footpaths blocks away. Twenty-two people were injured in the blast. One of them, a policewoman Angela Rose Taylor, remained in a critical condition in hospital for four weeks before she died. On 13 July 1988 Stanley Taylor, aged 51, was convicted of murder and later sentenced to life. He was convicted mainly on the evidence of Paul Hetzel, a former H Division prisoner who, when the pressure became too much for him, had a habit of swallowing metal utensils so that he would be transferred from H Division to hospital.

During my stay in H Division, Taylor and I became friends. One Monday morning, a public holiday, all prisoners in H Division were ordered to work.

When I came into the workshop Taylor looked at me. "Are you going to cop this shit, John?"

Already angered by the arbitrary order to work on a public holiday, Taylor's attitude was enough to push me beyond the point of caution. "They're not getting any work from me," I said.

"Nor me," Walker said.

The other prisoners stood around, waiting to see what O'Mealley would do. He went to the sink and, while everyone including the screw on the gallery watched, spent a few minutes washing and drying his hands.

I looked at Taylor; he grinned. What was the point of washing your hands before you started work?

After O'Mealley had finished, he walked across to the table, sat down and mumbled, "You can't win. I've been fighting them for 11 years. You can't win." He picked up a broom head and placed it in his vice.

With the exception of Taylor, Walker and me, the others guys sat down and began working. If the Iron Man of Pentridge was prepared to work on a holiday, so were they.

The screw in the gallery, a big, blonde-headed guy who had a reputation for bashing prisoners, stared down at Walker. "Walker! Sit down and start working."

"It's a public holiday," Walker said. "We don't have to work on public holidays."

"I'm giving you a direct order, Walker. Get to work!"

Ignoring him, Walker began to pace the yard. Taylor and I joined him.

"Killick!" the screw yelled. "Are you going to work?"

"I'm not working on a public holiday."

"Oh, aren't you. We'll see about that." He paused. "What about you, Taylor?"

"I'm not working!"

"I'm ordering the three of you to work! This is the last chance you've got!"

"You can't beat 'em fellas," O'Mealley said. "For 11 years I've stood up to them and look at me."

I looked at him. I knew this little man with the giant ego was attempting to save face. "We understand, Bill. You've done your bit." I meant it. He often told anecdotes about how he had single-handedly stood up against the screws, and, although he was an habitual liar, I knew they wouldn't have confined him in H Division for more than ten years unless he had bucked the system.

The screw went away. Taylor began to laugh.

I failed to see the humour in the situation. "We're going to get flogged over this."

"If they flog me," Taylor said, "I'll put an ice pick through their backs the first chance I get."

I wondered where he would get an ice pick.

About five minutes later a group of screws came to the door and ordered Taylor to step out.

Taylor looked at me and grinned. "Just as well my insurance is paid up." He stepped outside.

The screws closed the door. I heard someone order Taylor to march. I turned to Walker, "At least they aren't going to bash us in the passageway."

Walker gave me a solemn look. "A bashing's a bashing, no matter where it happens."

We continued to walk up and down until the screws returned and told me to step out.

Winking at Walker, I stepped out into the passageway. Four screws stood there with batons.

"Right turn, quick march!" one of them yelled.

I was escorted to the chief's office. Carrolan, a thickset, swarthy man who was almost bald, stood behind his desk. He gave me a menacing stare. "You won't do a bit for a bit, eh, Killick?"

"We were ordered to work on a public holiday, sir."

"That's right. And in return you get Friday off. We have to meet a quota by Wednesday and we're behind."

"No one said anything about getting Friday off. We were simply ordered to work."

"Well you should have been told! Don't ever ask me for any favours, Killick."

He had to be kidding. "No, sir."

"Put him in his cell."

Surprisingly, that was the end of the matter. Later, one of the screws told Taylor that it had been a test by Carrolan. To my knowledge it was the first time anyone had refused to work in H Division and got away with it.

53
She's Still Got My Photo

After a few years in H Division I developed severe dandruff and my eyes began to deteriorate. I was convinced that these maladies were a legacy of the food on which I had to exist. Often I had been forced to live for weeks on half-rations, which mainly consisted of bread. During all my time in H Division, I hadn't seen either a piece of fruit or fresh milk.

Concerned about my health I requested the doctor to allow me to buy shampoo and vitamins. The doctor told me I was in a punishment Division, not a holiday resort. Eventually my hair, which had been exceptionally thick, began to thin out.

When my eyes became so painful and inflamed that I couldn't open them the doctor was obligated to arrange for me to immediately be taken to hospital to see an eye specialist.

Handcuffed, I was put in the back of a van and taken to hospital by three of the biggest guards in H Division. As the four of us walked through the hospital waiting room I was aware of the inquisitive stares.

At least we didn't have to wait around. A nurse immediately ushered us into the doctor's surgery.

After an extensive examination of my eyes the specialist informed me I had iritis. Unless it was correctly treated I could go blind.

When I told him how I often had to subsist on half-rations he was genuinely outraged.

"I thought those days were long gone in our penal system," he said, looking at the guards.

He prescribed me some special eye drops, fresh fruit and a course of vitamins. From that point, although I had an occasional mild attack of iritis, my eyes were generally okay. But the dandruff persisted.

One of the most inhumane aspects of life in H Division, particularly while in solitary confinement in the labour yards, was the sensory deprivation resulting in a gradual erosion of emotions. Existing for long periods of time without talking to someone can psychologically damage people and all of us, even the hardest of men, needed to be able to occasionally touch another person.

The importance of touch was one day emphasised to me during one of my spells in the labour yards. I heard the screws hassling a prisoner in the yard next to mine.

"You little queer," one of them said.

"I'm sorry, sir," the prisoner sobbed. He sounded very young.

"No use being sorry. Why do you let other men fuck you?"

"I don't know, sir."

I heard a whack and the prisoner cry out.

"Because you're a little fuckin' queer!"

I glanced up at the screw in the gallery. He was staring down at the proceedings in the next yard, an amused look on his face

Before they departed, I heard the screws hit the sobbing prisoner a few more times.

Waiting until the screw in the gallery had walked away, I used my large hammer to force out one of the bottom bricks of the wall. Kneeling down, I looked through the hole. A slightly built blonde-haired boy was sitting on a pile of rocks crying. He looked to be about 16.

"Hey, kid," I said, softly. "Come over here."

Startled, he looked across to the hole in the wall.

"Quick, come over here," I said.

He stopped crying and hurried over. Apart from a red welt on his cheek, he was unmarked. They must have hit him around the body. He was pretty enough to be a girl. What chance did he have in a maximum security gaol? How could they justify sending a kid like this to H Division and bashing him?

I glanced up at the gallery, the screw wasn't in sight. "Listen, kid, how long are you down here for?"

"Two weeks."

"Well, they'll be tough on you for a few days, then they'll drop off. They didn't hurt you badly, did they?"

He thought about it. "No…but I'm scared. I'm really scared." He again started to cry.

"Give me your hand." I put my arm through the hole. He gripped my hand; I held his hand for about a minute than released my grip and withdrew my arm. I looked through the hole. He had stopped crying.

"Give me a smile," I said.

He smiled and I thought maybe he should have been born a girl.

"I have to go, kid. Don't be scared, you'll be all right. You've come through the worst of it. I'll see you tomorrow. Are you okay?"

"Yes. Thank you. I'll see you tomorrow."

I pushed the brick back into place. I didn't see him again. The next day someone else was placed in the adjoining yard. But the incident changed my attitude about homosexuals. Although I'd never be able to tolerate the deviates who loitered in toilets and parks with the intention of picking up boys, I realised that some homosexuals were born that way and no one had the right to criticise or harass them because of it.

One day while we were making brooms in the workshop, the door opened and Carrolan stepped inside. He was visibly upset.

"You men who have been in this Division a long time will be distressed to hear that Mr Clark passed away this morning."

The yard was silent. Carrolan nodded, then walked out. After the door had been locked and we could hear them walking up the passageway, Walker yelled: "Hooray!"

We heard the screws hurry back. The door opened. Carrolan stood there staring at us, his eyes narrowed, his face livid. I noticed that his hands were trembling. After about 20 seconds he slammed the door and went away. Although Carrolan never mentioned the incident again, for the next week everyone in the workshop was put on half rations.

Most people would consider Walker's actions callous and reprehensible, but I could understand what motivated him to cheer at the news of Clark's death. For more than ten years Clark had been the commander of an autonomous regime that had abused its power by unlawfully inflicting violence, terror and humiliation on its oppressed victims. Walker had spent nearly three years under Clark's regime. I wondered how many other men in the workshop silently identified with Walker's cheering.

In May 1970, O'Mealley was transferred to B Division. He had survived eleven-and-a half-years in H Division. Although we shook hands before he left, we both knew it was a charade. I despised him and I knew the feeling was reciprocal. After his release in 1979 he had a book published that nearly became a bestseller. In one of the chapters he took the opportunity to publically malign me. He also plagiarised word-for-word nearly 40 pages of American author Willard Motley's *Knock On Any Door*, a bestseller in the early '50s. Unfortunately for O'Mealley I recognised the text and exposed his plagiarism to the media. O'Mealley, lampooned by the media, went into hiding in Queensland. His book, *The Man They Couldn't Break* was taken from the bookshelves and pulped. *The Man They Couldn't Break* had been well and truly broken.

Not long after O'Mealley went to B Division, Ponton was transferred to A Division. Cormick, who couldn't take the pressure of H Division life, had again been sent to J Ward.

O'Mealley had been gone a few months when I received a letter from Cathy. Included with the letter was a large coloured studio photo. Although I hadn't seen a photo of her for over four years, she was almost as I had imagined she would be at 23. She wasn't beautiful in the true sense of the word; the pretty girl face had matured to display character and determination. Her figure had filled out perfectly and the short hair had been allowed to grow almost down to her waist.

She wrote that she had forgiven me for what had happened and if I still wanted to be friends she would correspond. Although she had been going with a guy for three years, it was over. She was working at two jobs and had an apartment of her own and a kitten named Chow and she had to pay an extra $20 a month to keep Chow. Mildred was now 18 and engaged. How long would it be before I was released?

After reading her letter and studying the photo, my emotions were in turmoil. Although I was ecstatic that she had written, all the old memories, hopes and dreams came rushing back. It had taken a long time, but after four years in Pentridge, the majority of it in H Division, I finally had managed to erect a barrier between her and my thoughts. Her letter had not only penetrated the barrier, it had shattered it. Confronted with the knowledge that for three years she had loved another man, I again cursed myself for having been such a fool. My only consolation was she hadn't married.

I immediately replied to her letter:

> Dear Cathy,
>
> It's good to hear from you. I was getting worried. I know there have been a lot of mail strikes over there, but even so ...
>
> Let's have a look at this photo. Hmm ... not bad. Oh, all right, I admit it, you're beautiful. But don't get a swollen head over it because you are still an imp – I can see it in your eyes. When I picked you out at fifteen I figured you'd grow up to look the way you do now. Wish I could judge racehorses as well.
>
> I don't know what to say about you going with someone for three years. I've no right to be jealous but I think I am a bit. I'm also a bit of an idiot. Anyway, how did he manage to keep all the other guys away? He must have been a special guy. Are you sure it's over?
>
> I've got two years to go. Time has passed fairly quickly. I've managed to stay out of trouble of late.
>
> Did you keep any of the letters or tapes I sent you?"

A few weeks later I received the reply.

> Dear John,
>
> I'm so glad you wrote. When I checked my mail and saw your letter my hands were shaking. I wasn't sure how you would react to hearing from me after so long.

> John, after what happened, I destroyed all your letters, but I've still got your photo and the ridiculous tapes you sent me. No matter what happened, you were my first love and no one can take that away from either of us.
>
> If there is anything you need while you are in there, let me know and I'll do my best to get it to you.
>
> It's a shame you still have two years to go. I suppose if you hadn't had that trouble a few years ago you would nearly be due out!
>
> When I was going with Paul he took me to the Playboy Club, where he is a member, and I was given membership as an honorary playmate. And yes, it's definitely over.
>
> John, no matter what you've done, I give you credit for picking yourself up and trying again.

For a while we corresponded regularly and with great enthusiasm. I was only permitted to write one four-page letter per fortnight and I crammed as much optimism, humour and reminiscing as I possibly could with minute printing. She usually replied with long letters and the rapport we once had in abundance quickly returned. But although I was again hopelessly in love with her, I was reticent about expressing it. The pending extradition to Sydney with the prospect of another long prison term weighed heavily on me. I was concerned that if I made her cognisant with all the facts she would become disillusioned and give up on me. But I also sensed that she was puzzled as to why I didn't write my usual love letters.

In April 1971 she wrote that she would be visiting Australia in 1972 and that she would arrange her holiday to coincide with my release.

I had no choice. I had to tell her. Whatever else I did, never again would I lie to her. That night I wrote and explained to her that I would be extradited to Sydney for numerous bank robberies and that I could be in gaol for another seven or eight years. Under the circumstances there was no point in her coming to Australia. It tore my heart out to write that but for once in my life I was putting someone else's interests before my own. I loved her and didn't want her to suffer because of me.

When she replied, she was to the point.

> Dear John,
>
> Just how many banks have you robbed? And I didn't say I was coming to Australia just to see you. I was going to visit my grandmother in Fairfield …

This time I knew that she was lying. I lost my cool.

> Dear Cathy,
>
> Sorry! I don't know how many banks I've robbed, I haven't got a calculator.
>
> Gee, I'm sorry about the misunderstanding. I thought you were coming to Australia to see me. I didn't realise you were actually coming on a family safari to see your grandmother. But why talk in past tense? 'I was going to visit my grandmother.' I know I've been a naughty boy, but what did your grandma do to make you cancel that trip?
>
> Oh well. Maybe you'll go back to the guy who made you an honorary bunny.

It didn't take her long to reply.

> Dear John,
>
> There is no point in us corresponding, apparently we can't communicate.

I had expected that letter. I hadn't left her much choice. But the way I felt about her wasn't something that could be turned on and off like a tap. The emotional pain of losing her became physical in its intensity. Crying uncontrollably, I fell to the floor, oblivious to everything but the pain that seemed to be tearing out my insides. Then it was gone and I knew that something inside me had finally died. That gut-wrenching pain and uncontrolled sobbing had been the death throes of a dying love. Replacing the pain was an emptiness that would remain with me for the rest of my life. The young man and the innocent girl who had fallen in love with each other at the bingo game an eternity ago were both gone forever. The girl now a liberated young American who wanted a lot more from life than I could offer; and the young man…well, he was long gone…and I dreaded to even contemplate what he had become. But I knew that if I was to remain sane, I had to forget about Cathy.

At least she still had my photo and the ridiculous tapes.

54
Riots In H Division

Under the command of Carrolan and Lindgren, a new form of work was introduced in H Division. Termed 'doing buttons' by the prisoners, it consisted of putting metal pins in small, plastic electrical components. Not only were the men in the other workshop given the task of doing buttons all day, but half of the labour yard prisoners were given the choice of doing this menial job instead of the more physically demanding breaking of rocks. After a while pressure was applied on prisoners to do buttons at night in their cells. Although most of them assented, Taylor, Walker and I refused to work in our cells. From that point the quantity of our meals decreased until we were eventually existing on half-rations. We persuaded the other men in our workshop to refrain from working at night in their cells. We also passed word to the other workshop, trying to convince the men that doing buttons at night was slave labour.

It wasn't long before Taylor, Walker and I were relegated to the labour yards. When I asked Lindgren why we were being punished he regarded me with undisguised hostility: "You and your mates are playing a dangerous game, Killick. That's all I'll say."

I requested to see Grindlay. After a few days I was taken to Carrolan's office where Grindlay was sitting behind the desk.

"What's your problem, Killick?"

"I've been put in the labour yards and I don't know why, sir."

Grindlay smiled. "I think you do know why."

I stared at him. "I haven't been charged with anything."

He met my gaze, his eyes implacable, hard. "We received information that you, Taylor and Walker were going to take over the Division, put on the officers' uniforms and walk out of here."

"Whoever told you that should be doing a short story course," I said, stunned.

Grindlay wasn't amused. "You'll be down the labour yards long enough to write a novel."

I tried to contain my rage. "We're down in the labour yards because we won't do buttons in our cells at night like all the others."

"You are confined to the labour yards for conspiracy to escape." He turned to Carrolan. "Return him to the yards."

Although Taylor, Walker and I were never charged with an offence, we spent the next three months in the labour yards.

When the Royal Commission into *Allegations of Brutality and Ill Treatment at H.M. Prison Pentridge* was concluded, the commissioner Kenneth Jenkinson QC commented in his Report (page 82): "… Watson had been refusing to do buttons in his cell at night, perhaps at the urging of S B Taylor or Killick, who did not deny neophytes in H Division the benefit or their advice…"

He went on: "… Watson and Giles were publicly rebuked in an industry yard by Senior Prison Officer Lindgren for inciting other prisoners to decline the nocturnal cellular work on buttons (as Killick was also rebuked on other occasions) …"

For some reason the screws in H Division (particularly Lindgren) were obsessive in their desire to coerce prisoners into doing buttons, not only during the day, but in their cells at night. Although many of us suspected that the screws must have been in receipt of some form of incentive bonus for increased production, it was never proven.

To my knowledge, the first man to openly display total disregard for the regimental order of H Division was Steven Sellars. From the moment he arrived in the Division he ignored all orders, despite being bashed. That night he abused the night screw for hours, laughing at his outraged demands to be quiet. The following morning I heard him again being bashed. This absurd situation went on for about a week. Every night he would yell out that he again had been bashed. He refused to march, he refused to salute and if they wanted him to go to the labour yards they had to carry him. His stubborn refusal to comply in any way with the rules presented a major problem to the authorities and, considering that he had broken nearly every rule in the book, he didn't remain in H Division for long. Although it's doubtful if he would have got away with it during the Clark/Hitler regime, Sellars had demonstrated through sheer guts, determination and a touch of madness that there was a chink in the armour of the dreaded H Division.

Another guy to hammer a chink in the armour was Christopher Dale Flannery, the two-bit crim who was later to gain notoriety as a feared hit man, earning the nickname Mr Rent-A-Kill.

On entering H Division Flannery began a hunger strike. Each night he would yell out, as Sellars had done, claiming to have been bashed. He vowed he would remain on the hunger strike until he either died or they let him out of H Division. But his resolve soon dissipated and he began accepting meals. Although he later told people that he had been the first person to categorically challenge the system in H Division, that person was, in fact, Steven Sellars, not Christopher Dale Flannery.

On 13 January 1972, five prisoners were brought to H Division after a fight on a farm. If Sellars and Flannery found chinks in the armour of H Division, these five guys were responsible for it being stripped to its underwear - an embarrassment from which it never would recover. The men, M Buhlert, A Donnini, D Kane, L Prendergast and W Prendergast were, at the time of their entry into H Division, intoxicated on a home brew made mainly from potatoes on the farm. From the moment they arrived in the Division they noisily proclaimed their intention to flout the rules and discipline.

That night they called out for every prisoner to join them. "It'll be the end of H Division!" they proclaimed.

Beginning with the first cell, they began calling out the cell numbers, demanding to know if the occupants would join them. Those in the first five cells, including Taylor and Walker, accepted the invitation. Then it was my turn.

"Number six?"

"This is Killick," I yelled. "Count me out!"

For a few moments there was stunned silence, then someone shouted: "You mean you're not going to support us?"

"It's too late for me," I yelled. "I get out this year, then I've got extradition to Sydney."

"We've all got something to lose!" an outraged voice bawled.

"Ahh, fuck him!" someone else shouted. "If he's lost his nerve leave him out."

"I haven't lost my fucking nerve! I've been down here for three and a half years! Where were you guys then? When me, Taylor and Walker jacked up about working on a public holiday no one gave us support. When we jacked up about doing buttons in the cell at night we were thrown down into the yards for three months. I've done my fucking bit!"

"John's right!" Taylor shouted. "He's done his bit. If he fucks up now he could get another 20 years in Sydney. You stay out of it, mate."

"Yeah, you don't have to prove anything, John!" Walker yelled.

"Yeah, okay," one of the instigators yelled. "Killick's out. That's fair enough; he's done his bit. What about you number seven?"

"I'm with you!"

Although some of the prisoners later reneged on their avowed allegiance to the rebellion, only one other guy, Donald Thompson, categorically refused to join the rebels claiming that he was expecting to be transferred to A Division. A few weeks later he was transferred.

From that night, with almost the entire Division united in rebellion, H Division was never the same. The doors of the cells opened inwardly; many of the prisoners barricaded their cells by wedging their beds in the doorframes effectively jamming the doors. To gain entry to the cells the screws were forced to use oxy welding equipment to cut the hinges from the doors.

Another ploy adopted by the prisoners was to allow their taps to run all night. The water rushed out from under the doors, drenching the

Division. Screws were insulted, abused, ridiculed and laughed at. Some of the prisoners mockingly pleaded to be bashed – so that they could instruct their lawyers to issue writs for unlawful assault. One of them, Robert Bertie Kidd, was in regular contact with top shelf lawyers and continually challenged the screws to bash him.

I once heard him say: "I'll see you in the cell next to me. That's where you belong you mongrels."

The possibility of having to defend, in a court of law, the questionable administration of H Division prompted the authorities to instruct that a no bash policy be implemented in H Division. But the belief that they had outside support gave the rebels boldness.

A few nights after the rebellion began, Grindlay came to the Division. Using a microphone, he demanded to know what the men thought they could achieve by their actions. Taylor, who had elected himself as spokesman for the rebels, proclaimed their intention of continuing the revolt until H Division was closed down.

"That will never happen," Grindlay said. "But if you stop this mutinous behaviour, I promise you I'll arrange for a meeting between the Minister for Welfare and an elected representative for the prisoners. We'll sit down at a table and discuss in a civilised manner any complaints that you have about H Division."

"What good would that do?" Taylor asked.

"It would do a lot of good. I can assure you that the authorities are prepared to give you men some concessions, but not until you stop this nonsense."

"We wouldn't believe a fucking word you said, Grindlay," someone shouted. "Up with the rebellion, down with H Division!"

A roar of assent went up.

"Wait a minute!" Grindlay cut in. He sounded piqued. "Why don't we ask Killick if I keep my promises or not? What have you got to say about it, Killick?"

Fuck this. No matter how hard I tried, people wouldn't leave me alone. Here we were, in the middle of the most serious rebellion in the history of Pentridge and the Governor wanted me to give him a character reference!

"What about it, John?" Taylor yelled. "Can we trust him?"

I came to the door. "I can only say what happened to me!" I shouted. "On the night I tried to escape and finished up barricaded in E Division, the Governor gave me his assurance that I wouldn't be bashed if I handed myself in. I know that he did everything in his power to ensure that that promise was honoured."

"But was it honoured?" someone queried.

"Yes, it was."

"There you are, men," Grindlay said. "I'm a man of my word. Let's settle this dispute at the conference table."

Eventually the men agreed to stop the rebellion pending the outcome of the proposed meeting. Taylor was elected as spokesman for the prisoners.

The Minister of Welfare did come to H Division and talks were held. Prisoners were permitted to declare their complaints and requests for the Minister through Taylor.

An order dated 28 January 1972 and signed by Grindlay, gave the following concessions:

> Prisoners will be permitted to write one letter per week. Formerly it was one a fortnight.
>
> Prisoners will not be required to wear hats.
>
> Prisoners will work five days a week.
>
> Prisoners will be issued with two clean shirts each week.
>
> Prisoners will not be employed to do buttons in their cells.
>
> All medical treatment and tablets at H Division will be administered by a Hospital Attendant who will attend H Division on all occasions when prescribed treatment is to be administered.
>
> Labour yard prisoners will shower on all working days.

Security prisoners will shower daily.

A Governor will attend one run-in or run-out each day and see all prisoners.

No movement of prisoners will take place unless the Chief Prison Officer or the Senior Prison Officer is in attendance.

Other changes were introduced. Saluting was abolished and prisoners were not required to swing their arms shoulder high when marching.

Although these changes were important, they avoided the two main issues: the bashing of prisoners and the confinement to H Division for trivial matters such as possession of a race guide.

The rebellion continued.

On my 30th birthday, 13 February 1972, I was granted an interview with Grindlay. I came straight to the point. "I'm requesting to be transferred to B Division, sir."

Grindlay raised his eyebrow. "What makes you think I'd grant you such a request?"

I'm sure he was waiting for me to mention I had refrained from joining the rebellion and that I had supported his assertion to the rebels that he was a man of his word. I knew that if I referred to these matters as a reason for me to gain release from H Division, it would be marked on my papers that I had done these things solely to get out of H Division.

I had decided to try another tack. "Well, as you know, sir, I'll be extradited to Sydney in another seven or eight months. I'm concerned that if I arrive at Long Bay straight from H Division it will be sufficient reason for the authorities to send me to Grafton. I've made every effort to rehabilitate and I don't think I deserve to be sent to Grafton."

Grindlay nodded his agreement. "You've got a point there. Grafton is the last place you need." He hesitated, then said: "Yes, I'm inclined to agree with you. You can go up next week."

Trying to conceal my exhilaration, I said: "Thank you, sir."

On 22 February, I was transferred to B Division. Although, with automatic remissions, I had less than eight months remaining on my sentence, I was allocated a cell in the high security Six Tier. A lot of prisoners, some of whom I didn't know, gave me items such as chocolates, tobacco, tea, sugar, books, magazines, etc, to "put you on your feet". One guy even gave me a race guide. There are various ways of being popular among fellow prisoners; apparently hitting a screw with an iron bar is one of them.

On 23 May 1972, Kenneth Jenkinson QC was appointed by Order in Council to head a Board of Inquiry into *Allegations of Brutality and Ill Treatment at H.M. Prison Pentridge*, an important stipulation being that only allegations of events having taken place since 22 May 1970 would be considered. Whether by accident or design, this ruling effectively prevented from giving evidence the man who had the most to reveal: William John O'Mealley had been released from H Division on 4 May 1970.

With the announcement of the intended Inquiry, solicitors and their assistants came to Pentridge to interview potential witnesses, both prisoners and screws. After learning of the decree prohibiting the giving of evidence about events in H Division prior to 22 May 1970, I decided to abstain from testifying. I would be unable to mention either the savage beating I had received in 1966, or the persecution and ill treatment I had undergone during the Clark/Hitler regime. It would be almost impossible for prisoners to prove allegations of brutality in H Division. It would be their word against the word of the screws. As far as I was concerned, the Inquiry would be little more than a whitewash of the Victorian penal system.

But with Peter Walker refusing to give evidence and O'Mealley ineligible, a lot of pressure was applied on me to testify. Excluding O'Mealley and Walker, I had spent more time in H Division than anyone else. Most of the prisoners felt it was imperative for me to give evidence. Conceding that I might be able to achieve something for the prisoners' cause, I consented to give testimony. I was called to give evidence on 18 September 1972. I told the Inquiry: "There is no place like H Division to illustrate man's inhumanity to man." I also stated that no one could spend a few months in H Division without undergoing a change in personality. "Some may become bitter, revengeful, others unstable and suffer breakdowns," I said.

Despite having answered truthfully and without exaggeration all questions put to me, I was unable to substantiate my claims that since 22 May 1970, bashings and ill treatment of prisoners had occurred in H Division.

The following day *The Age* gave a brief account of my evidence under the heading 'Man's inhumanity to man'. The article mentioned that I had described the NSW Black Peter system of punishment where prisoners were locked in a darkened cell and starved. I told the Inquiry that I would prefer to spend three days in Black Peter than several weeks in H Division. This article was to later cause me problems in NSW.

Although more than 100 prisoners gave evidence at the Inquiry, very few were able to substantiate their claims of ill treatment and brutality in H Division. In his Report, Jenkinson QC stated:

> ... A campaign of disobedience, threat, abuse and provocation was instituted and, with intermissions, maintained by H Division prisoners for the succeeding nine months ... (p. 84)
>
> Some moderation of the misconduct of H Division prisoners might have been detected after April, but violent and quite irrational indiscipline, as well as cunningly executed torment of prison officers continued during the middle of the year ... (p. 85)

In support of the revolt in H Division there were disturbances and an occasional fire in both B Division and C Division. Protests also were held outside the gaol by an ever-increasing body of supporters demanding an inquiry into the entire Victorian Penal System. Eventually, the authorities succumbed to the pressure.

As Grindlay later commented at the Royal Commission:

> ... the prisoners, when they felt at long last they had somebody outside working for them, gained a hell of a lot of confidence. (Transcript p. 2168)

In his Report, Commissioner Jenkinson stated:

> ... the Governor and his senior officers insisted, the Board infers, that the use of force be avoided by the officers. On several occasions force was used by prison officers against prisoners, but not unlawfully or imprudently. Finding themselves conceded so many inches, the rebels took miles. Their behaviour became more outrageous. Labour yard walls were smashed with hammers, they barricaded themselves in their cells for several days, smashed cell windows and furniture and screamed foul abuse which they knew was being recorded by tape recorders." (p. 85)

The report proved conclusively that when prisoners are isolated in special gaols ostensibly for security but, more often than not, for punishment, there will always be warders who will take advantage of the powers granted to them to abuse, humiliate, degrade and unlawfully assault prisoners. The report also revealed that many people subjected to even a short period of humiliation, degradation and violence become suicidal.

The rebellion demonstrated that sooner or later prisoners would revolt against oppression and inhumane conditions.

Not one prison officer named in the report spent a day in gaol.

55

Long Bay
(1972)

A few weeks after testifying at the Inquiry, I was extradited to New South Wales. While I was on the plane the two escorting plain-clothes cops from Sydney refused to remove the handcuffs. When I complained to the hostess, one of the cops, a solidly built young guy who played football for Penrith, said: "If we take the handcuffs off him we'll finish up in Cuba."

The hostess gave me a horrified look and walked away.

Probably for security reasons, I had been allocated the window seat. The senior cop, who seemed an amiable type, tried a few times to involve me in conversation, but I didn't reciprocate. It was the first time I had been on an aeroplane and after six and a half years in maximum security I found the sights enthralling.

Approaching Sydney the senior cop said: "Take a good look at Sydney by night. It could be another seven years before you see it again."

On arrival at Mascot, another cop was waiting for us. As the four of us walked towards the exit I saw an old man with a walking stick approaching us. Shocked, I realised it was Dad. Apart from having aged considerably, he seemed to have shrunk in stature. Although I had written to him the previous week informing him of my impending extradition, I hadn't expected him to be at the airport.

Stopping, I turned towards him. "Good day, Dad!"

He gave me a sad look. "You've aged, Johnny."

I realised the last time he had seen me, my now predominantly white hair had been jet black. I was reminded of the classic line in Ricky Nelson's recent comeback hit *Garden Party*:

"… we didn't look the same …"

The footballer pushed me towards the exit. "Come on, let's go."

"That's my father! I haven't seen him for seven years!"

"He can visit you when you get to the Bay."

"Why don't you take the handcuffs off him, you mongrels!" Dad yelled. At least he hadn't lost his spirit.

I was half-shoved, half-dragged through the exit. A car drove up and I was bundled into it. I looked out the window and saw the forlorn old man who was my father waving as we drove away. A cold rage surged through me. For a while I nurtured it. One day they would have to turn me loose and then it would be my turn.

After spending the night in a cell at Central Police Station I was taken to court the following morning and charged with the armed robberies in 1966 of two banks (Canley Heights and Cabramatta). The magistrate remanded me in custody.

On arrival at Long Bay I was taken to the MRP (Metropolitan Remand Prison) which, during my last stay at Long Bay, had been a women's gaol. It consisted of three large cell blocks, but I wasn't given the opportunity to see much of it. I was escorted to a cell in one of the wings and locked up. A cardboard sign had been taped on the outside of my door. It read: 'To be fed only by the CPO' (Chief Prison Officer).

For some reason I had been placed in solitary confinement.

The next morning the door was opened and a CPO handed me a bowl of porridge and a tin mug of black tea. I noticed two other screws standing nearby.

"I want to see the Governor," I said.

"If he wants to see you, he'll let you know about it," the CPO said, and slammed the door.

I might as well be back in H Division. I had to keep my cool. It was possible they were trying to push me into a confrontation to enable them to justify sending me to Grafton. It would have been marked on my papers that I had assaulted a prison officer with an iron bar. I would have to be careful.

About an hour later the screws escorted me to the MRP front yards, which were almost identical to the segregation yards at both Bathurst and the other section at Long Bay where I had spent time. Although some of the yards were occupied by several prisoners, I was given a yard to myself.

After the screws had gone, one of the guys in the adjoining yard called out: "Hey, mate! What have they got you in the yards for?"

"I don't know. I've just been extradited from Pentridge. Maybe they think I'm a security risk."

"Ha ha. Aren't we all! I'm Bobby Merrit. My mate's name's Warwick."

I soon discovered that Bob, an athletic, light-skinned Aborigine a few years my junior was, unlike Warwick, an intelligent guy. During the next few months, although we never occupied the same yard, we managed to have numerous conversations. I related in detail some of the stories I had written. He told me of some of the ideas he had for a book he wanted to write about Aborigines. A few years later he wrote a brilliant play entitled *The Cakeman* which received rave reviews in Australia and overseas.

During my first day in the yards I received a visit from Dad. Although we were separated by wire mesh and a screw stood listening to everything we said, I was elated to see him. During my long confinement in Pentridge I had steeled myself in preparation for the day when I would be informed that Dad had died. A few times I had been unexpectedly called to the Governor's office and my heart had been thumping with fear as my mind tried to prepare for the dreaded news.

Now I savoured the fact that the tough old bugger had survived. Although 'we didn't look the same', we were soon talking as though I'd never been away.

"Your old man nearly did something silly the other night when those bulls were shoving you around," he said. "I was close enough to the first bull to go whack, whack with the walking stick! Would've broke both his kneecaps. But I didn't want to get you into any more trouble than what you're already in."

The screw was staring at Dad, uncertain whether he was joking or not.

I smiled. "It would've been something to see, but it's just as well you didn't do it, Dad."

"How are they treating you, Johnny?"

"Can't complain."

"How many bank jobs have they got you on?"

"Only one. That's all I did." I intended pleading not guilty to robbing the Cabramatta bank.

Dad gave the screw a conspiratorial wink. The screw's face suffused with colour and he looked away. I nearly burst out laughing.

"How long do you think you'll get, Johnny?"

"Probably three or four years," I lied.

The tight security that had been placed on me augured for the imposition of a heavy sentence.

Dad gave me a solemn look. "Whatever you get, I promise you I'll be there when you come through those gates."

A sadness permeated my being. I met his gaze. "I'll hold you to that, Dad."

For a few moments we stared at each other.

The screw looked at his watch. "You'll have to finish up in a couple of minutes."

"I'll leave you some money," Dad said. "How much do you need?"

"Nothing. I managed to save a couple of hundred in Pentridge."

"It took you seven years, Johnny." He made it sound as though I'd gone whaling and returned with gold fish.

"Not quite, Dad. Not quite."

When I returned to the yard I calculated that for the past six and a half years I had managed to save sixty cents a week.

A few days later I was escorted to an office where a tall, distinguished-looking man who appeared to be in his fifties sat behind a mahogany table. On his left sat a middle-aged minister of religion. Next to the minister a guy dressed in an ill-fitting suit, who looked to be just out of college, sat staring curiously at me. The only items on the table were a small tape recorder and a manila folder.

The distinguished-looking guy introduced himself as Mr Stuart, head of the Long Bay Prison Complex. He told me to sit down. Switching on the tape recorder he introduced the minister and the young man who was a reporter for the *Daily Telegraph*.

Puzzled and wary, I nodded acknowledgement but remained silent.

"Now, John," Stuart said. "I'm going to ask you a few questions about some statements you made at the Prison Inquiry in Victoria. The questions and answers will be recorded." He paused and with a nod indicated the minister. "The reverend is here as a neutral witness to see that your answers are made of your own free will and that no threats or inducements are made. Have any threats or inducements been made to you since you entered the prison?"

"No, sir."

He nodded with satisfaction. "Some of the evidence you gave in Victoria was erroneous and has caused the department some embarrassment." Pausing, he opened the manila folder.

"It was reported in an article I have here from the *Daily Telegraph*, 19 September. I'm going to give you the opportunity to rectify the mistakes so that the reporter can print a retraction."

I stared at him. "I told the truth at the Inquiry, sir."

"You're in the front yards at the moment, aren't you?" Although his voice was calm, his look was intimidating.

"Yes sir, although I have no idea why."

"You are there for security reasons." He paused. "You told the Inquiry in Victoria that prisoners in New South Wales were put into solitary confinement stark naked. The fact is that no prisoner in this

State is forced to spend time in the pound or anywhere else without clothing."

"It happened to me at Bathurst, sir. I'll never forget it. I nearly froze to death."

I glanced at the reporter. He was smiling. The minister looked embarrassed.

Stuart stared at me. "I want you to think hard about this, Killick. It's very important. It was, after all, a long time ago."

He paused, his eyes narrowing to slits. "Now, are you sure you couldn't be mistaken about this?"

I calmly held his gaze. "I'm absolutely positive. I remember every minute of it."

Switching the recorder off, he looked at the two screws standing by the door. "Take him back to the yards."

As I was escorted to the yards one of the screws, a young guy with freckles and buckteeth said, "You should have told him what he wanted to hear."

The last thing I needed was a lecture on how to survive in gaol from a screw that looked like Bucky Beaver. "I'll bet you do the psychology quizzes in the *Women's Weekly*," I said.

The other screw grinned; Bucky flushed. "You'll finish up in Grafton, fella," he said. "They'll soon teach you some respect."

I didn't comment. The way things were going, I was a first class candidate for Grafton. No point making it easier for them by clashing with this guy.

As predicted by Bucky, I remained in the yards without an explanation as to why I was being punished or any indication of the amount of time I would have to spend there. Every morning I requested to see the Governor.

After about a week I was escorted to his office where he was seated behind a desk cluttered with papers and documents. He wore glasses, had thinning grey hair and looked to be in his sixties.

He gave me a benign smile. "Ah, Killick. I've been meaning to see you for a while."

His friendly attitude surprised me. He seemed more like an elderly neighbour whom I'd known for years, rather than Governor of a maximum security prison who had me confined in segregation. "I've been trying to see you since I got here, sir."

"Yes, I'm not always here you know. And if I saw everyone who wanted to see me, I'd never get any work done."

"I simply want to know why I'm in segregation. I came from Pentridge where I was in a normal routine part of the gaol."

He nodded sadly. "I'm afraid it's out of my hands. You are classed as an unacceptable risk in the mainstream of prisoners."

"But the authorities in Pentridge didn't see it that way."

"I'm afraid they did."

Pausing, he picked up a document on his desk and handed it to me. He said, "I shouldn't be doing this, but under the circumstances I feel justified in showing you this report."

As I read it, I had to contain the rage inside me. It was a report about me by the head of security at Pentridge. It began by claiming that I was the most dangerous man he'd ever met. Apart from listing the escape attempt at Hawthorn Court and the later attempt in E Division where I had assaulted De Boer, he attributed to me a number of serious offences committed in Pentridge that I hadn't done. One of these, the stabbing of a gaol bookmaker in B Division had occurred in 1970 while I had been in H Division. If any one man had committed the offences listed in the report, the authorities would have been justified in chaining him to the wall. No wonder they had put a sign on my cell door stating: "To be fed only by the CPO."

I handed the Governor the report. "Most of the things listed there are outright lies. They actually happened but were committed by other prisoners. This report is a payback for my having testified at the Inquiry."

He held out his hand in a placating gesture. "Unfortunately we can only act on information received. I've got six months to go before I retire. I can't risk having someone with your reputation doing something that could ruin my career."

"I suppose I'll go to Grafton after I'm sentenced."

"That's not my decision. But I give you my word that if you behave yourself and don't cause any trouble, I'll recommend that you be placed in routine maximum security after you are sentenced."

Opposed to the malicious report from Pentridge and, no doubt, an adverse report from Stuart, I doubted that this man's qualified recommendation would carry much weight. Might as well try for something tangible. "Could I be put in the same yard as Bobby Merrit?"

He gave me a shocked look. "I couldn't do that. If I put you two together I could have a mass escape on my hands."

I stared at him, trying to will him to understand the frustration and disgust I felt at the entire farcical situation.

He lowered his gaze. "Just go along quietly," he said softly. "Things are never as bad as they seem."

When I returned to the yard I called out to Bob. "Hey, Bob! Why are you in the yards?"

"I escaped. They had a lot of trouble catching me. The little piggies reckon I'm a baddie."

I laughed. He probably had a fictitious report in his file similar to mine. The false malicious report on me was just another example to me of what the authorities could do to people in gaol.

56

A Good Judge
(1972)

Being back in Sydney, even if it was in solitary confinement, had me reminiscing about the old days and how I had met Cathy at the housie game after the split with Irene. I decided to write to Maureen, the then voluptuous teenager who had unwittingly triggered the blow up with Irene. Maureen would be about 25 now. Maybe she would visit me? There had always been an attraction between us.

A few weeks after I had sent the letter I was called to the visiting area. It was Maureen's elder sister, Joye. Although I hadn't seen her for nearly seven years she, at 31, looked much the same to me: pretty rather than beautiful.

I could see she was a bit shocked to see me with mostly white hair. Probably, to her, I had aged 20 years.

The guard stood nearby, watching and listening as we stared at each other through the wire mesh.

"Hello, John. I've come about the letter you sent to Maureen."

"Well, it's great to see you, Joye. You look great. What's with Maureen, she married or something?"

"John, I've got some bad news: Maureen's dead. She died of cancer a few years ago."

The past seven years had inured me to accept bad news as a part of life, but this time I felt as though I'd been hit in the solar plexus. When I spoke my voice sounded cracked and dried, as though it was someone else talking. "I just can't believe it. She was so vibrant and full of life."

"It was terrible, John. She wasted away before our eyes."

I shook my head, not wanting to picture it. "My letter must have upset the family."

"No. We knew you didn't know. But it was weird seeing a personal letter written to her years after her death."

I nodded. So many things had happened in the past seven years of which I had no knowledge.

"She was beautiful, John. She had so many guys chasing her."

For a while we talked about Maureen, then I asked her about her marriage.

"Bob and I split up years ago. He's in Queensland. I'm moving there next month so the girls can see him."

"You're going back to him?"

"Definitely not. It's just for the girls."

I thought that would be the last time I would see Joye, but we still had a few more chapters to play out.

In the yards the weeks passed slowly. Dad visited me a few times, but after a while we found it difficult to keep a conversation going, particularly with a screw listening in. Instead of visiting me, Dad settled for sending an occasional letter.

When Labor won the Federal Election on 2 December, Bob was ecstatic. "Old Gough's going to look after the Aboriginal people," he said.

"Yeah, he'll do a lot for this country," I said. "But it won't help us."

A few weeks after Gough Whitlam became Prime Minister I was taken to Darlinghurst District Court for sentencing on the Canley Heights bank robbery.

Although I pleaded guilty, the prosecutor emphasised to Judge Hicks that my accomplice in the robbery had not been brought to justice and that I had refused to reveal his identity to police. The prosecutor also pointed out that, during the robbery, a shot had been fired and that someone could have been killed or seriously injured.

My legal aid appointed barrister had decided that my best chance of receiving a lenient sentence would be for me to make a personal plea to the judge explaining what I had been through since my arrest in April 1966.

I had expected my address to the judge to be impeded by nervousness but immediately I began speaking, the words flowed easily and with conviction.

I simply told the truth. I made no excuse for what I'd done. I said that I honestly couldn't say whether I was rehabilitated or not and that I felt rage inside me for what had happened in my life. But if I was ever going to be a useful member of society rather than a liability, I needed to return to society soon while I was still capable of love and empathy towards others. Prison was a great destroyer of relationships, of self-esteem, of dignity and of people. It desolated emotions.

After my barrister made a few remarks in support of my monologue, Judge Hicks commented at length about the seriousness of the offence but he didn't mention my mystery accomplice.

"The time you have spent in custody is quite substantial," he said. "Under difficult circumstances you have made attempts to rehabilitate yourself by enrolling for and completing correspondence courses. To your credit you have not chosen the course taken by many who come before these courts, with claims of having undergone remarkable personality changes and who point to themselves as paradigms of rehabilitation.

Rather, you have asked for a chance to become a useful member of society. I have no doubts that, if you chose to do so, you could become an asset to the community. I intend to give you that chance. I sentence you to two years and six months imprisonment with a recommendation for parole after six months. Your future is now in your own hands."

As I was taken down through the trap door of the courtroom dock and escorted along the subterranean passageway to the holding cell, every nerve in my body tingled with excitement. In six months time I could be free! Judge Hicks had demonstrated that not all persons in authority were unmerciful and vengeful towards people with my background.

But I still had one major hurdle to overcome: the Cabramatta bank robbery.

57

The Final Hurdle
(1972-1973)

The recommendation for parole after six months must have persuaded the prison authorities that I was now an acceptable risk in a normal maximum security prison. Instead of being returned to the MRP, I was taken to the section at Long Bay where I had spent time in the '60s; it was now named the CIP (Central Industrial Prison). Since my last visit, a few changes had been made. There were no remand prisoners, nor were there separate wings for the boys who were now integrated with the men. But, overall, conditions had improved, as had the quality of the meals. Occasionally, they even served steak and chips. One of the old workshops had been refurbished into a gym and games room. Five days a week two education officers worked at the gaol, and a small number of prisoners were classified as full time students. Every Saturday morning a debating class was held. Visitors from outside, including females, attended and sometimes competed in the debates. Naturally, a number of screws maintained strict surveillance on proceedings.

I was given employment in the book binding shop where my job was to operate a machine that embossed gold or silver lettering on books. After a few weeks, Bobby Merrit was given a job in the shop. He was placed on the machine next to mine. I wondered what the Governor at the MRP would say about it if he found out.

I wrote a short letter to Dad informing him that I had been sentenced to only two and a half years. Mindful of the charge still pending, I didn't mention the recommendation of parole.

Dad replied that after he had read my letter he went to the pub to celebrate. When the barmaid asked him what he was celebrating he had replied: "My son just got two and a half years for robbing a bank."

She thought he was joking.

A few weeks after I'd been sentenced my solicitor visited me to discuss the Cabramatta bank charge. Although he had a flattened nose that gave him more of a resemblance to a boxer than a lawyer, he spoke precisely and with the confidence of a man who knows he is right.

I believed I had a good chance of winning a trial, but he pointed out that if I pleaded not guilty and was found guilty, the judge might consider I had lied in court and was unrepentant, thus increasing the chances of receiving a heavy sentence.

Aware of what he was leading to, I asked him what he suggested.

"It's your decision, not mine," he said. "I can only advise. But Judge Hicks was quite impressed with you. If we could get you before him again, I'm certain he would be lenient."

"What are the chances of getting before him?"

"Because the circumstances are quite exceptional, I would say the chances are excellent."

"All right. Get me in front of Judge Hicks and I'll plead guilty."

Realising I'd probably have to make another speech to the judge, I joined the debating group. I had no qualms about speaking before an audience and I scored reasonably well in debates. But after the debates, when everyone stood around drinking tea, eating biscuits and talking trivialities, I became apprehensive. With rare exception, it had been nearly seven years since I'd spoken to a woman. When women approached me after the debates and wanted to indulge in conversation, I found myself nervous and self-conscious in their presence.

But after a while I became friendly with a regular visitor, Liz Fell. An attractive blonde woman in her mid-thirties who had a penchant for wearing funny little hats, Liz was a university lecturer who spoke to the crims in their own idiom, punctuating her conversation with profanities. Oddly, I found it an endearing quality in a woman whom I soon discovered possessed a higher IQ than any woman I'd known.

When I mentioned to her that I had completed a few writing courses she declared that I was the man she was looking for. She had been trying to persuade the authorities to grant permission for a prisoner-produced gaol magazine and I could be the editor. Although there was opposition from some quarters in the prison department, the education department lobbied for the magazine and, in March 1973, permission was granted for the production of a prison magazine subject to censorship by the head education officer.

One day I received a letter from the publisher at Angus and Robertson, Richard Walsh, informing me that Ian Mudie had spoken highly to him about my work and he would be interested to see anything I considered worthwhile,

Good old Ian Mudie, he hadn't forgotten me. I immediately replied to the letter, promising to contact him after I was released.

When I went to court for sentencing on the Cabramatta bank robbery, Judge Hicks stunned everyone, including me, by placing me on a three-year bond. My barrister told me he believed it was the first time in Australia that anyone had received a bond for the armed robbery of a bank.

Ebullient with my good fortune, I cheekily informed the barrister that it had been Australia's first C-Day robbery and what price did he estimate the bookies would have laid about the double?

Back in the holding cell, I thought of Cathy and the irony of it all. My decision a few years ago to be honest with her and confess that, after my release from Pentridge, I'd be in gaol for many more years, had been the catalyst leading to the termination of our relationship. Amazingly, I now would probably spend only a few more months in gaol than she had expected. She could have postponed the family safari for a few months. *She would have waited!*

I shut the thoughts from my mind. The Cathy affair was a closed book. I was a human time bomb. Would I be any different if I knew she would be waiting for me at the gate?

Maybe, but I doubted it. I had worked too hard at picking the scabs.

Within a week of receiving the bond I was called before the

Classification Board. To me, the people on the Board looked much the same as those who I had first encountered thirteen years ago. Although I knew these were different individuals, the fundamental procedure of the Board remained the same. The professional staff was there to make up the numbers. The senior prison official made the decisions.

The SPO, who had a fleshy, hooked nose and bloodshot eyes, immediately went on the attack. "Your prison record is atrocious, Killick."

I sighed. "I've been blamed for a lot of things I didn't do." I looked around the table. It was obvious no one believed me.

"That's the wrong attitude to take, Killick," Hooknose said. "Haven't you got any remorse for the things you've done?"

"I've got a lot of remorse."

"Well, you're not displaying it," a fat guy with horn-rimmed glasses said.

"Sorry about that," I replied.

"The fact is you could be out in less than four months," Hooknose said, making it sound tragic. "What do you intend to do when you are released?"

"I'm going to try and get a job as a journalist. I also intend to write a book. I've received a letter from a publisher who is interested."

"Don't you think you are flying a bit too high?" an immaculately dressed guy asked. "With your background you'll be fortunate if you can get a job in a factory."

I had been prepared for this and I controlled the rage. I had to learn to accept this type of attitude. These people assumed that factory work was all I was capable of, all I deserved. My hard-earned writing qualifications were meaningless. They couldn't see beyond my record or past their presumptions of what type of person a man with my record must be. For all their dealings with criminals, they knew next to nothing about the individuals they interviewed and judged. The person's record was the yardstick by which these people gauged the worth of the man.

They were suspicious of any prisoner with intelligence and skills, as he didn't fit into their preconceptions of what a prisoner is.

Surprising myself, I said: "Perhaps you're right."

A few of them nodded their approval. I was learning. If I were going to survive outside, these were the types of games I'd have to learn to play.

I gave what I hoped was an engaging smile and said: "Now that I'm close to release, I'd appreciate it if you would classify me minimum security and send me to Emu Plains or some other prison camp."

For a few moments there was shocked silence. Hooknose was the first to recover. "That's out of the question. For a start there's no guarantee that with your record you'll be given parole."

"But the judge recommended it."

"It doesn't matter. As I told you, your record is atrocious."

"But I've spent nearly seven years in maximum security. I honestly feel the need to be eased back into society via minimum security. There is constant tension and stress in maximum security. I could walk out of my cell one morning and find myself in the middle of a riot or some thug with nothing to lose could attack me because he got out of bed on the wrong side."

A delicate-looking, middle-aged guy said: "You should have thought of these things before you assaulted an officer **with an iron bar**."

Stuff this! I was sick of playing these stupid fucking games. "I did," I said, softly.

"What do you mean, you did?"

I met his gaze. "In 1968, I thought, 'What will the Classification Board at Long Bay in 1973 think, if I hit this officer on the head with this iron bar?' And then I thought, 'What the hell, I'll take the punt'."

Hooknose looked as though he was choking on a peach seed. "That's enough, Killick. On your way. You'll remain in maximum security until the day you are released."

Thanking the Board for its time, I left the room.

While I was at the CIP I formed a friendship with the Church of England minister, the Reverend Spencer. One day he had called me to his office where he told me it was his policy to have an informal chat with all C of E prisoners when they arrived. A kindly looking man in his late forties, he had receding grey hair and clear blue eyes that invited you to confide your innermost secrets to him. We had some long discussions about gaol, life and religion. He became determined to convert me to Christianity, but I was adamant that the man I had become couldn't accept God. He wouldn't give up and gave me books to read that put forward persuasive arguments that Christ had been resurrected. But you can't convince someone who doesn't want to be convinced. I read the books and remained sceptical. Nevertheless, we remained friends and I gave him my word that after I was released I would stay in touch with him.

About a month after my meeting with the Classification Board, the hypothetical situation I had put to them of being attacked by another prisoner became reality. A hot-tempered Aborigine serving life for murder became upset about my comments on his choice of music; without warning, he ran at me throwing punches. A savage fight ensued before the overseer was able to enlist the aid of a number of screws to break it up. Both my opponent and I were copiously bleeding from cuts to the face and head. The old wound above my eye had burst open and I had to be taken to the clinic for stitches.

On the way to the clinic I told myself I could forget about parole. I wondered why these things happened to me.

The nurse in the clinic was young, blonde and attractive. As she leaned over me to stitch the wound her hips pressed against my arm. Unable to control myself, I immediately became sexually aroused. If she was aware of the effect she was having on me, she gave no indication.

After she finished stitching, she stepped back and smiled at me; her skin was flawless. "There we are, nearly as good as new."

"Come on, Killick," the screw said. "Let's go."

I surreptitiously glanced at my lap. I was still aroused. "I feel a bit dizzy," I said.

The nurse grinned and turned to the screw. "Maybe he should rest for a few minutes; he's had quite a shock."

I concentrated on what the Parole Board would say about the fight when I applied for parole. I was soon ready to walk without embarrassment.

After the screw had escorted me to my cell and locked me up, I thought about the nurse. She must have known, the little vixen.

The next morning I was escorted to the Governor's office. Although he was thinner and his hair had turned totally grey, I recognised him as a former two-striper from my days at Goulburn Gaol. Even in those days he had been a strict disciplinarian.

If he remembered me, he gave no indication. "Killick, I'm not going to waste time lecturing you. You are charged with fighting. If you plead guilty, I'll deal with it, otherwise I'll assign it to the VJ."

Conscious of the stitches above my eye and my cut and bruised face, I said: "I can't deny I've been fighting, sir."

"Who started it?"

"No one, really. He's doing life and I've been in gaol for seven years. Tempers became frayed."

"An understatement, I'd say. Your temper seems to have gotten the better of you a few times." He paused and rubbed his hands against the back of his neck. "This could cost you your parole. The Parole Board might consider you are too violent for the community. But if you give me your word this is the end of it, I'll let you both off with a caution and you can return to work. No conviction will be recorded."

I was momentarily perplexed. This man, a renowned hard-liner, had me cold and he was going to let me off. First Judge Hicks, now the Governor. Maybe luck did really run in seven year cycles and my seven years of bad luck had ended. "You've got my word, sir."

"Good. Then it's settled. I've already spoken to the other bloke." He paused. "I remember you, Killick. You were the best 440 runner we ever had at Goulburn. Now take my advice and stay out of trouble and you'll get your parole."

When I returned to the shop I shook hands with my opponent. Noting with satisfaction his black eye. "I still don't like your taste in music," I said.

"And yours is up to shit, brother."

Grinning, Bobby Merrit came over. "If there's a rematch, there'll be no music up at Grafton."

That was the end of the matter.

A few weeks later, I heard on the radio that James Bazley had been shot outside his home at Clifton Hills, Victoria. Although he had been struck by two .38 bullets, he survived. I wondered if he had returned to bookmaking and had been shot by an irate punter.

After head office sanction for the prison magazine became official, the head education officer, a plump, fuzzy-headed guy of about forty, called a group of six prisoners, including me, to his office. We were, he told us, to be responsible for the production of the magazine which would be a monthly publication named *Inside Out*. He then announced that a guy named Robert would be the editor.

I nearly fell off my chair. "But Liz Fell told me I'd be the editor," I protested.

He gave me a disapproving look. "Liz Fell isn't responsible for this magazine – I am. I've always had Robert in mind as editor."

"Look, I don't want to sound egotistical," I said, "but I'm the best credentialed person in the gaol for this job. I've completed two writing courses with distinction and I even have a letter from Angus and Robertson wanting to see my work."

The education officer was unimpressed. "I've made my decision and it's not negotiable. You can be the assistant editor."

I stood up. "You know what you can do with your assistant editorship." I walked out.

Later, I paced the yard with Bobby Merrit who tried to counsel me. "You should have played it more cunning," he said. "Let him be the editor for the first few issues and you submit a few of your best stories;

once everyone reads them and realises you're the real writer, you'll be able to apply more pressure. We'll get the whole gaol behind you."

"I won't have time," I said. "I might be out in a few months."

"So you edit the second issue and do it better than the first. Then you'll be remembered as the man behind our history-making magazine."

I laughed. "Don't lay it on too thick, Bob. It's not a contest. I'd simply like to get this magazine off the ground and make it a good one. I know I'm the right man for the job. I'm always getting stuffed around by bureaucracy."

Liz Fell had inaugurated a weekly course at the CIP entitled 'Crime and the Criminal'. The day after my discussion with Bob, I attended Liz's class.

After the session had concluded, she called me aside. "What's the bullshit about you walking out of the room yesterday and refusing to help with the magazine?"

"You told me I'd get editor."

"I was wrong. I didn't realise old Buggerlugs had promised Robert the job."

"He and I don't get on. His ideas about the format of the magazine are in contrast to mine."

"Well, it's not up to you, Killick." She always referred to me as Killick. "I thought you were tougher than this. If you can't cope with a minor setback like this without reacting the way you did, you won't last a month in the real world." She poked me in the chest. "Lower that bloody pride of yours a bit." She walked away and began talking to a good-looking young guy who was serving five years for rape.

Although I nearly choked on my words, I apologised to the education officer. I added that I would help with the production of the magazine.

A few days later I gave Robert two of my best short stories, a feature article and a short article. "If you need any typing or editing done, let me know," I said.

Robert, who was in his forties, reminded me of a rough-looking version of the actor, Rex Harrison. He gave me a patronising look, "Sure."

Although he sought the aid of the other four staff, he didn't ask for my help to compile and produce the first edition.

Perusing through it, I discovered that Robert had published the shorter of my two stories and had ignored my feature article, although he had included the short article. Overall, the magazine was professionally done, but it had fewer pages than I'd expected and it could have done with more varied content. When I read through my story, I nearly blacked out. He had replaced semi colons with commas; twice he had eliminated semi colons and added 'and'. In the fourth paragraph he had omitted an entire sentence! The first story I'd ever had published and the guy had mutilated it! If he thought he was going to get away with it he had to be insane. I'd walk straight into his office and break his jaw! But, enraged as I was, self-preservation soon took control. After seven years, I was close to freedom. If I assaulted the editor I could imagine the scene as I stood before Judge Hicks.

"Well, Killick, before I pass sentence, would you like to explain why you put this man in hospital after I'd given you a bond for bank robbery?"

"Well, sir, he published one of my stories in the gaol magazine and he replaced semi colons with commas."

The thought of such a ridiculous scene made me smile. My best option would be to ensure the mutilation of one on my stories didn't happen again.

Later that day I accosted Robert. "Why did you mutilate my story, Rob?"

"What are you talking about? I didn't have the space to print all your stuff."

"I'm talking about the story you published. You left out a sentence and you changed the punctuation."

"If I changed anything," he said, "it would have been because I deemed it necessary. That's the editor's prerogative."

It took all my willpower to refrain from attacking him. I measured my words. "It took me a long time to write that story. Every word, every comma was there for a reason. Then someone like you comes along and arbitrarily decides to do it differently. We're talking about my story!"

"As editor, I've got the right."

"Shut up! We're prisoners, we haven't got any rights. Now I'm telling you, that if you ever change just one comma of one of my stories again, all the rights and prerogatives in the world won't help you because I'll break your fucking neck!"

Though he tried to appear calm, his eyes registered fear. "Don't you think you're over-reacting?"

"There's no point in discussing this any further. You've been warned. Just one comma." I walked away.

A week later Robert was transferred to Bathurst. I was promoted to editor of *Inside Out*. The next issue was a bumper edition, containing almost twice as many pages as the first issue. All semi-colons remained unchanged.

Early in June I was notified that I had been granted parole; I had 15 days to go.

Until that moment, I had refrained from thinking about the outside world. Now, freedom was a reality. I would have to start making plans.

Although I had tried, not altogether successfully, to conceal it, I was a man filled with bitterness and rage. It was impossible for me to gracefully accept that my youth was gone, the girl I loved was gone, my credibility and respect were gone.

The fact that I was mainly responsible for what had happened to my life was something I refused to or couldn't accept. I had been severely punished, sometimes unlawfully, for my crimes, while my oppressors remained unscathed. Society had classified and branded me as belonging to a particular class of human being regarded by some as sub-human being. I had been inculcated to accept without questions the harsh retribution demanded by society for my crimes. Retribution was something I had learned to understand as being an acceptable and justifiable part of life. But I also believed that those people who had inflicted unlawful punishments on me should suffer retribution.

The part of me that took control in crises demanded of myself that, if society refused to do it, I would have to be the one to perpetrate the punishments.

The beast that raged within was ready to take control.

The part of me that was still normal, that somehow had retained all the decencies and sense of fair play which had been an integral part of the young John Killick, fought against the raging beast.

Good decent people, who were a part of society, had helped me. Judge Hicks had given me a chance that few criminals received; even the Governor had shown mercy. Ian Mudie, the Reverend Spencer and Liz Fell, all people of principle and respected members of society, had taken a genuine interest in me. And Dad…he was still there, old and unwell, hoping, but not really believing that I would come good.

Surely I owed all of these people something, to at least <u>try</u> to make a useful and meaningful life for myself. I couldn't blame society for what had happened to me, because society didn't exist. It was an impersonal abstraction.

I would have to try to maintain a tight rein on my emotions and subdue the rage and hold it inside. I had proven that, if I tried hard enough, I could discipline myself. But I knew that if I had to live my life this way, controlling that turmoil inside, I would never know peace of mind…

The final two weeks passed slowly. I had learned that time was complex. To a person awaiting execution in the morning, twelve hours could seem fleeting; to a person being physically tortured, twelve minutes could seem to be an eternity. It was all relative.

The morning of my release, 22 June 1973, I shook hands with Bobby Merrit and a few others, signed for my few meagre possessions and walked to the main gate.

When the screw opened the first gate, I turned and looked back. I was almost overcome by a sense of loss. No matter what I might do from here on, the seven years and two months were gone, nothing could bring them back.

As the screw unlocked the last gate between me and freedom, he turned to look at me. "How long have you done, fella?"

"Seven years."

"Phew ... that's a big one. Still, it could've been life."

Without answering, I stepped through the gate and began walking down the paved road that was still inside the prison complex. There were no feelings of euphoria, only sadness.

Yes, it could've been life.

Maybe it still would be. The consequences of later escaping from another prison in a hijacked helicopter would make the past seven years pale by comparison...

www.ingramcontent.com/pod-product-compliance
Lightning Source LLC
Chambersburg PA
CBHW070009010526
44117CB00011B/1481